Renaissance Configurations

Voices/Bodies/Spaces, 1580–1690

Edited by

Gordon McMullan
Reader in English
King's College London

First published in hardcover 1998

First published in paperback (with new Preface) 2001 by
PALGRAVE
Houndmills, Basingstoke, Hampshire RG21 6XS and
175 Fifth Avenue, New York, N.Y. 10010
Companies and representatives throughout the world

PALGRAVE is the new global academic imprint of
St. Martin's Press LLC Scholarly and Reference Division and
Palgrave Publishers Ltd (formerly Macmillan Press Ltd).

ISBN 0–333–67665–3 hardback (*outside North America*)
ISBN 0–312–21348–4 hardback (*in North America*)
ISBN 0–333–67666–1 paperback (*worldwide*)

This book is printed on paper suitable for recycling and
made from fully managed and sustained forest sources.

A catalogue record for this book is available
from the British Library.

The Library of Congress has cataloged the hardcover edition as follows:
Renaissance configurations : voices/bodies/spaces, 1580–1690 /
edited by Gordon McMullan.
    p. cm.
Includes bibliographical references and index.
ISBN 0–312–21348–4
    1. English literature—Early modern, 1500–1700—History
and criticism. 2. Literature and society—England—History–
–17th century. 3. Literature and society—England—History–
–16th century. 4. Gender identity in literature. 5. Space and
time in literature. 6. Body, Human, in literature. 7. Sex role in
literature. 8. Renaissance—England. 9. Voice in literature.
I. McMullan, Gordon, 1962–
PR423.R44 1998
820.9'003—dc21
                                        97–49889
                                          CIP

10   9   8   7   6   5   4   3   2   1
10   09   08   07   06   05   04   03   02   01

Printed in Great Britain by Antony Rowe Ltd, Chippenham, Wiltshire

Contents

v

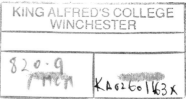

III NAMING/LOCATING

IV VOICING THE PAST

Notes on the Contributors

Ros Ballaster is Fellow and Tutor in English at Mansfield College, Oxford. She is the author of *Seductive Forms: Women's Amatory Fiction 1684–1740* (1992), editor of Delarivier Manley's *New Atlantis* (1992) and Jane Austen's *Sense and Sensibility* (1995), and has published several articles on seventeenth- and eighteenth-century writing by women.

Mark Thornton Burnett is Reader in English at the Queen's University of Belfast. He is the author of *Masters and Servants in English Renaissance Drama and Culture: Authority and Obedience* (1997), the editor of *The Complete Plays of Christopher Marlowe* (1999) and *The Complete Poems of Christopher Marlowe* (2000), and the co-editor of *New Essays on "Hamlet"* (1994), *Shakespeare and Ireland: History, Politics, Culture* (1997) and *Shakespeare, Film, Fin de Siècle* (2000). His new book, *Constructing "Monsters" in Shakespearean Drama and Early Modern Culture*, is forthcoming.

Kate Chedgzoy is Professor of English at the University of Newcastle upon Tyne. She is the author of *Shakespeare's Queer Children: Sexual Politics and Contemporary Culture* (1996), *Writers and Their Work: 'Measure for Measure'* (2000), and *Shakespeare, Feminism and Gender: New Casebook* (2000), and editor, with Suzanne Trill and Melanie Osborne of *Lay By Your Needles, Ladies, Take the Pen: English Women's Writing, 1500–1700* (1997) and, with Suzanne Trill and Melanie Hansen, *Voicing Women: Gender and Sexuality in Early Modern Writing* (1998). She has recently edited, with Emma Francis and Murray Pratt, *In a Queer Place: Sexuality and Belonging in British and European Contexts* (2001).

Helen Hackett is Senior Lecturer in English Literature at University College London. She is the author of *Virgin Mother Maiden Queen: Elizabeth I and the Cult of the Virgin Mary* (1995), *Writers and Their Work: 'A Midsummer Night's Dream'* (1997), and *Women and Romance Fiction in the English Renaissance* (2000).

James Knowles is Reader in English at the University of Stirling. He has published extensively on masques, notably Jonson's *Entertain-*

ment at Britain's Burse. He is currently working on the entertainments and some of the masques for the forthcoming Cambridge *Works of Ben Jonson*, on an edition of *Four Citizen Comedies* for Oxford University Press and on his monograph, *The Theatrical Closet*.

Gordon McMullan is Reader in English at King's College London. His publications include *The Politics of Unease in the Plays of John Fletcher* (1994) and a collection of essays, *The Politics of Tragicomedy: Shakespeare and After*, co-edited with Jonathan Hope (1992). His Arden Shakespeare edition of *Henry VIII* was published in 2000.

Amanda Piesse is early modern drama specialist in the English Department of Trinity College Dublin. She is editor of *Sixteenth-Century Identities*, co-founder of Early Modern Forum Ireland, and is currently preparing an original spelling edition of *The Obedience of a Christian Man*.

Michael Pincombe teaches English Literature at the University of Newcastle upon Tyne. He is the author of *The Plays of John Lyly: Eros and Eliza* (1996) and *Elizabethan Humanism: Literature and Learning in the Later Sixteenth Century* (2001). He is also Convenor of the Tudor Symposium, and has edited *The Anatomy of Tudor Literature: Proceedings of the First International Conference of the Tudor Symposium* (1998).

Sasha Roberts is Lecturer in English at the University of Kent at Canterbury. Her publications include *Women Reading Shakespeare, 1660–1900: An Anthology of Criticism* (co-edited with Ann Thompson, 1997), *Writers and Their Work: 'Romeo and Juliet'* (1998), and articles on early modern reading. She is currently completing a book, *Reading Shakespeare's Poems in Early Modern England*.

Ann Thompson is Professor of English Language and Literature at King's College London. She is one of the General Editors of the Arden Shakespeare, third series, and is co-editor, with Neil Taylor, of *Hamlet*, forthcoming in that series. She is the author of *Shakespeare's Chaucer* (1978) and co-author, with John O. Thompson, of *Shakespeare, Meaning and Metaphor* (1987). She edited *The Taming of the Shrew* for the New Cambridge Shakespeare and is co-editor, with Sylvia Adamson, Lynette Hunter, Lynne Magnusson and Katie Wales, of *Reading Shakespeare's Dramatic Language* (2001).

Suzanne Trill is Lecturer in English Literature at the University of Edinburgh. Her publications include *Writing and the English Renaissance* (1996), co-edited with William Zunder, and *Voicing Women: Gender and Sexuality in Modern Writing, 1500–1700* (1998), co-edited with Kate Chedgzoy and Melanie Hansen.

Susan J. Wiseman teaches at Birkbeck College, London.

Preface to the First Paperback Edition

Thanks to the efforts of Eleanor Birne and Josie Dixon, this paperback edition of *Renaissance Configurations* is being published in 2001 by Palgrave, the new imprint for Macmillan's academic output. It seems a fair while now since the contributors first turned up at the University of Newcastle upon Tyne to give the papers from which these essays developed, and we have all moved on a little since then and since the hardback was first published in 1998 – in several cases quite literally, to new institutions and/or to promoted posts. The issues raised in the essays in this collection remain sharp and current, however, and the contributors as a group continue to be, as well as friends, a coherent cohort of early modernists working in Britain and Ireland. We hope the wider readership the paperback affords – both within and beyond the geographical area represented by the contributors – will enjoy these essays, learn from them, and perhaps respond to them in books and collections to come.

G. M.
King's College London

Acknowledgements

It is no less true because it is a commonplace to say that a collection such as this is distinctly a collaboration, and that it is in several ways inappropriately served by the title-page implication that it was singly edited. This volume has its origins in a course on writing by and about women in Jacobean England that I taught at the University of Newcastle upon Tyne in spring 1994, a course of a kind that is now becoming a familiar component of English departments. The days when the only edition of poems by Æmilia Lanyer was to be found under the spectacularly misleading title *The Poems of Shakespeare's Dark Lady* already seem long ago, but it is necessary to recall just how recently such courses have made their way into university syllabuses. Certainly, few if any of the present contributors were invited or expected as undergraduates to read Lanyer, Wroth or Cavendish. Even in 1994, several of the texts of women writers that are now available in paperback were effectively unobtainable for teaching purposes. And it was partly out of a recognition that teaching these writers would be the best way to learn about them that I offered the new course at Newcastle. For various reasons – my ignorance of some of the material to be studied as well as my sense of the complex issues embodied in my own situation as a male lecturer addressing a roomful of (largely) undergraduate women on the subject of Renaissance writing by and about women – I decided to organise, as a resource for the course, a series of papers by a number of my contemporaries or near-contemporaries from English Departments in Britain and Ireland whom I perceived to be producing interesting work in the field. As the speakers visited Newcastle one by one over a period of months, it became increasingly obvious that there were connections and shared interests amongst them, which might usefully be recorded by way of a plenary conference and a publication. We thus reconvened some months later in the company of Professor Ann Thompson, who has been over a number of years a source of tremendous encouragement and support for many of us, and of Charmian Hearne, energetic and enthusiastic senior commissioning editor at Macmillan. The result is this volume.

I am grateful to the contributors both for the readiness with which they responded to my original suggestion that they come to Newcastle to give a paper (despite the logistic awkwardness that was sometimes involved) and for their considerable patience with the inevitable delays in the production of this volume, not the least of which was the effect of my inconveniently changing institutions in mid-flow. I have many debts to my erstwhile colleagues in the Department of English Literature at the University of Newcastle upon Tyne: to Rowena Bryson and Margaret Jones for much-appreciated organisational assistance with the initial seminars and particularly with the plenary colloquium; to Jerry Paterson, the then Dean of the Faculty of Arts, for suggesting the idea of the plenary; and to Linda Anderson, Tom Cain, Judith Hawley, Claire Lamont, Mike Rossington and John Saunders for turning up to hear an apparently endless series of papers without (much) complaint at my presumption.

The contributors wish singly and as a group to register their gratitude to a range of people for friendship, debate, encouragement and influence: these include, for me, Lorna Hutson, Margaret Healy, Tom Healy and Peter Stallybrass; for Helen Hackett, Anne Button, Katherine Duncan-Jones, Steve Hackett, Margaret Healy, Paul Salzman, Sue Wiseman, Henry Woudhuysen, and colleagues and students at UCL; for James Knowles, Alan Stewart, Graham Allen and Lois Potter; for Amanda Piesse, John Pitcher (for initial thoughts on *Pericles*), John Scattergood (for introducing her to Mercator and Ortelius) and Thomas Docherty (for new thoughts on Irigaray); for Mike Pincombe, Ewa Dąbrowska; for Suzanne Trill, the various members of the postgraduate seminars at Belfast and at Southampton for valuable comment on and discussion of her paper. I should perhaps add that one of the frustrations of editing a collection of essays such as this is that one inevitably gets to know people late in the day whom one would have wished originally to incorporate, had one only known. I should make it clear, then, that this collection includes only some, and by no means all, of the members of the particular cohort it represents.

Finally, we are all enormously grateful to Charmian Hearne for her enthusiasm and support well beyond the call of duty. The task of putting together a collection such as this is made vastly more enjoyable by the opportunity to work with someone as professional, cheerful and (let's be honest) patient as Charmian.

University of Newcastle upon Tyne and King's College, London 1994–7

Preface: Renaissance Configurations

Gordon McMullan

I

Renaissance Configurations is a collection of essays on cultural formations in early modern England which focuses on questions of gender, sexuality and politics in the relations of public and private,
verbal and spatial, material and textual. It is the work of a particular
cohort of early modern specialists teaching in university English
Departments in Britain and Ireland who began their professional
careers in the late 1980s and early 1990s and who work in the
broad field delineated by feminism, cultural materialism, new historicism, psychoanalysis and poststructuralism. Their desire to
extend the literary canon by interpreting works – especially works
by women – which have not to date received the attention
they deserve is balanced by a commitment to the reinterpretation
of works by canonical figures – reading, in other words, both Æmilia
Lanyer and William Shakespeare from a shared critical perspective.
No single, monolithic critical approach is represented, though: the
differences between the essays are as important as the similarities
and congruences, and there is a conscious pluralism of agenda and
attitude throughout. It is this heterogeneity, this diversity of focus,
that most clearly differentiates the present volume from the representative collections of the mid-1980s (Jonathan Dollimore and Alan
Sinfield's *Political Shakespeare,* for instance, and John Drakakis's
Alternative Shakespeares). The present volume has less specificity, is
less politically focused, but it takes its cue from the kinds of reading
performed in those collections to examine the canonical and the
uncanonical in light of each other, and it shares with them a firm
commitment to cultural studies, particularly as embodied in the
investigation of the often interconnected questions of the sexual
and the political. The title of the present collection aims to embody
both this point of origin and this relative diversity, delineating a
strong shared interest both in the verbal, physical and spatial stra-

tegies of early modern culture, and in the realignment of certain contemporary critical concerns as a result of investigations into those strategies over the last three decades.

Renaissance Configurations expresses the contributors' desire to produce work that is (in the sense in which these terms, in Britain at least, are understood) both 'scholarly' and 'theoretical'; in other words, to perform cultural criticism from the perspective of philosophical, anthropological and political critique, but always in ways that can be demonstrated to be historically and textually appropriate. They read closely and they historicise that close reading – a process that operates diachronically and is undertaken in the hope of making larger assertions about the construction and configuration of early modern culture. There is, for instance, a general preference for teasing out the political resonances of a text rather than for seeking direct political allegory; and the focus on sexuality and on the self – its creation and nurture, and its relations to space and event – serves to reinforce the contributors' wish to confront complex social and cultural formations. There is a particular concern with issues of space and place, with the crucial role of the sites of production and consumption of written texts, and with the problem of the gendering of those sites. Typical of the strategic moves in these essays is James Knowles's analysis of the early modern closet as a 'gendered space', noting in some detail the differences between the male and female closet and refusing inadequately theorised definitions of such cultural phenomena. The collection, in fact, offers a general resistance to uncritical dualisms, to unqualified binary oppositions – whether of gender (male/female), race (white/black), individual (self/other) or space (public/private) – and several of the essays focus quite closely on the interconnections of the verbal and the spatial, on the relations, for instance, between domestic and public architecture and literary texts, on the encoding practices involved in the configuration of domestic space, and on what Sasha Roberts calls 'the interweaving of textual and material culture'.

Above all, issues of gender and sexuality are central to the work of all the contributors, and their debt to both feminist critics and the founding figures of gender studies is substantial. The influence of Luce Irigaray and of Eve Kosofsky Sedgwick, for instance, in the analysis of the patterns of exchange that determine the relations of gender and power has been considerable. Sedgwick's deployment of the Irigarayan analysis of patriarchy as a system within which women become the objects of an exchange process that takes place

between men offers an understanding that both impels and under-
pins several of the essays. For Ros Ballaster, Lorna Hutson's analysis
of the particular Renaissance configuration of the homosocial economy described by Sedgwick serves as a starting point for outlining
the differences between the Renaissance viewed contempora-
neously and from the perspective of the Restoration; for James
Knowles, 'Marlowe's works embody a sixteenth-century "moment
of the closet" as significant as Sedgwick's nineteenth-century epoch
of closet-formation'; and, for my own work on early modern dramatic collaboration, Sedgwick's work has been immensely helpful
in illuminating the homosocial exchange processes embodied in the
writing of male collaborators.

It is, I think, especially important to note that, though this collection registers developing attitudes and outlooks in the analysis of
gender and culture, it has been put together by a group of people
keenly aware of the debt they owe to those British and American
critics – mostly women – who fought over a sustained period to give
a voice and a place to women writers and women's history in the
syllabuses of university departments long before any of the present
contributors were appointed to teaching posts. This debt to an earlier cohort is, perhaps paradoxically, sometimes acknowledged here
by way of critique, but it is a critique that operates in the recognition
both that the essays collected here could not have been written
without their prior work and that they have provided an intellectual climate and a level of practical encouragement upon which
they themselves were not able to depend when they began their
own work in these areas. At the same time, the contributors to the
present volume work within a context of considerable and continuing institutional change, change which – in the United Kingdom at
least – involves substantially increased professional obligations both
in terms of teaching and administrative workload and of pressure to
publish. The care with which they approach and negotiate the
subjects that concern them is perhaps reflective of an institutional
environment which makes unalloyed certainty about the configurations of the future, as well as of the past, an elusive commodity.

II

The principal general concern of this collection is to map the
cultural configurations of early modern England and in particular

to analyse the crucial role played by conceptions of gender and sexuality in the construction and development of culture. The collection is divided into four parts connected chronologically and thematically. Part I broaches the broad issue of the relations of selfhood and gender by way of questions of enclosure and privacy and a focus on that most ostensibly interior of domestic spaces, the closet. Encouraged by the work of D. A. Miller on modern notions of secrecy and of Alan Stewart (another British early modernist early in his career) on the Renaissance closet, James Knowles examines the 'historical distance between modern and pre-modern conceptions of privacy and interiority' in order to seek a broader cultural implication for the textual and biographical 'dialectic between the enclosed and infinite' he finds in the work of Christopher Marlowe. For Knowles, Marlowe's writing embodies 'a culture, politics and aesthetics of the closet', and his provocative achievement lies in his dis-covery to the theatre audience of some of the key 'open secrets' of post-Armada society. Knowles deploys the theatrical representation of the closet in Marlowe's plays to suggest that a rigorous public/private binary is an inappropriate basis for the study of early modern culture, since for Renaissance man and woman, at certain crucial moments, the public and the private were indistinguishable. As Knowles observes, in several important contexts, 'being private is an announced state, an inescapably public gesture', and such paradoxes put into question modern assumptions of distinct and separate public and private spheres.

Sasha Roberts extends the critique of the public/private divide by resisting the essentialising that tends to be the product of simple critical dualisms. She offers arguably the most material focus of the contributors to the volume, focusing on the particular physical circumstances of the consumption of literary culture by women readers, and noting the anxiety with which seventeenth-century men viewed the domestic spaces associated with women reading. Privacy in this context becomes bound up with cultural resistance: as she observes, 'enclosure is not necessarily restrictive; it may, in some circumstances, be enabling'. She provides considerable detail about the physical organisation of the Renaissance house, noting, like Knowles, the closet's status as the 'most private' space in the building; she examines the apparent male assumption of a link between textuality and sexuality embodied in the resistance to women reading 'seductive' books; and she describes the highly charged cultural status of the physical conjunction of these issues in the woman's private reading space.

Helen Hackett's essay sustains this interest in public and private through her study of Mary Wroth's *Urania,* as she seeks to histor-icise the configuration of the gendered self in relation to Renais-sance discourses of melancholia. Noting that Wroth invests her female protagonist Pamphilia with certain habits usually associated with male melancholics – describing her tendency to retire not only to her closet but also to private gardens which combine 'externality with inaccessibility' in a potentially threatening manner, and pro-viding her with the peculiarly eloquent voice associated with male melancholia – Hackett proposes that 'the established association of melancholy with secrecy and privacy rendered it a legitimating mode' for women's writing. By way of close analysis primarily of the second part of the *Urania,* she demonstrates the development of the woman's adoption of melancholic modes from the claim to 'the verbal giftedness of the male melancholic' to the withholding of female eloquence as a (paradoxical) means to establish power over the male lover.

Each of these essays, in questioning the adequacy of the public/private divide, implicitly brings into play other dualisms habitually deployed in the analysis and description of culture. This is perhaps at its clearest in respect of sexuality, the area of primary focus for Part II. Michael Pincombe's essay takes issue with recent expres-sions of frustration at the apparent absence of representations of lesbian desire on the Renaissance stage by examining the discursive possibilities available to John Lyly in his depiction of the figure of Sappho, best known to modern scholars as the '*ur*-lesbian', in his play *Sappho and Phao.* Drawing on the classical tradi-tions of female sexuality inherited by Tudor readers, Pincombe distinguishes between lesbian and what he calls 'Lesbian' desire, the latter implying Lyly's dependence upon the ancient association of the women of Lesbos with 'obscene' but none the less phallic sexual practices. In this light, it would appear not only that Renaissance playwrights did indeed address questions of what we might call lesbian desire, but also that the discourses available to Tudor writers premised a more complex spectrum of sexuality than can be addressed by way of a simple homosexual/heterosexual division.

Kate Chedgzoy complicates the volume's analysis of the con-struction of sexuality still further by broaching the related issue of race, examining the intersection of discourses in operation in the configuration of racial and sexual difference both in Renaissance writing and in current critical analyses of that representation, and resisting the assumption common to both that, in the determination of difference, blackness is the principal 'object of scrutiny', whilst whiteness is treated as 'an unproblematic, effectively invisible given'. She sets out to provide a productive visibility to whiteness 'by considering white woman's stake in the construction of racially and sexually marked identities'; and by way of readings of Shakespeare's *Othello* and Behn's *Oroonoko*, she demonstrates the reciprocal nature of the construction of the discourses of race and sexuality in the early modern period. For Chedgzoy, Behn's status as author of *Oroonoko* locates her 'between cultures', a position 'in many ways characteristic of the white woman's location *vis-à-vis* the intersection of racial and sexual difference', and she examines the reception of Behn's work across the centuries, noting the way in which Behn's own strategies and those of her critics have combined to erase the possibility of parallels between Behn herself and her black female protagonist, Imoinda.

Difference, or, perhaps better, differentiation, is at the heart of my own essay on the relations of authorship and sexuality in Shakespeare and Fletcher's collaboration, *The Two Noble Kinsmen*. I suggest that the *Kinsmen* offers a vastly more productive model for the analysis of collaborative playwriting than does the current critical tendency either to 'disintegrate' the text into cleanly attributable divisions or else to reject such specific attribution in a general celebration of the social text without examining what such decisions might imply for interpretation. The homosocial economy of *The Two Noble Kinsmen*, which equates virgin and stageplay as objects of trade and negotiation, 'foregrounds a series of equivalences between the sexual transactions that are the subject of Jacobean theatre in general and of this play in particular and the processes of collaborative production which sustained that theatre'. In particular, the female protagonist Emilia's inability to differentiate between the kinsmen at crucial moments of the play, and the inability she shares with them to assert her own agency in face of cultural imperatives, can be seen to figure the complex relations between collaborative authors and their text. Differentiation – the 'attempt to extract the individual from the relations of difference that provide the illusion of individuality' – thus appears simultaneously both necessary and impossible.

The construction – and fragmentation – of the self is the focus of the two essays that comprise Part III of the volume, both of which are concerned with the cultural renegotiations which marked the beginning of the reign of James I. Amanda Piesse is ostensibly the most indebted of the contributors to the volume to American New Historicism, opening her analysis of *The Comedy of Errors* and *Pericles* with a provisional assertion of the contrasting styles of Elizabeth and James – '[w]here Elizabeth is multiplicity and diffraction, James is unity and singularity of purpose.' By way of sustained close reading, she relates the quest for the self in these plays to the quest for certain significant physical locations, building up a detailed sense both of the development of the characters of Adriana and Marina and of the two plays' contrasting modes for the creation of personality; and she concludes by deconstructing her initial contrast of the rhetorical modes of Elizabeth and James from the perspective of contemporary feminism.

For his analysis of the discursive reconfiguring initiated by James's accession, Mark Burnett turns to the remarkably unstable world of Marston's city comedy *The Dutch Courtesan*, in which locations and situations may at any moment be reconstituted as their opposites, and in which prostitution becomes the key trope for the play's broader 'political unconscious'. Avoiding direct political allegorising, Burnett locates certain covert political ramifications for the play, which quietly, hesitantly, ironically even, reveals itself as militantly Protestant in loyalty and apocalyptic in tone, rehearsing, for instance, 'the same tropes that underscored the campaign' against James's wish to rehabilitate the memory of his mother, Mary, Queen of Scots, and drawing much of its linguistic force from the language of Revelation. He demonstrates the play's relation to and influence upon the proliferation of 'disguised ruler plays' on the early Jacobean stage, notes the possibility that Marston withdrew the play prior to performance because of the notoriety it had already gained, and concludes by returning to the troping of the prostitute Franceschina, whose metaphoric disintegration in the course of the play serves ultimately to 'affirm male wholeness and completeness'.

The concluding part of the volume offers a series of perspectives, both critical and chronological, on writing by early modern women. Suzanne Trill takes issue with the role of Virginia Woolf's mythical Judith Shakespeare in determining the ways in which current criticism imagines Renaissance woman. Noting the definition of Judith as 'the sister of a famous brother (exemplifying difference) and "our" [i.e. feminist women's] sister (exemplifying continuity)', Trill questions the relevance of Woolf's model for interpreting the work of a Renaissance woman writer also known for having 'a famous literary brother', namely Mary Sidney, sister of Philip Sidney. As she observes, while Mary Sidney's 'identification as "Sidney's sister" does not have the same . . . consequences as the tale of "Shakespeare's sister", it is certainly double-edged', since while her family connection gave her legitimate access to print, it has subsequently distorted the way she has been perceived. Noting the importance accorded to Sidney's work by her contemporaries, Trill rejects the assumption that for a woman to write religious texts was to adopt the most culturally submissive of forms, and she argues that only when critics have moved beyond limiting definitions both of 'oppositional' writing and of the 'specifically female voice' will Sidney's achievement be fully appreciated.

Susan Wiseman's essay revisits two writers already broached in the collection, Sidney's daughter Mary Wroth and the Royalist writer Aphra Behn, and returns also to the question of the voice, particularly of the female voice, by way of an analysis of the role of Echo in seventeenth-century poetry. She sees E/echo as a key, and paradoxical, trope, 'meaningless, involuntary and yet filled with meaning'; and she traces its/her deployment across the century as competition for the subject – and in particular the gendered subject – in a range of contexts and locations. Wiseman reads the poetry of echo by Wroth and especially by Behn as an articulation of desire which is both sourceless and supplementary, producing a series of interventions, 'ideological as well as sonic', in the poems, and inviting a political understanding of echo 'as a voice which announces the inability of language . . . fully to orchestrate and suppress meaning'. In Behn's hands, the echo provides a curious (non-) space in which the female voice is empowered to reply to authoritative discourse while claiming to remain silent, thereby troping that discourse 'from within a discursive self-positioning as secondary' and thus establishing a position while ostensibly not doing so.

This double movement is a characteristic strategy of the writers who are the focus of Ros Ballaster's essay, which concludes the collection by looking back at the English Renaissance from the perspective of the Restoration, or at least from the perspective of two Restoration writers, Margaret Cavendish and Katherine Philips. Philips, for instance, withdrew a volume of poetry from the press after it had been advertised, a decision which can be read 'as a complex ploy to appear in print while appearing to deny the desire to do so'. For Royalist women, Ballaster argues, the new political configurations of the 1660s presented a peculiar problem: they wished to celebrate the restoration of court culture while retaining the agency acquired for women in the period since the beginning of the Civil War and avoiding a return to the kinds of discursive pattern described in Mark Burnett's essay. As a result, Philips and Cavendish developed 'a fantasy ... of a Royalist return to Renaissance values in which women figure the possibility of a "restored" economy of literary-social relations without the underpinning of a patriarchalist belief in the divine "fatherhood" of sovereign power', which they delineated as superseded by events. Their achievement was thus consciously to reconfigure the Renaissance 'retrospectively for their own historical moment'.

Contemporary criticism, of course, inevitably performs a similar manoeuvre, rereading the past with the present in mind. Such refigurings are bound both to distort and to tell a particular kind of truth, and the logic of a collection such as this is to reflect on and to offer a degree of order to certain shared concerns and strategies at a particular critical moment. It is the task of others to determine the motivations and innovations, as well as the successes and failures, of these strategies, but the contributors hope that this collection will be seen as a useful addition to the ranks of a criticism concerned equally with the configurations of English Renaissance culture and with the late-twentieth-century analysis of that culture and that it will be read as the work of a cohort of critics who, by virtue of roughly coincident career dates and a certain geographical proximity, seek to make sense of their relations to the professional discourse they inhabit at a time of considerable institutional unease.

I
Turning the Key

1

'Infinite Riches in a Little Room': Marlowe and the Aesthetics of the Closet

James Knowles

> Privacy is the seat of *Contemplation*, though sometimes made the recluse of *Tentation* ... Be you in your Chambers or priuate Closets; be you retired from the eyes of men; thinke how the eyes of God are on you. Doe not say, the walls encompasse mee, darknesse o're-shadowes mee, the Curtaine of night secures me ... doe nothing *priuately*, which you would not doe *publickly*. There is no retire from the eyes of God.
>
> (Brathwaite, *The English Gentlewoman*)[1]

> I have grown to love secrecy. It is the thing that can make modern life mysterious and marvellous. The commonest thing is delightful if only one hides it.
>
> (Wilde, *The Picture of Dorian Gray*)[2]

The 1590s, which closed with the invention of the water closet, was a decade obsessed with the closet, closetedness, enclosure and problematic and rapidly developing senses of privacy, interiority and inwardness, across wide cultural and political fields, but especially in its dramatic productions. Marlowe's works are no exception and the purpose of this essay is to explore how the aesthetics of the closet, the 'infinite riches' of the 'little room' resonate within his writing.[3] The two opening quotations suggest the concerns of this essay, secrecy, privacy, surveillance, the closet and sexuality, while their differing tones capture the ambivalent attitudes towards the dangers and pleasures of privacy and secrecy and represent the historical distance between modern and premodern conceptions of privacy and interiority which lie at the heart of this study.[4]

3

The 'infinite riches' of the closets and chambers of this chapter endow with greater materiality and specificity the dialectic between the enclosed and the infinite, aspiration and entrapment, previously traced by Marjorie Garber in the intellectual structures, metrical and formal dimensions of Marlowe's play.[5] Even in Henslowe's property list for these plays Garber found 'enclosing and restraining artefacts emblems of a constant attempt... to imprison, and wall up one another, whilst maintaining the fiction of breaking boundaries.' This essay considers how Marlowe depicts a 'culture of closet' necessitated by the post-Armada, anti-Catholic paranoia; a 'politics of the closet' which invests his plays and which informs his secondary activities as a government agent; and an 'aesthetics of the closet', where texts are imbricated in concealed, semi-concealed and revealed meanings, constantly alluding to unspoken secrets, hidden motives and desires. From the translation of *De Bello Civili* to *Edward II*, Marlowe explores the impact of social and self division, which shapes, but also demonises, a political closet, which as the king's closet in *Edward II*, constitutes the crucial locale of political intimacy. Even *Hero and Leander* is shaped by this aesthetics of the closet, not only in its subject-matter, but in its unstable and productive metaphoricity: infinite riches in little verbal rooms.[6]

Examination of the Marlovian closet invokes the contemporary resonances of such terminology, and particularly D.A. Miller's famous formulation, the 'open secret', which frames many of the modern concerns around the closet: secrecy, privacy and knowledge.[7] Like the emperor's new clothes, the 'open secret' depends on a recognition which no one articulates, so that the secret becomes not the fact, but the knowledge of the fact. For Miller, this process of secrecy (the continual performance of knowing/not acknowledging) constitutes a subjectivity which is predicated upon the 'open secret' that the very privacy and secrecy we claim as constitutive of our autonomous individuality derives from and reinforces the dominant power structure. Indeed, we define our identity 'as a resistance' to the dominant ideology, the belief that we can be secret or private, but in fact the very binary of public/private which appears to shelter us from social determination, is both a product of and productive of the dominant ideology.[8] So privacy becomes not escape from the dominant ideology, but the tool of self-policing, an irresolvable 'double bind of a secrecy that must always be rigorously maintained in the face of a secret that everybody already knows, since this is the very condition that entitles...subjectivity in the first place.'[9] Although Miller's essay concentrates on nineteenth-century texts, his 'open secret' captures the complex paradoxicality of early modern subjectivity as defined by the closet, suggesting some of the implications of the discourses of secrecy, privacy and interiority in early modern society. As used by Eve Sedgwick and others, the formulation of the 'open secret' as 'not to conceal knowledge, so much as to conceal knowledge of the knowledge' allows us to explore the coded and half-heard discourses which typify Marlowe's plays.[10]

Marlowe creates a charged world, alluding to secrets (whether real or imaginary, actual or hollow) and the process of secrecy, localised through the closet.[11] My approach to the Marlovian closet is also deeply indebted to Alan Stewart's 'The Early Modern Closet Discovered', which outlines an early modern epistemology of the closet, rooted in its social, cultural and architectural formations.[12] Stewart depicts the gendered closet as the site of powerful transactions and relations (overtly indebted to queer analyses of the 'closets of power'),[13] tracing the genesis of the early modern closet, its political, social and textual manifestations, to emphasise its *relations*, transactions and utilisations, and to argue that the early modern closet draws attention to and marks out those relations, not as secrets, but compulsively to reveal them as 'socially and even ethically problematic'. Such arguments also underpin this essay, although it centres less upon early modern (or current) epistemologies, and more upon the interactions of Marlowe and 1590s theatre with those epistemologies. In particular, I want to suggest Marlowe's works embody a sixteenth-century 'moment of the closet' as significant as Sedgwick's nineteenth-century epoch of closet formation, and to show how the theatre of this period stages the closet in multiple and complex ways. Secrecy and theatre (which might seem opposites) emerge as mutually interconnected, the theatre using and disclosing secrets in the concealments and dilations of the plot and in its theatrical devices, whilst the 'open secret' is itself inherently theatrical, centring upon a performance of knowing unknowingness.[14] The radical power of Marlowe's theatre is to take 'open secrets' so central to the demarcations of society, order and subjectivity and to discover them to the theatregoing public. It is precisely this playing along and across these boundaries that generates the provocative transgressions of Marlovian theatre.

THE CULTURE OF THE CLOSET

The immediate context of Marlowe's plays can be traced in the post-Armada paranoia over Catholic invasion and infiltration and the horror of civil war: 'outrage strangling law' as Marlowe describes it in *Lucan's First Booke* (?1587).[15] Faced with external and internal threats, the Elizabethan polity used coercion, surveillance and terror to achieve its own continuance. Intelligence operations, such as the abduction of Dr John Story, showed the would-be rebel how 'he is no where safe from his prince' and that the authorities would exercise 'wonderfull vigillancye'.[16] The Elizabethan state was highly policed, requiring obedience through publicly sworn oaths of office and loyalty (such as the Bond of Association, 1584), and enforced religious conformity, patrolled by the Lords Lieutenant and the episcopal pursuivants.[17] Many members of the Elizabethan intelligentsia served as government 'intelligencers', supplementing a tiny professional service,[18] some willingly (unemployed graduates), others coerced, often through entrapment. It is unsurprising, therefore, that the service was riddled with double agents of confused or contradictory loyalties.[19] Indeed, the uncertainty surrounding the nature and extent of Marlowe's implication with Walsingham's intelligencers reflects the shadowy and duplicitous looking-glass world of government service, even in the early modern period.[20]. The 'Rainbow Portrait', which combines mystical symbols and state power coded into the rich fabric of the dress, embodies this climate. Elizabeth appears as Irene, but her cloak, embroidered with eyes and ears (emblems of 'reason of state'), represents prudent monarchical surveillance.[21] The operation of such surveillance in the post-Armada era is demonstrated in the case of the satirical verses pinned to the door of London's Dutch Church, which denounced the stranger community as 'intelligencers' seeking 'alteracion' in the state, having been 'infected' with Spanish gold. Its author, 'Tamberlaine', predicts a massacre of London against the Catholics to surpass the massacre of Paris.[22] Marlowe's plays share these concerns, staging the culture of the closet, a treacherous world, full of intelligencers, covert messages, hidden motives and plans.[23]

The Massacre at Paris links war, Catholicism, court politics and the dangers of inwardness, all focused through the central symbolic space, the closet. Superficially a brutal *commedia apocalyptica*, the play's tortive ironies allow a counter-representation of the parallel inhumanities of Catholic and Protestant powers.[24] It also dramatises the Elizabethan nightmare of conflicted confessional and political regimes (notably in scene 1), justifying the regimes of surveillance and coercive belief which hedged religious observance. Faced with potential subversion (treason was 'compassing or imagining' the monarch's death), the authorities struggled to track the 'inward disposition' of the subject.[25] The production and verification of the necessary circumstantial evidence for treason prosecutions generated deep epistemological problems, since imagination, 'a secret thing hidden in the breast of man ... cannot be known but by open fact or deed' requiring 'some thing or means to notify the same ... before it can be discovered and punished.'[26] So the authorities sought to track hidden 'passions and inclinations' in unreliable 'effects and external operations', ultimately relying on mystical arguments:

> Wish the King no evil in thy thoughts, nor speak no hurt of him in thy privy chamber; for all the birds of the air shall betray thy voice, and with her feathers shall bewray thy words.[27]

Discourses about interiority in this period are characterised by an awareness of its potential dangers, which homilies and treatises sought to regulate. Indeed, a major element of state executions was the ritually expiative display of the 'bowels and inlay'd parts' of the traitor, reversing treachery's concealments.

The Massacre discovers all manner of inward spaces, from the Admiral's bed, through Ramus's study, to Spain as the 'council-chamber of the Pope'.[28] These inner spaces, sites of potential security for their inhabitants, are invaded by violence, the invasive gaze of the audience and by royal surveillance. Thus Guise's dominion over his wife is described in spatial terms (Mugeron's adultery has ' fill[ed] up his [Guise's] room that he should occupy', using 'a counterfeit key to his privy chamber' (MS scene 19, lines 5–6, and scene 19, line 2). The play parallels Guise's infiltration of her closet to discover her secrets (scene 15), with Henry III's use of the royal cabinet to destroy Guise. In both scene 15 and scene 21 the private space tempts self-exposure, so the Duchess writes her desires (scene 15, lines 18–21), Guise opens his treacherous designs (MS scene 19, lines 33–6), while in the royal closet, he articulates his ambitions (scene 21, lines 48–55), pre-empted by Henry's own plans to entrap Guise. Each incident instances the false security engendered in the (apparently private) closet, summarised in Guise's plan:

> When thou think'st I have forgotten this
> And that thou most reposest on my faith,
> Then will I wake thee from thy foolish dream
> And let thee see thyself my prisoner.

> (MS scene 19, lines 33–6)

Guise not only encapsulates both his and Henry's strategy, he voices the potential deceptiveness and dangers of inwardness, both to the occupant and to the observer. In part such anxieties about privacy echo Protestant anti-confessional propaganda (scene 15 is structured as a confession, culminating in the request for pardon), but it also reveals the danger of believing in our own privacy and secrecy in a society which seeks to institute total surveillance.

Secrecy's dangers are illustrated in Guise's death in the 'royal cabinet' (scene 21).[29] Like his wife before, Guise, lulled into security by the closet, displays his ambitions (lines 48–55), echoing his earlier 'confession' (scene 2, lines 49–52), but ironised by the audience's knowledge of Henry's own pre-emptive plotting and the three concealed murderers, whose presence becomes a visual manifestation to the audience of the surveillance and punishment which the scene then enacts (1–27 and 50.1). Indeed, the scene mirrors the whole process of treason, from 'imagining and compassing', through to confession as Guise 'disgorge[s]' his breast, to his death, a grisly realisation of the 2nd Murderer's prayer (line 6: 'Oh that his heart were leaping in my hand'), to Guise's scaffold speech (lines 77–87) and finally to the display of the body before his son. It becomes a dramatisation of the judicial process of trial and expiation through disembowelment, but crucially located in the royal cabinet.[30] Henry comments:

> Come, Guise, and see thy traitorous guile outreach'd,
> And perish in the pit thou mad'st for me.

> (lines 33–4)

The closet becomes both trap and also a hell ('pit') for the subject, so that the secrecy which 'traitorous' Guise used to conceal his plot becomes the means and the locale which the monarch uses to frustrate him.

THE POLITICS OF THE CLOSET

The closet in *The Massacre* reveals a nexus of ideas. On the one hand, the closet as the symbol of the inaccessible, hidden places, either of religious belief or treacherous design, represents a site of intense anxiety for the authorities and on the other, as a symbol of royal power, figures the desire of monarchs to know the minds of their subjects and the elusiveness of that information. In its use by Henry to entrap Guise, it also envisages the possibility of revealing hidden designs and the king's use of power and surveillance (literally his occluded prerogative, physically manifest in the spying murderers) to punish those who disrupt the peace. This ambivalence is central to the closet as a representation of dangerous seclusion/potential liberation, and also, paradoxically, for the monarch, the site of royal power. The closet in *Massacre* permits a double inflection, where on the one hand the play demonstrates the right of lawful kings to exercise authority, whilst on the other hand, it juxtaposes the subject's and the king's closet, suggesting that the very prerogative power claimed by the king is analogous to the interiority denied as subversive to the subject.

The material nature of the closet in early modern England helps elucidate Marlowe's presentation of this intensely paradoxical locus. The early modern closet was a gendered space, being the inner room, or innermost room of the lord or lady's suite of rooms, a place for retirement from public gaze.[31] Both male and female closet develop from earlier uses (notably the storage of documents or for private devotion),[32] but whereas the female closet tends to retain its functions as a site of private devotion, and as a storage place for household goods or valuables,[33] for men, the closet functions as office, muniment room and library.[34] These differences can be seen from the contents, with women's closets filled with 'a dozen of pictures, litle baskets of boxes, bookes, glasse plates, drinking glasses and glasse bottles...',[35] while the male closet was dominated by business impedimenta, as in Smythson's design for a closet with shelves, dual desks and spaces for maps.[36] The growing number of these smaller, more secluded, often opulently furnished rooms belongs to the desire for privacy, which was spurred by the establishment of static households and facilitated by the increased incidence of architecturally unified house construction.[37]

Such architectural configurations manifest totally different conceptions of privacy.[38] Although the general pattern from the late sixteenth century onwards saw the retreat of the noble family into these smaller, 'private' rooms, larger formal rooms (for example, the great chamber used for entertaining) were also deemed to be 'private', that is, places of exclusive entrance differentiated from socially mixed areas such as the hall.[39] Privacy and status were intertwined and privacy was not principally individual but *familial*.[40] Equally, to *be* private, to enter into the closet, was a public statement. To facilitate this withdrawal, as the functionally mixed spaces of the late sixteenth century became more specialised, new rooms were added, culminating in the post-Civil War adoption of the French *en enfilade* arrangement.[41] So in the refurbished Ham House the 'White Closet' (a luxurious private room for entertainment) was separate from the private closet, which in turn differed from the dressing room.[42] These distinctions around privacy can be seen in Ford's *The Broken Heart* (*c.* 1633), first, where Bassanes wishes to enter Ithocles' chamber, only to be told 'your brother would be private' (III.2.29), a scene which is revealed moments later when Ithocles is discovered in 'a chair' with Penthea.[43] To be private is not simply to be alone, a point reinforced by another incident later when the King commands 'All leave us', holding back his counsellors saying, 'We would be private' (IV.3.5). Being private is an announced state, an 'inescapably public' gesture of withdrawal.[44] Such paradoxes radically disturb modern notions of distinct public and private spheres and create a social terrain in which the private and public interpenetrate in ways which are difficult to map.[45]

The closet generated much anxiety, largely because of its ambivalent status and the uncertainty which shrouds its relations and transactions. On the one hand, this room, apparently at the centre of the house, actually exists on the margins of the household, or in ambivalent relation to it, its occupants, the master and secretary both within but also in differing ways beyond the household's social structure. Its internal relations, too, fostered concern, since they hovered uneasily between two conflicting social discourses: patronage and friendship. These anxieties were compounded by further opacity about the nature of its transactions. Alan Stewart fruitfully associates these with the other 'transactive spaces' (market, theatre and so on), which exercised the Elizabethan authorities. It might also be added that the paradox of the closet – that this private and specialised space strangely replicated the socially and functionally mixed nature of the public rooms it embodied (withdrawal from cross-class relations, uncertain interactions and unclear functions) – only served to increase the concern.[46]

The royal closet carried particular resonances since it represented the pinnacle of power. During the Tudor period the separation of Chamber and Privy Chamber created a withdrawn space in which the monarch lived, surrounded by nobles who acted as personal servants and who, by virtue of their propinquity to the monarch's semi-divine aura, acted as royal substitutes on diplomatic missions and state business.[47] Royal palaces were constructed with a hier-archy of rooms, which required the gradual exclusion of larger numbers of people the closer to the monarch they were.[48] Indeed, even within the Privy Chamber a further hierarchy operated, whereby the supreme officer, the Keeper of the Privy Stool, derived great influence from his unlimited access to the monarch even in the most exposed moments (a key symbolised his office). Although, due to Elizabeth's gender, the influence of these private servants (the Ladies of the Bedchamber) was reduced, the politics of inti-macy, where closeness marked favour, still operated.[49] In fact, Eliza-beth carefully regulated the right of entrée while she skilfully manipulated her gender and the politics of intimacy to stage grad-uated revelations of herself in the presence chamber, privy gallery, privy chamber, private garden and, occasionally, the bedchamber.[50] The Scots ambassador, Melville, was invited to her bedchamber to view her 'little cabinet' to demonstrate the Queen's esteem for his master.[51] Proximity symbolised power: proximity was power.

In *Edward II* the moments when Gaveston sits with the King (I.4.7.1–2) and when Mortimer and Lancaster are denied access to the King (II.2.129–98) dramatise the operations of the political closet.[52] In the latter case, the refusal of entrée symbolises the breakdown of the correct relationship between monarch and aris-tocracy, just as the earlier description of Gaveston as 'ignoble vassal' (I.4.16) marks the usurpation by the favourite of the nobles' position as counsellors. Indeed, at the opening of I.4 the barons' outrage centres less upon the open flaunting of a sexual relationship than upon the political relationship that Gaveston's *position* implies. To be placed by the King's side (I.4.10) is not simply to be secure; it is a manifest mark of favour. This is the import of the exile of Mortimer and Lancaster from the King's chamber, of Gaveston's access, and of the exchange of portraits as Gaveston departs for Ireland to act as governor in the King's place (I.4.125). He rules by virtue of his intimacy with the King, just as he ruled through the Seal, commanding in the King's name (I.1.167–9). His walking 'arm in arm' (I.2.20) symbolises precisely this intimacy, and equally, when Edward is reconciled to the barons (I.4), he offers each an office, promising to listen to Warwick's counsel, whilst Lancaster is enticed by the offer, 'Live then with me as my companion' (I.4.342).

Embedded in the issues of service, in patronage and faction, *Edward II*'s opening emblem of the poor men figures the caprice of these systems, as Gaveston's selection of the 2nd Poor Man illustrates:

> Let me see; thou wouldst do well to wait at my trencher and tell me lies at dinner time...
>
> (I.1.30–2)

This point is restated in Spencer's question to Baldock (II.2.1) and, indeed, Baldock and Spencer, although often dismissed as shadowy repetitions of Gaveston, illuminate the self-interested operations of patronage, so Spencer occupies a 'place of honour and trust' (III.1.143) in opposition to the barons' insistence on their right to places at the council table. Similarly Mortimer starts as a counsellor and favourite of the Queen, and as with Gaveston, his route to power is through his access to Queen and Prince (later significantly denied to Edmund).

Mortimer's grasp of the court system is illustrated in the exchange with his father (I.4.390–410), who argues the inevitability of favourites ('The mightiest kings have had their minions' [I.4.390]), to which young Mortimer replies that he objects not to Gaveston's 'wanton humour', but to the power and favour he has accrued, and he specifically comments upon the favourite's usurpation of the noble idea of livery:

> He wears a lord's revenue on his back,
> And, Midas-like, he jets it in the court
> With base outlandish cullions at his heels,
> Whose proud fantastic liveries make such show
> As if Proteus, god of shapes, appeared...
>
> (I.4.406–10)

His objections to the intimacy, power and wealth that Gaveston has amassed, and to his debasement of liveries and his acquisition of a faction (the 'outlandish cullions'), depend on his own exclusion.[53] The liveries signal the fear of other powerful factions at court and the debasement of the aristocratic position, an anxiety Kent also voices (I.1.157–8) when he reprimands Edward's honours to Gaveston. *Edward II* resonates with the tones of an aggrieved nobility faced with a 'basely born' (I.4.402) 'peasant' (I.4.7), 'lown' (I.4.82), 'groom' (I.4.291) or 'night-grown mushroom' (I.4.284), and the fear of Protean, uncontrollable social transformation.

Edward II demystifies the patronage system, anatomising the politics of the closet, whereby access to the monarch's body determines power. At one level the play dramatises a conflict of modes of power, in which the old system based upon 'place' (rank) is menaced by a new order rooted in the gaining of 'place' (position) through ability or cunning.[54] Mortimer may be a noble, but he actually gains power through skilful political manipulation, differing little from Gaveston or Spencer (as the repeating structure of the play suggests). These parallels are most striking between Gaveston's proclaimed title, 'Master Secretary' (II.2.68; 'Chief Secretary' at I.1.154), holder of the Seal, and Mortimer's exultant description of his dominion over the council chamber (IV.5).[55] Both these allusions mark the growing significance of the secretariat in governmental structures, which became a matter of controversy during the 1590s. Day's *The English secretorie* laid out the possibilities for rapid advancement in the office and instructed in the necessary skills, while Cecil (a controversial Chief Secretary) and lesser members of the secretariat, Robert Beale and Nicholas Faunt, wrote treatises partly designed to define and defend the office.[56] Several connect the principal secretary's power to his access to the monarch, stressing the etymological links between secrecy/secretary, advising that beyond a good university education, skill in languages and a dextrous pen, a secretary should specialise in ciphers and codes.[57] Beale advises that the secretary should keep all the monarch's secret business in a 'speciall Cabinet' with coded drawers to classify papers.[58] Strikingly, Day's phrasing imagines the secretary as a living closet of his master's arcana.[59]

Gaveston's and Mortimer's functions as secretaries articulate the anxiety that attended the role. On the one hand, we find admiration for the power and manipulativeness of secretarial skills, as in Mortimer's adroit manipulation of politics or his use of the 'secret token' (V.4.19). On the other hand, we can trace the concern of the nobles over their exclusion from royal councils and fear at the ascendancy of base-born but better educated civil servants. These are gathered together in the figure of Lightborn, the least secretarial of all figures in the play, but also what lies 'within ... [the] ... room' (V.4.17) of Mortimer's power. Even as Lightborn boasts a foreign education (he learned the use of poisons in Naples), his secret assassinations mirror the skills of the new rulers in secret writing. This closet, with its puns, unpointed sentences and unspoken motives, conceals death, while the letter images the increasing brutality of the play, where destruction hangs upon mere jots, points and tittles. The moment parallels the murderous surveil-lances in *Massacre*, embodying the monstrosity within Mortimer's power. It is literally a demonstration: a '*de-monstrum*', a showing of the horror within.[60]

The secretarial discourse of the period lends *Edward II* a particular historical resonance, echoing many of the attacks on Cecil, the Queen and her favourites. Indeed, given the frequent allusions to Elizabeth as Edward II, the parallels would have been inescap-able to an Elizabethan audience.[61] *A Declaration of the Causes* (1592) condemns Cecil as a 'traitor... far more sore and pernicious to the realme, then euer were the *Spencers*, *Peter* of *Gauestone*, or any other that abused either Prince or people', whilst the *Copy of a Letter* (1584) compared Elizabeth with Edward, making Leicester her Gaveston.[62] Hubert's *Deplorable Life and Death of Edward II* (1628), which circulated in manuscript in the latter part of Eliza-beth's reign, implicitly compared Edward's minions with the current monarch's parade of favourites.[63] Such allusions suggest *Edward II* uses the monarch's closet and the minions of a male king as a reflection upon the male favourites of a *female* monarch to voice contemporary anxieties around the Queen's secretariat.[64]

In *Edward II*, the system of closet government, the absolute dom-ination over an apparently confined area, becomes an image of the terrifying and pervasive power that reaches to 'some nook or cor-ner' (I.4.72) where the subject might wish to escape. The play also establishes a series of parallel interior spaces and closets, linking the King's closet to the confinement at Teignmouth, to the cloister, the imprisonment in the 'cave of care' at Killingworth (V.1.32) to the closet that conceals murder, to the dungeon ('the lake' [V.5.25]) where Edward dies. We move from metaphors of confinement to actual imprisonments with frightening rapidity, but the analogies between the spaces also holds historical specificity, perhaps suggesting the connection between the occluded power of the royal closet and the imprisonment of those subjected to it.

THE AESTHETICS OF THE CLOSET

The most pointed of these metaphorical-made-literal little rooms comes as Edward bewails his fate in the dungeon. He describes his grief as a 'diet [of] heart-breaking sobs' that 'almost rends the closet of my heart' (V.3.21–2), the pericardium. The closet of the heart provides a spatial metaphor for interior spaces and consciousness of inwardness. Edward implicitly imagines his heart as the closet of a body assembled from the various rooms, moving from the exterior as public chambers to the interior as the 'closet'. The use of the 'closet' in this metaphorical sense connects the actual physical closet of monarchy, the place where secrets are stored and power operated, and the 'closet of the heart', where other secrets are concealed, and which provide further resonances to Gaveston's secretarial role.

Secretaries were often regarded as friends, not simply privileged servants. Angel Day extols the 'measure ... of *Fidelitie, Trust,* or *loyal Credit* ... in which place our *Secretorie,* as you see, standeth bounden by first degree of his seruice', requiring that 'hee ought for the residue of that which to his attendance appertaineth, bee accompted a Friend.'[65] The discourse of friendship fixes the secretary between two contradictory discourses, patronage and friendship, one implying relations of parity, the other of hierarchy. The treatises tackle this in the argument that the master and servant should be close in rank so that correct decorum can be maintained, but the contradiction accentuates uncertainty over the status of these male relations behind closed doors, which generates much of the anxiety and the desire to explain and contain the closet.[66] Indeed, the infiltration of friendship points up the implicit homoeroticism of secretarial relations. The 'coniunction' and 'perfect vniting' of master and secretary in private counsel are described by Cecil as 'the mutual affections of two lovers, undiscovered to their friends': a secret bond between men.[67] The closet and the secretary were widely associated with illicit sexuality, but *Edward II* stages these relations, discovering to the audience erotic and homoerotic implications previously restricted to the literate classes.[68]

Marlowe continuously reappropriates relations and their discourses which are implicit to the social structure and reshapes them, as in the charged moment in *Edward II* when both Isabella and Gaveston claim Edward as their 'lord' (I.4.160–1), the phrase, unstably located between rank and married status, further intertwining erotic and political significances.[69] The discourses of patronage, friendship, service, secretarial duty could all be reinflected, both to uncover their implicit eroticism and also to juxtapose the erotic and the political in disturbing ways. Such double-coding, endemic to Elizabethan society, creates a fertile uncertainty which permits the construction of a politically or erotically illicit meaning, whilst shielding the author. So, allusions to Ganymede or Jove may simply demonstrate erudition or act as 'open secrets', allowing illicit ideas and discourses to shelter half-heard on the margins of the text.[70] These processes are heightened in *Edward II* by the constant allusion to the idea of the 'closet', the secretarial service, the continuous inference that secrets exist, and the repeated reference to concealed significances (hidden in imprese, ambiguous letters and secret tokens), and which are focused in Gaveston's metaphor of the boy actor, concealing his genitalia while acting as Diana surprised by Actaeon. To depict the King's progress from royal closet to cave of care, from dominion to subjection, was to open the secret and discover the process of secrecy, playing along and emphasising the very boundaries of the open secret which provided the foundation of power.

Further appropriations operate throughout Marlowe's *oeuvre* as dominant literary forms, or key cultural myths, are refashioned in new ways, a strategy that itself rewrites the Protestant 'reformation'. *Lucans First Booke* counters the traditional Virgilian imperialist view of Caesar's *coup d'état*, whilst *Dido* demythifies the Aeneas of Augustan propaganda, reading him as 'famous through the world/ For perjury and slaughter of a queen' (V.1.293–4). Each inverts traditional ideal models, central cultural symbols, providing a series of counter-readings of the canonical texts and moments of Renaissance culture. Nowhere is this clearer than in the playful reinscription of *Hero and Leander*, regarded in the Renaissance as an archetypal narrative. Coded into this key myth, in a poem filled with narratives written into the pavements and walls, inside the inset narrative of Leander's underwater tour with Neptune, nests another narrative of the shepherd and the 'boy so faire and kind' as if resting inside the cabinet in the privy chamber.[71] Each narrative layer allows the reader to open another door into another inward space, so that closeted inside this myth of heterosexual eroticism another eroticism plays.

The Chinese-box structure of *Hero and Leander* highlights the interconnection of the spatial and verbal, what I want to term the 'aesthetics of the closet', embedding textually the transactive space of the closet, literally *figuring* the 'betweenness' of closet, its transactions and relations, in the radical transformative emphasis of the writing and in the unstable metaphoricity of Marlovian writing.[72] In this period, analogies between verbal tropes and physical spaces and inset narratives as verbal closets or cabinets, were the literal commonplaces of rhetorical and mnemonic treatises, which regularly recommended the use of places, spaces and particularly rooms as devices to enable the recall of orations, their content and rhetorical figures.[73] Indeed, many Renaissance fictions associate 'plot' with spatial and rhetorical organisation.[74] Thus *The Adventures of Master F.J.* carefully charts a geography of favour in which the lover, gradually, metaphorically and literally, penetrates the terrain of the house and his mistress as, simultaneously, the reader penetrates the frame narrative structure.[75] Similarly, the temple pavement in *Hero and Leander* becomes a place within a place, where the 'sundrie shapes/ ...headdie ryots, incest, rapes' (lines 143–4) of the gods are listed and ordered, marmorealised and memorialised, just as the narrative spaces of the poem act as little rooms, each containing a different story, nested one within the other. Key rhetorical texts, such as Erasmus' 'Sileni Alcibiades', develop these analogies, with complex meanings secreted within the 'ridiculous' statue of the flute-player, the proverb itself a verbal room, revealing its own hidden meanings.[76] Erasmus regarded Christ and Scripture as quintessential Silenian forms, and the potential for hidden or inverted meanings and truths under profane or frivolous exteriors, charges all utterance: 'the reversing of values brings about a reversed use of words.'[77] Rhetoric, often pictured as an opening or revelation (in contrast to the closed fist of logic), was seen as discovery, its key techniques of etymology and allegory rooted in the uncovering of occluded significances, its Protean verbal productivity the embodiment of newly discovered meanings: infinite riches in little verbal rooms.[78]

Marlowe's frequent allusions to Proteus capture the social and verbal transformations which underpin the fascination with margins and limens throughout his work. In *Edward II* the Actaeon/stag metamorphosis emblematises human liminality (between beast and god), while the 'pliant king' (I.1.52) is manipulated, in part by the Protean figure of Gaveston, who at the end of the play translates from lover to murderer.[79] In *Hero and Leander*, amidst a broader liminality, language embodies the betweenness of the 'seaborderers' (line 3), through its very metaphoricity, the frequency and intensity of the figurations of the poem. In the temple pavement sequence the inset narrative dominates the reader's attention, and art and nature become totally confused in the profusion of figures, culminating in the description:

> o'rehead,
> A livelie vine of greene sea agget spread;
> Where by one hand, light headed *Bacchus* hoong,
> And with the other, wine from grapes out wroong.

> (137–40)

The uncertain position of the adjective 'greene' (is it sea or agate it applies to?) is extended in the 'livelie' vine. Does 'lively' mean alive or simply life-like? These possibilities are bound up in the contrast between the solidity of the agate, the liquid movement of both Bacchus and the syntax, as the materiality of the agate apparently dissolves, heavy substance becoming light and lively. The line is caught between motion and stasis, just like the closing grapes from which Bacchus 'out wroong' wine. The compressed verb and the drops of wine caught still but forever in movement again capture the complex relation between motion and immobility. Marlovian metaphor continually creates a radical undecidability for the reader, so that neither reader nor figure can rest as either literal or figurative.

This transformative capacity enacts the Erasmian copiousness in both the proliferation of figures and significations, and the 'enargeia' (vividness) that verbal plenitude produced.[80] This vividness centres upon the discovery of hidden orders and meanings, so enargeia is required

> whenever ... we do not explain a thing simply, but display it ... as if it were expressed in colour in a picture, so that it may seem that we have painted, not narrated, and that the reader has seen, not read.[81]

Description and vividness act as forms of discovery, to conjure the real through the verbal, creating a fusion of *res* and *verba* which animates the description, and 'maketh vs beeleue that our eyes doe almost witnesse the same, and that our very sences are partakers of euery delicacy in them contayned...'.[82] In *Hero and Leander* the constant detail seeks this performative quality to the writing, paralleled in Tamburlaine's 'working words', whereby each description displays poetic virtuosity, but also the encoded significances of the objects portrayed, disclosing new layers or levels of meaning.[83] Thus the vividness and verbal dexterity of the copious text produced pleasure, fixed the text in the memory, and recreated the experience for the reader, through textual liminality which traverses the boundaries of *res* and *verba*. Each of these features embeds, verbally, dramatically, figuratively the betweenness of the transactive closet, playing across the demarcations of secrecy, knowledge and subjectivity, exposing the open secret and its operations: an aesthetics of the closet.

AND 'SO NOW' TO BED: THE CLOSET STAGED

In the theatrical context the closet has other important resonances. As has been shown, Marlowe's plays are filled with closets, which are then discovered to view, private places displayed to the audience, such as Ramus's study or the bed in which Coligny is murdered.[84] Like many plays of the 1590s (especially *The Spanish Tragedy* and *Arden of Faversham*) Marlowe's texts specialise in these moments of iconic discovery: Faustus in his study (*Faustus*, Prologue, line 28, and I.1.0.1),[85] Barabas in his counting house (*Jew*, I.1.0.1–0.2),or Jupiter 'discovered ...dandling Ganymede on his knee' (*Dido*, I.1.0.1–0.2). In *Faustus* the discovery place stages the 'place of execution' (I.2.25) or conjuration, a space which then reappears to frame key moments, such as Faustus's despair (V.1),[86] literally the place of execution as the tormented magician rushes towards it to burn his books, only to be confronted by the hellmouth.[87] Both from the stage directions and from the 1616 title-page (which may reflect contemporary staging practices) the discovery clearly reveals a study or closet.[88] In the 1616 woodcut Faustus carries a book for conjuration, while on the rear wall, pierced by a small window, hangs an armillary sphere, a crucifix, three heavily clasped books on a shelf, and another unidentified mathematical instrument, impedimenta which resemble the equipment seen in other stage studies and closets of the period.[89] The detailed furnishments of the scene further enhance the parallels between moral and scenic discovery as the closet/study, site of intellectual aspiration, becomes the place of a journey to nowhere but hell, 'for where we are is hell' (II.1.124).[90]

Although the closet was staged primarily using the discovery space, the fluidity of Elizabethan stage location allowed it to extend across the platform, so in both *Edward II* and *Massacre* the royal closet fills the whole stage.[91] In *Massacre*, scene 21, the inner apartments Guise enters to be murdered, with the King in his royal cabinet hard by, recreate the succession of interconnected closets of the royal palaces, each room concealing and then revealing its contents: murder and royal power. In *Edward II* (V.4) although the discovery space initially contains Lightborn, the staging and the interaction with Mortimer both suggest the closet. This exchange between men behind closed doors, based on the secret meanings of the letter, the blurred lines of the connection between Mortimer and Lightborn, and the latter's erotic insinuations, articulates the anxieties around the closet. Such concerns would be increased if Mortimer's closet is paralleled with the 'lake' in which Edward is confined and murdered (V.5.25).[92] The discovery then effected would link bureaucracy and brutality, displaying the monstrosity of power, just as Guise dies in the 'pit' or hell of the royal closet.

The 'lake' infiltrates a final series of ironies in the spatial rhetoric of the play, connecting the closet, the dungeon, the lair of a beast and, ultimately, the grave. Throughout the last section of the play, Edward is compared with a hunted beast, describing himself as 'chased' (IV.7.22), and as a deer and a 'kingly lion' (V.1.13), a pointed reversal of the 'hunt of the passions' which underpinned the play's opening.[93] Indeed, Edward's self-dramatisations in IV.7 and V.1 both figure himself as dismembered ('rip up this panting breast of mine/And take my heart' [IV.7.66–7]), and as a self-destroying wounded lion (V.1.13–14).[94] Such imagery has a profound resonance, not only in relation to Gaveston's erotic chase, but through the associations of hunting with monarchy and manliness. Edward's end in the 'lake' (literally, an underground dungeon, but figuratively also an animal's den),[95] increases the sense of the brutalisation of the King, his final moments like a beast gone to earth in its lair, yet unable to escape.[96]

Both *Edward II* and the *Massacre* discover the relations (bureau-cratic, erotic and political) of closet government, producing terrify-ing images of the operations of power. The heart of order and rule, the monarchical closet emerges as a central site of institutionalised brutality, which is exported to the margins, the caves and dungeons of *Edward II*, but which, as both plays suggest, emanates from the centres or closets of power. The discovery thus functions as a trans-gression of the decorum which separates power and the force which maintains it, just as the theatrical opening reveals the fracturing of order and security, be it in the desecration of the arbour (in *Spanish Tragedy*), Guise's chamber, or the monarch's bedchamber in *Edward II*. The potential moment of domesticity is spectacularly violated in the final discovery of *Edward II*, where the language uneasily moves between the erotic and inward (Lightborn even calls for a feath-erbed), and the king's desires to be loved, to play the boy, are grotesquely ruptured by the parody of anal penetration.[97]

The brutality of this death is both the antithesis but also the logical conclusion of the opening image of the play: man trans-formed to beast. Most interpretations emphasise Edward as Actaeon dismembered, yet the image is even more pointed, for as Bacon commented in *De Sapienta Veterum*, the hunter embodied 'the curiosity and unhealthy appetite of man for the discovery of secrets', especially those of princes.[98] In his *Ovid's Metamorphosis Englished* Sandys gives the fable a particularly erotic twist: 'This fable was invented to show vs how dangerous a curiosity it is to search into the secrets of Princes, or by chance to discover their nakednesse.'[99] Bacon's Actaeon, less erotic more politic, encapsu-lates the dangers of secrecy:

> For whoever becomes acquainted with a prince's secrets without leave and against his will, is sure to incurr his hatred: and then, knowing that he is marked and that occasions are sought against him, he lives the life of a stag: a life full of fears and suspicions. Often too it happens that his own servants and domestics, to curry favour with the prince, accuse and overthrow him. For when the displeasure of the prince is manifest, a man shall scarcely have a servant but will betray him; and so he may expect the fate of Actaeon.[100]

Ironically, at the end of this play it is the monarch who has become the hunted deer, betrayed by his own followers, yet the image

almost suggests that, in this discovery of monarchical secrecy, the
audience invokes the fate of Actaeon in its own 'unhealthy appetite'
in enjoying the play.

Yet, most powerfully, *Edward II* discovers both the 'secrets' and
the 'nakednesse' of princes by pointing towards the ways in which
their secrecy and surveillance denies the same secrecy to their
subjects, and how the subject's desire for secrecy may collude
with dominion.[101] Edward's literal 'nakednesse' (erotic and
destructive) is paralleled by the nakedness of the subject, the
image suggesting a further revelation, as the exposure of princes
is dangerous precisely because it reveals their humanity, just as the
play strips away the robes, images and words which surround
monarchy, an outing of the foundations of power in the human
subjectivity which power would deny to its subjects. The power
of the closet – and the potency of the parallel spaces established
by Marlowe's theatre, its aesthetics of the closet – lies both in the
strangeness it discovers at the heart of early modern subjectivity
and in the estrangement it effects upon the viewer from those
images of power at the very moment of apparent discovery and
intimacy.

NOTES

1. R. Braithwait, *The English Gentlewoman* (1631), sigs G2v and H1r.
2. O. Wilde, *The Picture of Dorian Gray*, ed. I. Murray (Oxford, 1981).
3. C. Marlowe, *The Jew of Malta*, ed N.W. Bawcutt (Manchester, 1978),
    I.1.37.
4. L. 'Of the Wisdom of the Ancients: the Concept of Privacy among the
    Elite of early Modern England', in *Rethinking Social History*, ed. A.
    Wilson (Manchester, 1993), pp. 78–96, explores these issues, particu-
    larly emphasising the difficulty of obtaining privacy in this period (p.
    82). This marks a major difference in the conceptions of public and
    private space and hence secrecy in the two periods.
5. M. Garber, ' "Infinite Riches in a Little Room": Closure and Enclosure
    in Marlowe', in *Two Renaissance Mythmakers*, ed. A.B. Kernan (Balti-
    more, 1977), p. 7.
6. 'Infinite riches' may allude to verbal productivity as well as (parodi-
    cally) to depictions of the Virgin Mary as a room, almsbox or treasury.
    Barabas's linguistic dexterity transforms material to verbal wealth,
    playing on the double meaning of 'thesaurus'. See, G.K. Hunter,
    'The Theology of Marlowe's *Jew of Malta*', *Journal of the Warburg and
    Courtauld Institutes*, 27 (1964), 211–40, esp. pp. 222–6.

7.   D.A. Miller, *The Novel and the Police* (Berkeley, 1988), chapter 6, 'Secret Subjects, Open Secrets'.

8.   'Secrecy would seem to be a mode whose ultimate meaning lies in the subject's formal insistence that he is radically inaccessible to the culture that would otherwise entirely determine him': *Novel and the Police*, p. 195.

9.   *Novel and the Police*, p. 195.

10. E.K. Sedgwick, *The Epistemology of the Closet* (Harmondsworth, 1994), p. 67, and *Novel and the Police*, p. 206.

11. Compare R. Rambuss, *Spenser's Secret Career* (Cambridge, 1993), p. 21, who sees Spenser creating a 'privileged interpretive community' around the half-spoken secret.

12. A. Stewart, 'The Early Modern Closet Discovered', *Representations*, 50 (1995), 76–100. I am very grateful to Dr Stewart for allowing me to see this paper in typescript and for several conversations about the early modern closet.

13. For example, M. Signorile, *Queer in America: Sex, Media and the Closets of Power* (New York, 1993; 1994).

14. Miller comments, 'I have had to intimate my secret, if only *not to tell it*; and conversely, in theatrically continuing to keep my secret, I have already rather *given it away*' (p. 194).

15. L.B. Smith, *Treason in Tudor England: Politics and Paranoia* (1986), pp. 32–6, and *Lucan's First Booke*, line 2, in *The Complete Works of Christopher Marlowe*, ed. R. Gill (Oxford, 1987), vol. 1.

16. R. Pollitt, 'The Abduction of Doctor John Story and the Evolution of Elizabethan Intelligence Operations', *Sixteenth Century Journal*, 14 (1983), 131–56, p. 155, and C. Breight, 'Cultures of Surveillance: Marlowe in the 1950s', *Research Opportunities in Renaissance Drama*, 32 (1993), 27–43.

17. D. Cressy, 'Binding the Nation: the Bonds of Association, 1584 and 1696', in *Tudor Rule and Revolution: Essays for G.R. Elton from his American Friends*, ed. D.J. Guth and J.W. McKenna (Cambridge, 1982), pp. 217–34, and G.R. Elton, *Policy and Police: the Enforcement of the Reformation in the Age of Thomas Cromwell* (Cambridge, 1972), esp. Chapter 8, 'Police'.

18. A. Plowden, *The Elizabethan Secret Service* (Hemel Hempstead, 1991), p. 55 describes the Elizabethan intelligence service as 'pitifully small and amateurish' with a maximum of twelve full-time agents. Others involved (in various ways) include John Dee, Giordano Bruno and Antony Munday, and both Kyd and Watson had intelligence-community connections. See also, C. Nicholl, *The Reckoning* (1992).

19. Plowden, *The Elizabethan Secret Service*, pp. 54 and 105, A. Gray, 'Some Observations on Christopher Marlowe, Government Agent', *Papers of the Modern Language Association of America*, 43 (1928), 682–700, p. 690, and R. Kendall, 'Richard Baines and Christopher Marlowe's Milieu', *English Literary Renaissance*, 24 (1994), 507–52.

20. See C. Breight, 'Cultures of Surveillance', for a considered assessment of Marlowe's role (probably as a confidential messenger, or perhaps as an agent of some kind). It is quite possible he was coerced.

21. R. Strong, *Gloriana: the Portraits of Elizabeth I*, (1977), pp. 157–61, and J. Arnold, *Queen Elizabeth's Wardrobe Unlock'd* (Leeds, 1981), pp. 81–4. The serpent and armillary sphere may symbolise intelligence and prudence, the heart, counsel: see F. Yates, *Astraea: The Imperial Theme in the Sixteenth Century*, p. 217.

22. A. Freeman, 'Marlowe, Kyd and the Dutch Church Libel', *English Literary Renaissance*, 3 (1973), 44–52: p. 51 (esp. line 15). Catholic plots were particularly feared in 1592, see R.B. Wernham, *After the Armada* (1984), pp. 453–4.

23. Following the Dutch Church libel the Privy Council ordered the strict search of 'anie ... chambers, studies, chests or other like places for al manner of writings or papers' (Freeman, 'Dutch Church Libel', p. 43).

24. J. Briggs, 'Marlowe's *Massacre at Paris*: A Reconsideration', *Review of English Studies*, n.s. 34 (1983), 257–78.

25. Pulton, *De Pace Regis et Regnis* (1610) and James I, *Basilicon Doron* (1603) cited by K.E. Maus, 'Proof and Consequences: Inwardness and its Exposure in the English Renaissance', *Representations*, 34 (1991), 29–52, pp. 29 and 34. I have drawn heavily on this essay in this paragraph.

26. Pulton, *De Pace Regis*, cited in Maus, p. 34.

27. *An Exhortation Concerning Obedience*, cited in L. Smith, *Treason in Tudor England*, p. 2.

28. Marlowe, *The Massacre at Paris*, in *Dido, Queen of Carthage and The Massacre at Paris*, ed. H.J. Oliver (1968), scene 16, line 12. All references are to this edition. Passages from the MS version of scene 19 are lightly modernised from the transcription given by Oliver, and prefaced by 'MS'.

29. Briggs, '*The Massacre of Paris*: a Reconsideration', p. 265 notes Marlowe's reshaping of the sources here to locate the murder in the closet and directly after Henry's assurances of goodwill (scene 21, lines 40–7).

30. The discovery space functions as the 'royal cabinet' and following Epernoun's description of the King 'mounted in his cabinet', Henry is revealed (line 34.1, 'The Guise comes to the King'). The use of the discovery space allows Henry to comment ironically on Guise's confession.

31. Stewart, 'The Early Modern Closet Discovered', p. 81, and A.T. Friedman, *House and Household in Elizabethan England: Wollaton Hall and the Willoughby Family* (Chicago, 1989), p. 147.

32. M. Howard, *The Early Tudor House* (1987), p. 118. For the devotional closet, which later developed into two-storey chapels with an upper closet for the nobles, see M. Girouard, *Life in the English Country House* (1978), pp. 56–7.

33. Emblem books depict good housekeepers holding keys for the closet, see *The Theatre of Fine Devices*, emblem 18, cited in G. Ziegler, 'My Lady's Chamber: Female Space, Female Chastity in Shakespeare', *Textual Practice*, 4 (1990), 73–90, p. 76.

34. Girouard, *Life in the English Country House*, pp. 165–70.

35. E. Peacock, 'Inventories Made for Sir William and Sir Thomas Fairfax, Knights, of Walton, and of Gilling Castle, Yorkshire, in the Sixteenth

and Seventeenth Centuries', *Archaeologia*, 48 (1865), Pt 1, 121–56, p. 140. This is closer to the cupboard/closets at Burley on the Hill, see J. Summerson, *The Book of Architecture of Sir John Thorpe in Sir John Soane's Museum*, *Walpole Society*, 30 (1966), p. 74. In fact, closets appear to have been very various, often puzzling architectural historians, for example, the closets (warming rooms?) in the chimney places at Worksop Manor (Girouard, *Robert Smythson and Elizabethan Architecture*, p. 132).

36.   M. Girouard, 'The Smythson Collection of the Royal Institute of British Architects', *Architectural History*, 5 (1962), 21–184, pp. 42 and 111 (II/13).

37.   P. Thornton, *Seventeenth-Century Interior Decoration in England, France and Holland* (New Haven, 1978), pp. 4, 10, 52 and 296–303. The Green Closet at Ham House (a cabinet of curiosities) and Henrietta Maria's painted closet at Denmark House illustrate this trend; see Girouard, *Life in the English Country House*, p. 174, P. Thornton and M. Tomlin, *The Furnishing and Decoration of Ham House*, *The Furniture History Society* (1980), pp. 25–6, and Thornton, *Seventeenth-Century Interior Decoration*, p. 298.

38.   Pollock, ' "Living on the Stage" ', p. 82 stresses the utterly different conception of privacy articulated in the early modern era, which did not consider that the family could or should be a place of retreat from the world.

39.   A.T. Friedman, *House and Household in Elizabethan England*, p. 151, and F. Heal, *Hospitality in Early Modern England* (Oxford, 1990), pp. 29–32, 37–42 and Chapter 3, passim; see also, M. Johnson, 'Meanings and Polite Architecture', *Historical Archaeology*, 26 (1992), 45–56, and R. Coope, 'The "Long Gallery": Its origins, development, use and decoration', *Architectural History*, 29 (1986), 43–85, p. 51. I am grateful to Philip Knowles for the Johnson reference.

40.   Ziegler, 'My Lady's Chamber', pp. 73–4.

41.   Thornton, *Seventeenth-Century Interior Decoration*, p. 3.

42.   Thornton and Tomlin, *The Furnishing and Decoration of Ham House*, pp. 77–87.

43.   J. Ford, *The Broken Heart*, ed. T.J.B. Spencer (Manchester, 1980). All references are to this edition.

44.   P. Fumerton, *Cultural Aesthetics* (Chicago, 1991), Chapter 3, 'Secret Arts: Elizabethan Miniatures and Sonnets', pp. 67–110, esp. pp. 69–71.

45.   Pollock, ' "Living on the Stage of the World" ', p. 82.

46.   The dangers of introspection, Braithwait's 'tentation' in *The English Gentlewoman*, illustrate the ambivalence even of solitary closetedness.

47.   D. Starkey, 'Representation through Intimacy: A Study in the Symbolism of Monarchy and Court Office in Early Modern England', in *Symbols and Sentiments*, ed. I. Lewis (1977), pp. 187–224, and 'Intimacy and Innovation: the Rise of the Privy Chamber, 1485–1547', in *The English Court*, ed. D. Starkey (1987), pp. 71–118.

48.   H.M. Baillie, 'Etiquette and the Planning of the State Appartments in Baroque Palaces', *Archaeologia*, 101 (1967), 169–99.

49. P. Wright, 'A Change of Direction: the Ramifications of a Female Household, 1558–1603', in *the English Court*, pp. 147–72.
50. Wright, 'A Change of Direction', pp. 159–60, and S. May, *The Elizabethan Courtier Poets: The Poems and Their Context* (Columbia, Missouri, 1991), p. 13.
51. Fumerton, 'Secret Arts', p. 67.
52. All references to C. Marlowe, *Edward the Second*, ed. C.R. Forker (Manchester, 1994).
53. 'Outlandish' suggests both the fantastical nature of the dress and the outsider status of the faction that has now become the insider and dominant grouping.
54. R. Cecil, *The State and Dignity of A Secretarie's Place* (1642), sig A4r recommends 'new' men for royal service.
55. Stewart, 'The Early Modern Closet Discovered', p. 89 comments on the uncertainty over whether Gaveston is secretary to the state or to Edward. One might add it is equally uncertain which body he serves: body politic or body natural?
56. See Rambus, *Spenser's Secret Career*, esp. Chapter 3, R. Beale, 'Instructions for a Principall Secretarie' (1592), in C. Read, *Sir Francis Walsingham*, 3 vols (Oxford, 1925), vol. 1, appendix, pp. 423–43; C. Hughes, 'Nicholas Faunt's Discourse Touching the Office of Principal Secretary, &c. 1592', *English Historical Review*, 20 (1905), 499–508.
57. A. Day, *The English secretorie* (1592), sigs O1r and T3r.
58. Beale, 'Instructions', p. 428.
59. *English secretorie*, sig O1r, and Rambuss, *Spenser's Secret Career*, pp. 47–8.
60. I am grateful to Mark Burnett for this point.
61. Two other (lost) plays dealt with 'mortymore' and 'the Spencers' (*Henslowe's Diary* ed. R.A. Foakes and R.T. Rickert [Cambridge, 1961], pp. 106, 107, 205). Jonson wrote *The Fall of Mortimer* some time in the late 1590s.
62. R. Verstegan, *A Declaration of the Causes of the great troubles* (Antwerp, 1592) [STC 10005], sig E2r, and R. Parsons (?), *A Copie of a Letter Written By A Master of Arte of Cambridge* (Antwerp, 1584), sig M7r.
63. F. Hubert, *The Deplorable Life and Death of Edward the Second* (1628) [STC 13900] and *The Poems of Sir Francis Hubert*, ed. B. Mellor (Hong Kong, 1961), esp. xxi and pp. 280–9. The 1628 text, based on BL MS Harl 2393(a), is shorter than the 1629 revised edition. Six copies of this text are extant, although we know at least nine other copies circulated in the seventeenth century.
64. Interestingly, Cecil made six pages of notes about Edward II from Holinshed, now PRO SP 12/255/82.
65. *The English secretorie*, sig R1v.
66. Ibid, sigs R1v–R2r.
67. Cecil, *State and Dignity*, sig A4r and Day, *English secretorie*, sig R1. On the imagery, see Stewart, 'The Early Modern Closet', pp. 87–9, and A. Bray, 'Homosexuality and the Signs of Male Friendship in Elizabethan England', in *Queering the Renaissance*, ed. J. Goldberg (Durham, NC, 1994), pp. 40–61.

68. Stewart, 'Early Modern Closet Discovered', p. 65 cites *Euphues*. Gascoigne's *Adventures of Master F.J.* (in P. Salzman, *An Anthology of Elizabethan Prose Fiction* [Oxford, 1987]) pp. 50, 58–61, and 69 describes the bedchamber, but the closet is also associated with sexual liaison (p. 69) while the secretary is depicted as a potential sexual partner, culminating in a description of his return after a long absence so that his 'quills and pens [were] not worn so near as they were wont to be, [so he] did now prick such fair large notes that his mistress liked better to sing faburden under him than to descant any longer upon F.J.'s plainsong' (p. 62).

69. Compare *Dido*, where Jove presents Ganymede with Juno's wedding necklace.

70. Compare A. Sinfield, 'Private Lives/Private Theater: Noel Coward and the Politic of Homosexual Repression', *Representations*, 36 (1991), 43–63, p. 49.

71. *Hero and Leander*, line 679, in *The Complete Works of Christopher Marlowe*, vol. 1.

72. Stewart, 'The Early Modern Closet Discovered', pp. 89–90 notices how 'to closet' began to be associated with 'textual consultation and plotting', and with information collection, retrieval and analysis.

73. F.A. Yates, *The Art of Memory* (1966, repr. Harmondsworth, 1969, 1978), passim. The currency of the metaphor can be seen in Erasmus, *Ratio vera theologiae* where the collation of places', the comparison of lucid passages with obscure ones, is recommended; cited in T. Cave, *The Cornucopian Text: Problems of Writing in the French Renaissance* (Oxford, 1979), p. 83.

74. L. Hutson, 'Fortunate Travellers: Reading for the Plot in Sixteenth-Century England', *Representations*, 41 (1993), 83–103, p. 86. The 'plat' or 'plot' could be a précis, summary or outline, either in the verbal or visual (architectural) sense. Walsingham, for example, compiled 'A Plot for Intelligence out of Spain' (*c*.1586); see Plowden, *The Elizabethan Secret Service*, p. 110.

75. Gascoigne, *The Adventures of Master F.J.*, esp. pp. 27, 29, 30, 31, 50, 58, 66, 69, 70, 77 and 78. Gascoigne borrows from the Renaissance dialogues, such as Erasmus' *Convivium Religiosum* where the progress through the differing vistas of house and garden suggest the varying theological perspectives and arguments, a technique developed from the house and garden settings in Ciceronian dialogue, see T. Cave, '*Enargeia*: Erasmus and the Rhetoric of Presence in the Sixteenth Century', in *The French Renaissance Mind: Studies Presented to W.G. Moore*, ed. B.C. Bowen, *L'Esprit Créatur*, 16 (1976), 5–19, p. 15.

76. 'The Sileni were small images divided in half…constructed so they could be opened out…when closed they represented some ridiculous ugly flute- player…when opened they…revealed the figure of a god…': M. M. Phillips, *The 'Adages' of Erasmus: A Study With Translations* (1964), p. 269. Marlowe may have known the Erasmian Silenus directly or through Bruno's *Spaccio*: see H. Gatti, *The Renaissance Drama of Knowledge*, pp. 122–3.

77. Ibid., p. 279. 'Sileni Alcibiades' also contrasts spiritual and material wealth: 'The kingdom of heaven has as its symbol a grain of mustard seed, small and contemptible in appearance, mighty in power; and diametrically opposite to this, as I have said, is the reckoning of the world' (p. 273).

78. P. Parker, '*Othello* and *Hamlet*: Dilation, Spying and the 'Secret Place' of Woman', *Representations*, 44 (1993), 60–95, p. 64. On Proteus as verbal productivity, see *Cornucopian Text*, p. 27.

79. Gaveston and Lightborn were probably doubled; see M. Hattaway, *Elizabethan Popular Theatre* (1984), p. 144.

80. See Cave, '*Enargeia*', pp. 7–9, and *The Cornucopian Text*, pp. 18–34.

81. Erasmus, *De Copia* cited in Cave, '*Enargeia*', p. 7 (Professor Cave's translation).

82. Day, *The English secretorie* (1586), sig D3r. Cave calls the result 'word-things', see '*Enargeia*', pp. 8–9, and *The Cornucopian Text*, pp. 18–21; Day uses 'forcible vtteraunce' (sig D3r) in a similar vein..

83. *Tamburlaine the Great*, ed. J.S. Cunningham (Manchester, 1981), Part 1, II.3.25. It is possible the conflation of 'enargeia' with Aristotelian 'energia' in *De Copia* influences this idea.

84. Coligny's bed could have been staged with either a portable bed or an arras over the discovery space, see Hattaway, *Elizabethan Popular Theatre* on discovery places (pp. 27–9), A. Gurr, *The Shakespearean Stage, 1576–1642*, 3rd edition (Cambridge, 1992), pp. 149–52, and R. Hosley, 'The Discovery-Space in Shakespeare's Globe', *Shakespeare Survey*, 12 (1959), 35–46. On beds, see Hosley,'The Staging of Desdemona's Bed', *Shakespeare Quarterly*, 14 (1963), 57–65.

85. *Dr Faustus: A-and B-texts*, ed. D. Bevington and E. Rasmussen (Manchester, 1993). All citations are from the A text in this edition.

86. Hattaway, *Elizabethan Popular Theatre*, p. 180, who also argues that I.3.79–84 is accompanied by tableaux of tormented devils in the discovery space but invisible to Faustus (p. 172).

87. Hattaway, *Elizabethan Popular Theatre*, pp. 183–4. This reconstruction allows for the dismembered limbs to be seen in the discovery space after the hell-mouth has been removed.

88. Reproduced in R.A. Foakes, *Illustrations of the English Stage, 1580–1642* (1985), pp. 109–11, and discussed in *Dr Faustus*, ed. Bevington and Rasmussen, pp. 42–3.

89. For example, *The Devil's Charter* requires 'Alexander in his study with bookes, coffers, his triple Crowne upon a cushion before him' (1.4) and 'Alexander in his study beholding a Magical glasse with other observations...', see Hosley, 'Discovery Space', p. 44. Hattaway, *Elizabethan Popular Theatre*, p. 29 cites *Friar Bacon and Friar Bungay* (*c.* 1592), scene xi, as a close parallel to the *Faustus* staging. Other Globe plays utilise displayed studies, while the Red Bull could stage equally elaborate closets in *If It Be Not A Good Play The Devil Is In It* and *The Devil's Law-case*, see Gurr, *Shakespearean Stage*, p. 187.

90. This sudden appearance of the hell-mouth compares with the cauldron in *The Jew of Malta* (probably staged by Barabas giving his final speeches on a upper stage, descending to the discovery space, where

the cauldron, a symbol of hell, would be revealed). See Hattaway, *Elizabethan Popular Theatre*, p. 36, and Hunter, 'Theology', pp. 233–4.

91. In *Faustus* I.1 and *Jew* I.1, the central characters quickly leave their tableau and the unlocalised stage space becomes absorbed briefly into their closet.

92. Some critics argue this scene used a trap, but the implicit stage direction 'So now' (V.1.38) suggests Lightborn draws a traverse to reveal Edward. See Hattaway, *Elizabethan Popular Theatre*, p. 159, and G. Wickham, '*Exeunt to the Cave*: Notes on the Staging of Marlowe's Plays', *Tulane Drama Review*, 8 (1964), 184–94, p. 185.

93. OED, 'closet' (5).

94. Also 'unbowel' (V.3.10).

95. OED, 'lake', 'a pit, den of lions' from Vulgate Latin '*lacus*' (3a); also 'an underground dungeon (OED, 3b), as in *Edward II*, V.5.2, a 'vault'. Occasionally, it may also mean 'a grave'.

96. Edward may, implictly, parallel Daniel at this point 'in lacum leonum', *Daniel*, 6.16 in *Biblia Sacra Vulgata*, ed. R. Gryson (Stuttgart, 1969).

97. Smith, *Homosexual Desire*, pp. 220–1. Hattaway, *Elizabethan Popular Stage*, p. 159 points out that the discovery may have been used earlier to display Gaveston and Edward entwined. If so, this increases the horrific echoes of the discovery.

98. F. Bacon, *De Sapienta Veterum* (*Of the Wisdom of the Ancients*) in *The Works of Francis Bacon*, ed. J. Spedding, R.L. Ellis and R.D. Heath, 7 vols (1857–9), vol. 6 (1858), p. 719.

99. E. Sandys, *Ovid's Metamorphosis Englished* (1632), cited in Fumerton, *Cultural Aesthetics*, p. 158.

100. Bacon, *Of the Wisdom of the Ancients*, p. 719. Interestingly, after his fall Bacon was himself described as Actaeon in an anonymous Latin poem (PRO, SP14/120/39).

101. L.A. Montrose, 'The Elizabethan Subject and the Spenserian Text', in *Literary Theory/Renaissance Texts*, ed. P. Parker and D. Quint (Baltimore, 1986), pp. 303–40, esp. p. 328 uses the Sandys passage to argue a demystification of the images of royal power in Spenser. It is possible that Marlowe effects the same thing in this passage.

2

Shakespeare 'creepes into the womens closets about bedtime': women reading in a room of their own

Sasha Roberts

While Shakespeare's women characters have long been the subject of literary criticism, his women readers have not. This is particularly so for the late sixteenth and seventeenth centuries: the historical record provides few clues for women's reading of Shakespeare. But although surviving accounts of women reading Shakespeare in early modern England are fragmentary, they can be used to question contemporary perceptions of women as consumers in the literary marketplace. My concern here is with notions of reading and private space articulated by male commentators on women readers of Shakespeare's most frequently reprinted text before 1640, *Venus and Adonis*. The poem was arguably Shakespeare's 'best-selling' text in the late sixteenth and early seventeenth centuries: nine editions had appeared before Shakespeare's death in 1617, with a further six reprints by 1640; it was the only work by Shakespeare to be printed by a woman in the seventeenth century (Elizabeth Hodgkinson, 1675), and published in Scotland before the eighteenth century (Edinburgh, 1623).[1] Although the poem has now fallen to the margins of what has become the Shakespearean canon, *Venus and Adonis* attracted considerable contemporary commentary, providing rare descriptions both of women and men as readers of Shakespeare and of Shakespeare's status as a writer.

Seventeenth-century accounts of women reading *Venus and Adonis* are discovered in a range of texts, including drama, poetry, prose and conduct-books, concentrated in the period 1610–41; they do not offer authentic records of actual reading acts, but rather fictional and rhetorical images of readers. My interest is in the *topos* male writers articulate of private space, female sexuality and reading Shakespeare; a *topos* that assumes the act of reading is shaped by the material habitat of reading, and that points to the fraught status of women's privacy in early modern England. In theory at least, private space allowed women to place themselves beyond the surveillance of their fathers and husbands, to define their own reading acts: turning the key of their bedchamber and closet doors against others, women could fashion for themselves some measure of independence. Personal chambers with the privacy they apparently afforded, are repeatedly revealed to be highly charged sites of reading: the Shakespearean text is reported to engage not only with the bodies of women readers, but with the spaces they inhabit. I explore this interweaving of textual and material culture by outlining domestic, private reading spaces commonly available to the elite; I then turn to the concerns raised in seventeenth-century accounts of women reading *Venus and Adonis* and question the examples of two seventeenth-century women readers of Shakespeare's poem. Finally, I return to the construction of privacy within the home by examining the use of locks and keys in elite houses, and the relationship between privacy and female subjectivity.

PRIVATE READING SPACES

Acts of reading take place in different material settings, whether institutional or domestic, metropolitan or provincial, public or private. The early modern home is conventionally described as 'the private realm'; a realm set apart from the 'public' arenas of politics, paid work, education and entertainment; a realm that was the province of women.[2] But the identification of the home with 'the private' can sometimes mask the many distinctions of communal and personal, open and secret, public and private space within the elite home itself. Country houses, in particular, had to meet both public and private needs: as Francis Bacon argued in his essay 'Of Building', 'I say, you cannot have a perfect Pallace, except you have two seuerall sides...the One for Feasts and Triumphs, and the Other for Dwelling.'[3] Halls and great chambers provided families with spaces in which to meet, entertain and administer hospitality to their guests, as well as an opportunity to demonstrate outwardly their taste and status through the use of furnishings and decoration. While the size and splendour of these formal rooms increased in the late sixteenth century, private space within the home also became more diversified. One of the key developments in late sixteenth-century architecture, Alice T. Friedman points out, was 'the creation of smaller and more private rooms in domestic structures of all types'.[4] In addition to existing withdrawing and bed-chambers, parlours, studies and closets were incorporated into elite homes, while in the newly built 'prodigy' houses, such as Elizabeth Shrewsbury's Hardwick Hall, private chambers became ever more detached from service areas and large formal rooms. The increasing specialisation of space in the elite house made it a complex domain, with different thresholds of communal and personal, private and public space.

Privacy, and so private space, is historically specific. James Knowles has already pointed out different conceptions of privacy in (or applied to) early modern England (pp. 3–22): the intertwining of privacy and status; the distinction between being 'private' in chosen company and being alone; privacy as principally familial not individual; and privacy as an 'inescapably public' gesture of withdrawal. Indeed, the opportunity for early modern men or women to 'achieve' privacy within their own homes has been questioned. Patricia Fumerton has argued that 'even the most private rooms in Elizabethan houses (and certainly the royal bedchamber) were sites where privacy could never be achieved. Private rooms were essentially public, readily open to servants and visitors.'[5] Moreover, the private rooms of the Elizabethan household were reached only through a series of public chambers, an act which, according to Fumerton, 'forever deferred any final arrival at innermost privacy'. Fumerton's concern is with what this means for the construction of private subjectivity – 'the truly "private" Elizabethan self': 'the incessant segmentation and recession of rooms, "houses," service, stuff, and eating habits – all of which accelerated towards the end of the sixteenth century – record a privacy whose resident identity was forever elusive, unlocatable' (pp. 74–6 and 130). Margaret Ferguson has questioned how far women, in particular were able to construct their own subjectivity in their own rooms given the 'experience of feeling themselves expropriated by a misogynistic discursive tradition'. She cites the examples of Christine de Pizan and Virginia Woolf: although both women belong to 'that historically small and privileged group of women who have actually had a room of their own, neither can find therein a refuge from her culture's definitions of her sex'.[6]

Both Fumerton and Ferguson raise the important relationship between subjectivity and space in early modern England. But how fragile or 'forever deferred' was private, female subjectivity is a matter open to debate; my sense is that the experience of privacy among early modern elite women was more diverse than Fumerton and Ferguson allow. While we can point to general patterns of architectural development in early modern England, it should be remembered that the sheer variety of houses across different regions with different internal structures and living arrangements make it difficult to draw broad generalisations about individual experiences of private and female subjectivity. Certainly private space within the home was important – and affordable – to the elite. Thus Sir Henry Wotton, advising gentlemen on the building of 'Lodging-Chambers' in his *Elements of Architecture* (1624), took issue with the Italian fashion of casting partition walls so that 'when all Doors are open, a Man may see through the whole House', for it put 'an intolerable servitude upon all the Chambers, save the inmost'. Instead of constructing private spaces, Italian families:

> must be forced to make as many common great Rooms . . . that thereby they want other Galleries and Rooms of Retreat, which I have considered among them (I must confess) with no small Wonder; for I observe no Nation in the World by nature more private and reserved than the *Italian*, and on the other side, in no Habitations less Privacy, so as there is a kind of Conflict between their Dwelling and their Being.[7]

Wotton articulates a subtle understanding of relations between subjectivity and space, between 'Being' and 'Dwelling'. Arguing for the importance of 'Privacy', located in 'rooms of retreat', he expresses surprise at the 'servile disposing of inward Chambers' as 'common' rooms in Italy. English houses, Wotton implies, do not demand of their inhabitants the same 'kind of Conflict between their Dwelling and their Being'. The paradox of 'private experience as inescapably public' (Fumerton, p. 69) was more applicable, so Wotton seems to suggest, to the Italian context than to English homes.

For the purposes of this essay, I shall consider privacy as a controlling act – the ability to choose your own companions, or to be alone – enabled by material conditions: the creation of with-drawn, hidden, personal or secure spaces. In many country houses of the late sixteenth and seventeenth centuries, "rooms of retreat" were placed beyond communal and public rooms; the corridor, which allowed individual access to rooms and therefore greater privacy for their occupants, was not in standard use until the eighteenth century. Leading off the great chamber was the withdrawing chamber which, argues Gervase Jackson-Stops, marked 'an entrance into female territory'.[8] Used as a private sitting-room for conversation, eating, work or reading, the withdrawing chamber offered more intimacy than formal rooms: Anne Clifford, for instance, reports in her diary that at Knole her husband 'dined *abroad* in the great Chamber and supped *privately* with me in the Drawing Chamber' (my emphasis).[9] Although the bedchamber (often found beyond the withdrawing chamber) could accommodate private activities, it was not necessarily a solitary room: it could be used for conversation and light meals with friends and family, while personal man- or maid-servants who accompanied gentlemen and women in their bedchambers often slept in the room at night on a truckle bed (in 1633, for instance, the fourth Earl of Huntingdon's bedchamber at Donington Park contained both the Earl's 'blacke bedstead' and a 'truckle bed').[10] Items of furniture recorded in inventories of elite bedchambers indicate the use of the bedchamber for sitting, working, reading or writing in comfort and warmth: Lady Arabella's bedchamber at the Countess of Leicester's residence (1634), for example, included a bedstead, a little table, two chairs and three stools, a court cupboard, a carpet and tools for the fire, while the 'Queens lodgings' at the Earl of Essex's house at Wanstead (1597) were furnished with a single folding table and a chair, a cupboard made of walnut, stools and footstools, a close-stool and chamberpot, and a gilt bedstead dressed in white taffeta (an appropriate colour scheme for a Virgin Queen).[11] Inventories seem to reveal few differences in the basic furnishings of elite bedchambers belonging to men and women. The probate inventory of Essex House (1601), for instance, lists footstools, quilts, rugs and blankets in both 'my Ladies Bedchamber' and in the Earl of Essex's bedchamber; the most obvious contrast between the two rooms lay in the value of their beds – 'my Ladies' bed cost £221; the Earl's bed was valued at £300.[12]

Where houses contained a study they were furnished for reading, writing and keeping confidential papers; there might even be room for a small fireplace – the Earl of Essex's study at Essex House (1601) contained andirons and tongs for the fire, likewise Henry

Earl of Huntingdon's 'writing chamber' at York House (1596).[13] But usually the most private, and smallest, room of the elite house was the closet. Closets were usually found leading off the bedchamber, or perhaps secreted into walls and passages: among the accounts for improving York House in 1607, for instance, are payments 'to make a little closet in the passage for the Lady francis'.[14] The closet was used for storing confidential papers, treasured objects (often locked away in desks or cabinets) and valuable household items, and for working, reading and religious devotions: 'when thou prayest, enter into thy closet, and when thou hast shut thy door, pray to thy Father which is in secret' (*King James Bible*, Matt. 6:6). They were typically furnished with reading, writing and storage in mind – with books and shelves, tables and stools, cabinets and chests, and Turkish carpets for comfort. For instance, the King's closet at Knole, decorated in sumptuous green mohair, was just large enough for a chest, a single chair and table, and a small day-bed, while the Earl of Essex's green velvet closet at Wanstead contained a bed, a chair and high stool, and a folding table.[15]

Alan Stewart and James Knowles have pointed to differences in the functions between men and women's closets in the period: while the woman's closet might be used for solitary reading, religious devotions, writing, sewing and storage of precious objects and domestic goods, according to Stewart the gentleman's closet was 'not designed to function as a place of individual withdrawal, but as a secret non-public transactive space between two men behind a locked door'. Stewart highlights the contrast between the items kept in Sir William More's closet and that of his wife at Loseley Hall (1556): whereas Sir William's closet contained numerous papers, writing implements and a large selection of English, French, Italian and Latin texts, his wife's closet 'is a room stuffed with household utilities, a room where she may retire to read a rather restricted selection of books alone'. Such gender distinctions in the use of the closet were, however, subject to considerable local variation in different households. Anne Clifford, for instance, used her closet as a personal retreat after 'falling out' with her husband – as in January 1616 when she went 'to see the things in the closet and began to have Mr *Sandy's* book read to me about the Government of the Turks, my Lord sitting the most part of the day reading in his closet' – but importantly she also had access to her husband's closet and the books within it, such as on 16 April 1617 when she 'spent the evening in working and going down to my Lord's Closet where I sat and read much in the Turkish History and Chaucer' (pp. 47 and 66). While Anne Clifford's closet (and her husband's) is associated with retreat and reading in her diary, in 1634 the Countess of Leicester kept her pictures and books in her 'drawinge chamber' and apparently used her closet for storing valuables – it contained a 'truncke of plate' full of precious items including "one gould case for a booke".[16] By contrast the closet in the garret of Thomas Hanbury's house at Buriton (1611) contained a still; as distilling was usually undertaken by women it seems likely that this particular closet was associated with women's household activity and productivity.[17] At Hardwick Hall in 1601, women's closets were variously furnished for storage, for sitting and for personal hygiene: the closet within 'the gentlewomens Chamber' contained an 'Iron bounde Cofer' and two trunks; Elizabeth Shrewsbury kept 'a great Cofer, a wood Chest', two trunks and 'a little Close stoole' in her closet; while the 'Closet within the Maydes Chamber' contained 'a great Iron bounde Cofer, a wood Cofer, trunckes' and a single 'Chare covered with lether and guilt', indicating the use of the room for a woman to sit in, and perhaps retreat to, alone.[18] Peter Thornton argues that Elizabeth Shrewsbury's withdrawing chamber, which adjoined her bedchamber, 'seems to have been more in the nature of a large private closet into which she could withdraw': it was furnished for comfort (with chairs and a fire) and storage (with cupboards and chests), while desks and chairs for writing were kept in her bedchamber, and it was probably from here that she carried out her extensive correspondence.[19] The broad contrasts that we may draw in men and women's use of their closets need, then, to be qualified by the diversity of spaces and living arrangements in early modern England; at the same time, we should not automatically relegate the objects women stored in their rooms – many of which are not detailed in inventories – to a lesser status than books: personal items and souvenirs can be a powerful means of self-expression.

The thresholds of the bedchamber, closet and study doors marked important boundaries between communal and personal space within the home. These rooms, as Roger Chartier points out, allowed for considerable privacy, 'hiding what could not and should not be seen (care of the body, natural functions, the act of love) and offering a place for practices more than ever associated with isolation'.[20] It was in these rooms that books were kept and where reading in the elite home commonly took place (libraries were not a standard feature of large houses until the eighteenth century). Thus in Shakespeare's *Cymbeline*, Imogen keeps a copy of the *Metamorphoses* (the source of Shakespeare's *Venus and Adonis*) at her bedside: books were usually found in the bedchamber, argues Chartier, because it had become common to read before going to sleep (p. 140). Similarly in *Titus Andronicus*, Shakespeare adds the contemporary detail of Lavinia retiring to her 'closet' with her father to read 'sad stories' from her sister-in-law's copy of the *Metamorphoses*.[21] The closet, study and bedchamber offered men and women an intimate and comfortable reading habitat inducive to long hours of uninterrupted and intensive reading, in which they could choose their own company; personal chambers represented distinct sites of reading, differentiated from communal rooms in the home and a marked contrast from an institutional reading space such as the university library.[22] Indeed, the privacy these rooms offered was sometimes deliberately sought out by readers: in February 1668, for instance, Samuel Pepys retired to 'my chamber' to read 'the most bawdy, lewd book that ever I saw', *L'Escholles des Filles*: he deemed the book too provocative for his wife but (seeking to justify his own double-standards) claimed it 'doth me no wrong to read for information sake (but it did hazer my prick para stand all the while, and una vez to decharger); and after I had read it, I burned it, that it might not be among my books to my shame'.[23] As Robert Darnton has argued, 'the "where" of reading is more important than one might think, because placing the reader in his [*sic*] setting can provide hints about the nature of his experience'.[24] Privacy allowed for a range of reading experiences not easily afforded in public habitats – above all devotional, melancholic (see Helen Hackett, pp. 64–85) and erotic.

In what we might term the gendering of private space, women were specifically encouraged to identify their closets and bedchambers as chaste spaces. As Richard Brathwaite put it in *The English Gentlewoman* (1631), 'we may be in *security* so long as we are sequestred from *society*. Then, and never till then, begins the *infection* to be dispersed, when the sound and the sicke begin to be promiscuously mixed.' Society, Brathwaite argued, posed a threat to women's chastity: thus he reminds women that 'You are taught to *Enter your Chambers and be still. Still*, and yet *stirring* still . . . . Make then your Chamber your private Theatre, wherein you may act some devout Scene to Gods honour' (in the space of her private chamber, devotional reading and contemplation acted as a signifier not only of a woman's faith but of her chastity: 'Let [meditation] bee your *key* to open the *Morning*, your *locke* to close the *Evening*').[25] As Georgianna Ziegler has argued, the woman's room comes to signify her chaste self – an 'association of woman with *room*', which stems from 'a long patriarchal tradition in which the chaste female is metaphorically an enclosed garden, vessel, or chamber' (as Richard Brathwaite put it, 'chastity is an inclosed Garden; and by no licentious foote to be entred').[26] Ziegler points out that in early modern England women were often confined to their rooms 'or kept apart within the household...a kind of domestic enclosure created by a patriarchal feudal society, afraid both of the weakness and of the insidious power of women' (p. 74). Yet as Brathwaite acknowledges, the still chastity of the woman's chamber cannot be guaranteed, for there exists a gap between theory and practice; open and secret space; public and private; how privacy *should* be used and how it *could* be used: 'PRIVACY is the seat of *Contemplation*, though sometimes made the recluse of *Temptation*' (p. 44). What troubles him is precisely the possibilities of sexual agency that women's privacy allowed: 'Be you in your Chambers or private Closets; be you retired from the eyes of men; thinke how the eyes of God are on you. Doe not say, the walls encompasse mee, darkenesse o're-shadowes mee, the Curtaine of night secures me: These be the word of an *Adulteresse*: Therefore doe nothing *privately*, which you would not doe *publickly*' (p. 49).

Brathwaite's attack upon the impropriety of women's privacy goes beyond the adulterous liaison itself, to include books and objects – artefacts which distract a woman from her devout devotions. The preservation of chaste female space is threatened by literary texts for words, Brathwaite explains, have the power to 'corrupt the disposition; they set an edge or glosse on depraved Liberty'; in particular, '*Books* treating of light subjects are Nurseries of wantonnesse: they instruct the loose Reader to become naughty' – especially 'Stories of Love' and 'licentious poeticall histories' drawn from classical mythology and avidly read by gentlewomen.[27] Brathwaite argues in *The English Gentlewoman* that, in their reading, gentlewomen 'reduce every period of Loves discourse, to a Scene of Action; wherein they wish themselves Prime-actors': acting out 'their Fancy' by taking on for themselves the lead roles in literary texts, he characterises women's reading as a wish fulfillment (p. 131). But a woman reader wishing to enact her 'Fancy' was threatening in a society which sought to circumscribe a gentlewoman's sexual desire and expression. Significantly, Brathwaite's discussion of appropriate reading matter for women is embedded in his analysis of the proper use of privacy: 'to you, *Gentlewomen*, I direct my discourse, whose privacy may enable you, if well employed, for better things than the toyes, tyres, and trifles of this age. How many (the more our misery) bestow their *private houres* (which might be dedicated to Contemplation, or workes of piety and devotion) upon light-feather'd inventions, amorous expostulations, or minting of some unbeseeming fashions' (pp. 44–5). For Brathwaite, such 'light-feather'd inventions' are part of a wider narrative of the corruption of gentlewomen's privacy and chastity, in which one text becomes singled out for its dangerous potential: Shakespeare's *Venus and Adonis*.

WOMEN READING SHAKESPEARE IN A ROOM OF THEIR OWN

Reporting on the 'unchaste practices' of the English Nunnery at Lisbon, Thomas Robinson declined to repeat 'all the obscene bawdry which I have seen [lest] I should make the Christian Reader blush'. But he did make a note of the Father Confessor's bedtime reading: 'after supper it is usuall for him to read a little of *Venus and Adonis*, the Jests of *George Peele*, or some such scurrilous Book: for there are few idle Pamphlets printed in *England* which he hath not in the house'.[28] Robinson identifies *Venus and Adonis* as 'scurrilous' – gross and obscene – and therefore appropriate reading matter for the sexually corrupt Father Confessor. The act of reading *Venus and Adonis* is precisely located in the 'dark' privacy of the bedchamber late in the evening, after supper, hidden behind closed doors. In *The Anatomie of the English Nunnery at Lisbon* (1623), published in the same year as the commemorative First Folio, Robinson makes Shakespeare's *Venus and Adonis* emblematic not only of obscene literature, but of illicit goings-on in private chambers at night.

Venus and Adonis was accounted scurrilous for Shakespeare's representation of sexual passion, especially in the figure of Venus. The poem adapts the tale from Ovid's *Metamorphoses* of a beautiful young man who rejects the forceful advances of a woman: while Adonis seeks to hunt the boar, he is himself pursued by Venus 'like a bold-fac'd suitor' (6); he tries (at times unsuccessfully) to resist her, and finally resumes the hunt – only to be killed by the boar; as Venus grieves over Adonis' dead body, he is transformed into an anemone. Shakespeare's *Venus and Adonis* dwells upon Adonis' effeminacy and Venus' 'quick desire', describing at length the strategies of seduction she employs to satsify her 'glutton-like' sexual appetite (548). In one notorious passage Venus presents her own body as an erotic landscape ripe for sexual exploration, inviting Adonis with her 'round rising hillocks, brakes obscure and rough', 'sweet bottom grass' and 'pleasant fountains' (229–40). Taking possession of Adonis' 'rich treasure', she makes him 'her object' (255): 'he now obeys, and now no more resisteth,/While she takes all she can, not all she listeth' (563–4). Venus dominates Adonis sexually, verbally and physically: the poem enacts a role reversal with a woman taking the part of seducer, making a 'siege' upon a man's body (423) – 'Would thou wert as I am,' she laments, 'and I a man' (370).[29]

The immediate success of *Venus and Adonis* helped fuel the vogue for Ovidian narrative poetry or *epyllia* (little epics), one of the most popular poetic genres of the 1590s. While the most obvious readership of Elizabethan epyllia were the classically educated young gentlemen of Oxford, Cambridge and the Inns of Court – elite institutions to which almost all writers and dedicatees of epyllia belonged (with the notable exception of Shakepeare) – the translation of tales from the *Metamorphoses* in the form of epyllia made a body of erotic myths available to a readership uneducated in Latin; a readership that included women. Elizabethan epyllia typically present 'bold' and beautiful women anxious for sexual gratification, but their lust is rarely condemned – merely described, like their bodies, in sometimes graphic detail. While Shakespeare adds the odd moral overtone to his description of Venus ('careless lust stirs up a desperate courage, / Planting oblivion, beating reason back, / Forgetting shame's pure blush and honour's wrack', 556–8), the poem does not attempt the instruction in 'the prayse of vertues: and the shame / Of vices' that Golding claimed was necessary for reading Ovid's *Metamorphoses*.[30] Indeed, in his dedication of the poem to the third Earl of Southampton, Shakespeare disclaimed the poem as lightweight, promising Wriothesley 'some graver labour' in the future (usually assumed to be his *Lucrece*). Contemporary commentary on *Venus and Adonis* repeatedly drew attention to the poem's lascivious subject matter. 'Who list read lust there's *Venus* and *Adonis*/True modell of a most lascivious leatcher', remarked Thomas Freeman in 1614; when asked 'what's thy judgment of *William Shakespeare*' in the anonymous *Returne from Parnassus* (performed at St John's College, Cambridge, *c.* 1601–2), the press-corrector Judicio replied, 'Could but a grauer subiect him content,/Without loues foolish lazy languishment'.[31] In *The Scourge of Folly* (*c.* 1611), John Davies of Hereford classed Shakespeare as one of the 'Paper-spoylers of these Times' for his *Venus and Adonis* – 'Fine wit is shew'n therein: but finer 'twer/If not attired in such bawdy Geare' – while in his marginalia Gabriel Harvey noted that 'The younger sort take much delight in Shakespeare's Venus and Adonis; but his Lucrece, and his tragedy of Hamlet, Prince of Denmarke, have it in them to please the wiser sort.'[32] Francis Johnson has argued that the poem was actually *priced* as erotica: apparently costing over three times the normal price of fiction in 1593, the expense of a copy of *Venus and Adonis* was, he claims, 'due to the book being classified under *erotica* rather than to Shakespeare's as yet relatively unmade reputation'.[33]

Certainly the seductive possibilities and erotic enjoyment of Shakespeare's text by male readers was dramatised by contemporary playwrights. In Jervis Markham and Louis Machin's *The Dumbe Knight* (1608), for instance, two male visitors discover a gentleman's clerk in his master's bedchamber, enthusiastically reading aloud from 'maides philosophie, or *Venus* and *Adonis*': at the bawdy lines 'Graze on my lips, and when those mounts are drie,/Stray lower, where the pleasant fountaines lie', he knowingly exclaims: 'Go thy way thou best booke in the world.'[34] Shakespeare's poem was shown to be used, like Ovid's *Art of Love*, as a seduction manual by its male readers – as Hic Mulier explained in *Haec Vir* (1620), 'a Man court[s] his Mistris with the same words that Venus did *Adonis*, or as neere as the Booke could instruct him'.[35] Thus in Thomas Heywood's *Faire Maide of the Exchange* (1607), Bowdler attempts (unsuccessfully) to seduce Mall Berry with lines from the same passage enjoyed by the gentleman's clerk in *The Dumbe Knight*; Heywood assumes that his audience would be familiar enough with Shakespeare's *Venus and Adonis* to develop a comic scene featuring considerable (mis)quotation from the poem. Similarly in *The Returne from Parnassus* (*c.* 1600), the gallant Gullio quotes supposedly 'pure Shakspeare' from the opening stanzas of *Venus and Adonis* to demonstrate how he would go about seducing a woman, and claims to keep his copy of the poem in an appropriate setting for a text of seduction – in bed, 'under my pillowe'.[36]

If men are shown to seduce *with* books, women are frequently represented as being seduced *by* books. Textual and sexual experience are assumed to be intimately linked in the body of the woman reader – thus Brathwaite characterises the act of women reading 'idle' texts as one of insemination, a travesty of the immaculate conception: 'My Lady here sits and reads, wonders at the ingenuity of him [the author], (a pregnant youth doubtlesse), and will make her *pregnant* too, if shee have any moving faculty in her.'[37] Among the 'light-feather'd inventions' that Brathwaite singled out as a particular danger to female chastity was Shakespeare's poem: '*Venus* and *Adonis* are unfitting Conforts [*sic*] for a Ladies bosome,' he concluded in *The English Gentlewoman*. 'Remove them timely from you, if they ever had entertainment by you left, like the *Snake* in the fable, they annoy you' (p. 139).[38] Brathwaite metaphorically maps Shakespeare's text onto the woman reader's body: her bosom. Intimacy is the keynote here, and addressing a male readership in *The English Gentleman* (1630), Brathwaite goes into more detail about his vision of women's erotic reading experiences when lamenting 'to what height of licentious libertie are these corrupte times growne':

> When that *Sex*, where Modesty should claime a native prerogative, gives way to foments of exposed loosenesse; by not only attending to the wanton discourse of immodest Lovers, but carrying about them (even in their naked Bosomes, where chastest desires should only lodge) the amorous toyes of *Venus* and *Adonis*: which Poem, with others of like nature, they heare with such attention, peruse with such devotion, and retaine with such delectation, as no subject can equally relish their unseasoned palate, like those lighter discourses.
>
> (p. 28)

Women are fashioned here as close-readers (and hearers) – perusing, retaining and relishing the 'amorous' text of the poem with particular 'attention'. They cultivate an intimate relationship with the poem, metaphorically keeping it 'in their naked Bosomes' and literally 'carrying' the book about their persons (in practice this could well have been possible: all editions published after 1594 of *Venus and Adonis* [Q2–Q16] are light and slim octavo volumes easily 'carried about'). The intimacy that Brathwaite evokes between 'the amorous toyes of *Venus* and *Adonis*' and

the body of the woman reader is also implied (and arguably par-
odied) in Thomas Middleton's *A Mad World, my Masters* (*c.* 1605).
Newly married and obsessively jealous, Harebrain tries to prevent
the possibility of his wife commiting adultery by policing the books
she keeps in her chamber: 'I have conveyed away all her wanton
pamphlets; as *Hero and Leander, Venus and Adonis*; O, two luscious
marrow-bone pies for a young married wife!'[39] *Venus and Adonis*,
Harebrain implies, will stimulate the sexual appetite of his young
wife – hence Shakespeare's text gets characterised as food (rather as
Brathwaite depicts the act of women reading the poem as relishing
an 'unseasoned palate'). Harebrain's behaviour is lampooned in
Heywood's play, but his wife is also shown to be sexually culpable:
with the help of a prostitute, she goes on to cuckold him in her own
bedchamber.

Women readers of *Venus and Adonis* are fashioned not only
according to notions of a woman's sexual appetite (her mental
and physical receptiveness to erotic advances), but to distinctions
of private and public space within the elite home: women's reading
is shown to be both sexually and spatially inflected. Thus in
The Scourge of Folly (*c.* 1611) John Davies of Hereford regrets
that the 'fine wit' of *Venus and Adonis* was 'attired in such bawdy
Geare':

> But be it as it will: the coyest Dames,
> In private reade it for their Closset-games:
> For, sooth to say, the Lines so draw them on,
> To the venerian speculation,
> That will they, nill they (if of flesh they bee)
> They will think of it, sith *Loose* Thought is free.[40]

Like Brathwaite, Davies assumes that women read Shakespeare's
poem not with their minds but with their bodies, 'if of flesh they
bee'. But Davies' distrust of women as readers of *Venus and Adonis* is
also motivated by their reading of the poem behind closed doors –
'in private' – beyond the surveillance of their husbands. Men might
seek to restrict their wives' personal freedom but (as Middleton's *A
Mad World, my Masters* dramatises) within women's private chambers '*Loose* Thought is free'. Thus the woman's closet is imagined as
the setting for her 'venerian speculation', and women's 'Closset-
games' become a particular source of patriarchal anxiety; the room
is effectively classed as a special site of reading.

Thomas Cranley's *Amanda or the Reformed Whore* (1635), similarly locates the act of women reading *Venus and Adonis*. Amanda's prostitution is signalled by the books she keeps by her bed:

> And then a heape of bookes of thy deuotion,
> Lying upon a shelfe close underneath,
> Which thou more think'st upon than on thy death:
> They are not prayers of a grieved soule,
> That with repentance doth his sinnes condole,
> But amorous Pamphlets that best likes thine eyes,
> And Songs of love, and Sonets exquisit:
> Among these *Venus* and *Adonis* lies,
> With *Salmacis* and her Hermaphrodite:
> *Pigmalion's* there, with his transform'd delight.

(p. 32)

The 'amorous' subject matter of Ovidian narratives – Shakespeare's *Venus and Adonis*, *Salmacis and Hermaphroditus* (1602) ascribed to Beaumont, and Marston's *Metamorphosis of Pigmalion's Image* (1598), censored by the Bishop of London in 1599 – as well as their physical position 'upon a shelfe close underneath' her bed, are symbolic of Amanda's sexual depravity; her misplaced 'devotion'. A woman reading *Venus and Adonis* in bed becomes, in Cranley's narrative, a prelude to her entertaining a lover, or client, in the bedchamber. (Similarly, in 1609, the Earl of Northumberland warned his son that wives often turn 'to an Arcadia, or some love discourses, to make them able to entertain a stranger upon a hearth in a Privy Chamber'.)[41] Thus when Amanda's spiritual and sexual reformation takes place, it is marked by her reading matter and use of space: 'she did abandon every earthly pleasure,/Delighting onely in religious bookes', enclosed herself within her room and 'forth of the house she seldom times would walke,/Unlesse it were to Church, and backe againe'.

The implied connection between *Venus and Adonis*, a woman's private chamber and female seduction is further developed in a curious fantasy of young women readers, John Johnson's *The Academy of Love describing ye folly of younge men and ye fallacy of women* (1641). Johnson recounts a dream in which he found himself in 'Love's University', presided over by its Vice Chancellor, Cupid. The University teaches 'women of several ages, witts and beauties' a '*liberall arts*' degree in the *ars amandi*, 'so that those who are most prompt in this faculty of liberality, with most celeritie proceede graduates' (p. 13). Cupid's guided tour of the University takes Johnson through various public halls and lecture theatres; they drop in on a seminar where Johnson observes that the female students 'were all perfect in their syllables, both English & Latine', hinting perhaps at contemporary concerns about the appropriateness of women learning Latin and reading classical literature (p. 13). Finally, they arrive at 'Loves Library, which was very spacious, and completely filled with great variety of Bookes of all faculties, and in all kindes of Volumes'. Cupid explains to Johnson that 'our courtly Dames' study the Library's books 'onely to exect or cut off their thread-bare curtesans, and induce fresh and new furnished ones': Cupid's 'courtly' women read in order to master strategies of seduction. Various authors are represented in 'Loves Library': two Spanish poets (unidentified), Dante, Massinger, Shirley and Sir Philip Sidney (perhaps the *Arcadia*, as mentioned by the Earl of Northumberland to his son in 1609). Their texts are represented as recreational, not scholarly: 'I have ordained many hours of recreation and as many sorts of pastime', Cupid explains, 'that our Tomes may always be imployed. O what a pitifull University should I have if I permitted vacations!' (pp. 96 and 101). Johnson singles out one writer for women's recreational reading in private:

> There was also *Shakespeere*, who (as *Cupid* informed me) creepes into the womens closets about bedtime, and if it were not for some of the old out-of-date Grandames (who are set over the rest as their tutoresses) the young sparkish Girles would read *Shakespeere* day and night, so that they would open the Booke or Tome, and the men with a Fescue in their hands should point to the Verse.
>
> (p. 99)

In their closets the girls choose to read Shakespeare's 'Verse': probably a reference to *Venus and Adonis*, given that the students are learning the *ars amandi* and that 'Loves Schoole of Poetry' in Cupid's Academy is replete with figures from Ovid's *Metamorphoses*. The girls are described as 'sparkish' (easily inflamed), while Shakespeare is personified as a closet-creeper: a surrogate lover, a pimp, or perhaps a voyeur, who sneaks into young women's rooms 'about bedtime' when they are preparing for bed and perhaps undressing. In the space of the woman's closet, the Shakespearean text implicates both the author and his woman reader in erotic innuendo. Admitting the Shakespearean text into their closets is akin to admitting a man; hence the sense of scandal surrounding reading *'Shakespeere* day and night'. Indeed, the girls are accompanied in their rooms by men who point to the verse 'with a Fescue in their hands'.

In his *Dictionarie of the French and English Tongues* (1611), Randle Cotgrave defined the fescue as 'a straw, rush, little staulke, or sticke'; the *OED* notes that the fescue was commonly used as a reading aid. But objects may not always be put to their orthodox uses. Cotgrave suggests a range of alternative uses for the fescue besides reading in his *Dictionarie*: 'fetuser. To touch, or wipe over with a feskue; also, to tickle by touching with a feskue'. The multiple uses of the fescue as both a reading aid and a tickler would seem to resonate in *The Academy of Love*; rather as Brathwaite characterises idle books as 'light-*feather'd* inventions', Johnson characterises the act of reading Shakespeare's verse as a 'tickling', implicitly erotic experience. In an earlier episode we learn that a young student 'departed to a private closet, as I thought to lay up her gold, whether it was so or not I am not certaine, because the young gallant traced her forth, and tickled her too, as a man would probably imagine, because she laughed so heartily': she had just been reading to the gallant 'a few straines' of her own poetry that featured figures from the *Metamorphoses* (p. 33). Johnson implies that women's familiarity with Latin, Ovidian literature and indeed with Shakespeare's verse prefigures their sexual familiarity with other men in their private rooms. Shakespeare's verse becomes cast as a key textbook of female seduction; part of a young gentlewoman's training in the *ars amandi*.

Cupid's female students studying the *ars amandi*, like the penitent Amanda, are, of course, fictional characters; rhetorical constructs ostensibly designed to inspire moral improvement among women while providing a salutory warning for men. But Johnson and Cranley tread uneasily between condemning illicit sexuality and playing the voyeur themselves ('thy swelling brests are not display'd enough,/Pull them up higher', instructs Cranley of Amanda. In turn, *The Academy of Love* and *Amanda or the Reformed Whore* arguably offer voyeuristic pleasures to the reader – a snoop at women's private rooms and sex lives. As Helen Hackett has observed for Elizabethan romance, the narrative foregrounding of the female reader by the male writer 'may not be so much about women reading, as about male readers deriving pleasure from imagining that they are watching women reading'.[42] In addition, both Johnson and Cranley perpetuate misogynistic stereotypes of women's sexual appetites. Cranley can only envisage extremes of female depravity or piety, while Johnson frames his dream with a vehemently misogynistic opening and ending, displaying his fear and revulsion of female sexuality. The dream was inspired, he explains, by his horror of the 'greedy desire' of his mistress who with 'that insatiable appetite of Sylla making me the *cadaver* of her love to feede her helluous gorge, never ceased to crave' (p. 1). Like Shakespeare's Venus, Johnson's mistress is never sexually satisfied.

The Academy of Love and *Amanda or the Reformed Whore* hinge upon the disparities between the orthodox use of a space or object and the actual use made by women of their material worlds. The status of women as subjects in their own rooms is fraught with difficulty for Johnson, Cranley, Davies and Brathwaite (as indeed for fictional characters like Middleton's Harebrain): for them, private space enables a woman to place herself dangerously beyond her husband's surveillance. The woman's closet and bedchamber are fashioned as sites of independent and illicit acts of reading – acts that compromise a woman's chastity – and it is to the closet and bedchamber that Shakespeare's verse is shown to belong. This does not mean that seventeenth-century women were furtively reading erotic literature in their private rooms: at work here is a *topos* of private space and female sexuality focused in the figure of the woman reader – a *topos* that reveals more about the anxiety women's privacy could evoke for men than about historical acts of reading. In articulating this *topos* women are imagined as a distinct readership for Shakespeare's poem – a readership that behaved differently from men, and responded to the text in particular ways, cultivating a dangerously intimate relationship with the poem and/or its author; a readership unable to impose sexual self-restraint, especially in private. The operating assumption here is that women cannot be trusted with literature open to erotic innuendo for it merely feeds their 'venerian speculation'. As Mary Ellen Lamb has argued, 'at stake both in their reading and their sexuality is the status of women as subjects, able to think, to desire, to produce meanings in their minds and bodies'.[43] While this characterisation of women reading Shakespeare spans a thirty-year period (1611–41) it seems to heighten in the 1630s (the decade in which Brathwaite and Cranley's texts appear, followed shortly by

Johnson's in 1641). For male commentators writing a generation
earlier in the 1590s and early years of James' reign, *Venus and Adonis*
seems more significant in terms of encouraging male effeminacy
rather than female sexual depravity; by the 1630s, the target of
commentators' criticism and concern became women readers. This
perhaps suggests a shift in the perception of the notional female
sexualised reader – and the literary markets supposedly supplying
her – in the early decades of the seventeenth century: an increasing
anxiety about women readers of erotic literature towards the 1630s.
How, then, might we begin to access seventeenth-century women's
contact with *Venus and Adonis*?

The frequent reprints of *Venus and Adonis*, especially in the early
part of the seventeenth-century, together with the allusions to the
poem in contemporary drama, poetry and prose, indicate the
poem's renown; it was 'one of the most popular books of its time',
argues Harry Farr (p. 235). Brathwaite's *English Gentlewoman* and
Cranley's *Amanda*, both texts targeted at women, assume their
readers would be familiar enough with *Venus and Adonis* for them
to casually refer to the poem. Examples exist in contemporary
literature of women displaying a careful knowledge of the text,
such as the young woman who recognises 'an old passage between
Venus and Adonis' used as a seduction-piece by her suitor in John
Taylor's *Divers Crab-Tree Lectures* (1639) – while the tale may not be
true, it had to be *credible* to Taylor's readers given his claim that the
'Lectures' were based on 'real life' episodes.[44] A similar claim is
made by the figure of Hic Mulier in *Haec Vir* (1620) when she
attacks the effeminate man's theft of women's proper 'inheritance':
'[you have] rauisht from vs our speech, our actions, sports and
recreations. Goodnesse leaue mee, if I haue not heard a Man
court his Mistris with the same words that *Venus* did *Adonis*, or as
neere as the Booke could instruct him' (sig. Cf). Hic Mulier implies
she can recognise passages from *Venus and Adonis*; moreover, she
effectively incorporates Venus' words, and by extension *Venus and
Adonis*, within a community of female readers and speakers – part
of women's 'inheritance'. The 'Man-Woman' figure of Hic Mulier
and her claim to *Venus and Adonis* is layered with ironies that can be
read in many ways, but the implicit reference to women readers of
Venus and Adonis in this and other contemporary texts suggest how
pervasive Shakespeare's poem had become.

The only seventeenth-century commentary on *Venus and Adonis*
by a woman that I have found confirms this sense of the poem's

ubiquity. In her commonplace book (*c.* 1631), Lady Anne Southwell copied out her short prose defence of poetry, originally written as a letter to her friend the Lady Ridgway (a maid of honour to Elizabeth I). 'To my worthy Muse' is interesting not only as a rare piece of poetry criticism by a seventeenth-century woman, but for the texts Anne Southwell mentions. 'How falles it out (noble Ladye)', she asks, 'that you are become a sworne enemye to Poetrie'?

> I will take uppon mee to knowe, what hath soe distasted your palate against this banquett of soules, devine Poesy. Some wanton Venus or Adonis hath bene cast before your chast eares, whose euill attyre, disgracing this beautiful nimph [divine poetry], hath unworthyd her in your opinion...To heare a Hero & Leander or some such other busy nothing, might bee a meanes to skandalize this art. But can a cloud disgrace the summer?[45]

Anne Southwell expects her woman reader to share her own familiarity with *Venus and Adonis*. Although this does not necessarily mean that Southwell actually read the poem (it was not listed among her books), her comments are revealing for her characterisation of the poem as wanton and for the authority she adopts as a reader of literature. While she concurs with the view Brathwaite puts forward in *The English Gentlewoman* that women should read divine poesy and not *Venus or Adonis*, she does not let a man speak for her: she appropriates for herself the ability to discern what makes good reading, and trusts her own literary judgement (in fact, her own library of over a hundred books included works of literary 'criticism', such as the 'Aduancement of Learning by Sr. frn: Bacon in quarto').[46] Moreover, unlike Cranley, Johnson or Brathwaite, Anne Southwell's concern about the 'wanton Venus or Adonis' is not with women's ability (or lack of it) to read the poem, but with its impact upon the status of poetry *per se*. For Southwell, *Venus and Adonis* is not so much a threat to women's chastity as it is to the reputation of literature.

Lady Anne Southwell's distaste for the poem, however, does not seem to be shared by Frances Wolfreston, who openly acknowledged her ownership of the poem: the only surviving copy of the first edition of *Venus and Adonis*, Q1 of 1593, is inscribed with her name and 'hor bouk' on the title page.[47] Frances Wolfreston

(1607–77) lived for most of her life at her husband's country estate of Statfold Hall, near Tamworth (Staffordshire), where she built up a library of nearly a hundred books. We know these were Frances' books because she wrote her name in them in order, suggests Paul Morgan, 'to distinguish this loan collection from other books at Statfold' (p. 200). Her collection comprised theology, history, current affairs, medicine, Latin and French, but was dominated by English literature – including plays by Chapman, Dekker, Heywood, Marlowe, Massinger and Shirley, poetry by Donne, Drayton, Greene, Gascoigne, and no fewer than ten Shakespeare quartos.[48]

Morgan argues that Frances Wolfreston's books 'represent the leisure reading of a literate lady in her country house, not considered important enough to be bound... the "idle bookes and riffe raffes" specifically excluded by Sir Thomas Bodley from his library'. But Frances seemed to place considerable value in her books and sought to make them available to her daughters; she made special mention of them in her will, instructing that they should remain in a single collection and bequeathing them to her eldest son 'conditionally [that] if any of his brothers or sisters would have them any tyme to read, and when they have done they shall returne them to their places againe, and he shall carefully keepe them together' (cited by Morgan, p. 200). The presence of *Venus and Adonis* in Wolfreston's library reveals how the prescriptions on women's reading put forward by writers like Brathwaite and Cranley were not necessarily followed by women – indeed, Paul Morgan concludes that Wolfreston's books 'may best be regarded as revealing the reading tastes of a literate lady of the mid-seventeenth century' (p. 210). Her example points to the disparity between the fashioning of a female readership for Shakespeare's poem in fictional and rhetorical texts, and the historical realities of women reading Shakespeare. Frances Wolfreston (like Lady Anne Southwell) seems to bear little resemblance to the 'sparkish Girles' or 'coyest Dames' reading Shakespeare for their 'closset-games': a quarter of her library was made up of religious texts, and she was commemorated (predictably perhaps) as 'a provident and vertuous wife' upon the tablet erected to her memory in the family burial plot at Statfold (Morgan, p. 199). She also took an interest in both the work of 'literary criticism' (she owned a copy, for instance, of Puttenham's *Arte of English Poesie*) and contemporary debates about the nature of women: her collection included Swetnam's *The arraignment of lewd, idle, froward and unconstant women* (1645), and

I.A.'s *The good womans champion; or, A defence for the weaker vessell* (1650?), upon which Frances wrote 'in prais of wemen a good one'.[49] Her sympathetic annotation to a 'defence' of women invites us to consider how a seventeenth-century gentlewoman might come to interpret a text, or indeed approach the act of reading itself, with a strong sense of her own authority as a reader.

In turn, the different responses of Anne Southwell and Frances Wolfreston to *Venus and Adonis* are a useful reminder of how early modern women readers might bring very different interests and agendas to their reading and should not therefore be universalised as a reading group (a strategy employed by Brathwaite, Davies, Cranley and Johnson). In fact, the two women's personal libraries were very different: while nearly half of Frances Wolfreston's library was made up of contemporary fiction, Anne Southwell's library contained only a handful of literary texts (among them 'Orlando Furioso in folio', 'Spensers Fayrie Queene in folio', 'Dr Donnes Poems in Quarto' and 'The Swaggering Damsell a Comedie in quarto') and was dominated by non-fiction – theological treatises and meditations, travel narratives, tracts on current affairs, books of reference, classical texts, critical works and, intriguingly, treatises on military strategy and conduct-books for men. Gentlewomen's libraries (made up of both newly bought, loaned and inherited volumes), and their access to books (such as Anne Clifford's use of her husband's Chaucer) varied widely, pointing to a more diverse picture of women's reading in early modern England than prescriptive texts generally allow.

This raises the question of early modern women's agency in their reading. Seventeenth-century commentaries on women reading *Venus and Adonis* fashion women as independent consumers in the early modern literary marketplace (while the printing of the poem by a woman, Elizabeth Hodgkinson, in 1675 indicates the possibilities for women as producers in the early modern literary marketplace): their unwritten premise is that women make their own choices about what to read, buying or obtaining books for themselves, and reading them in their own rooms. While we cannot assume that this measure of independence was commonly enjoyed by literate women, it does suggest that there was more flexibility for women as readers and consumers of books in early modern England than is normally granted by writers of conduct-books (such as Brathwaite's *English Gentlewoman*) or rhetorical, 'reforming' narratives (such as Cranley's *Amanda*), or indeed sometimes by historians of literacy.[50] It is important to remember that women's consumption of literature in early modern England was shaped by local differences, not only at the level of the household – with different material possibilities for private reading offered by different houses and different living practices adopted by different families – but in terms of the book trade. Frances Wolfreston might have acquired her books while visiting London, but she could equally have bought them from local booksellers such as John Brooke in Coventry or Thomas Simmons in Birmingham.[51] We know that *Venus and Adonis* was sold further north than the Midlands, Frances Wolfreston's territory: the poem is listed in an inventory of 1616 for a bookseller's shop at York.[52] Regional diversity in early modern literary culture (a subject which requires further research) must have afforded women different obstacles and opportunities in the consumption of erotic literature. While rhetorical texts such as Brathwaite's *English Gentlewoman* and Cranley's *Amanda* effectively treat women readers as a group and make generalisations about their patterns of reading, the fragmentary surviving records of women readers and the early modern book trade point instead to the locality and diversity of women's reading experiences.

TURNING THE KEY: THE MATERIAL CULTURE OF PRIVACY

There are two sides to a locked door: inside and outside. The locked door that encloses a woman within her chamber can also be used to shut a man (or woman) out: to exclude. The lock and key controlled thresholds of privacy: personal space was created not only by ways of thinking, but by material artefacts.

Locks and keys assumed considerable significance during the Elizabethan period. They had long been used as a metaphor for female sexuality; in *The Academy of Love*, for instance, Johnson writes that if a man brings one of Cupid's students 'the golden key, hee unlocks their modesties closet doore, and enters as freely, as a knowne Puritane into his owne Congregation' (p. 57). The key could also be used to denote housewifely thrift – a material as well as sexual control, as an emblem from *The Theatre of Fine Devices* (1614) explains: 'the key doth note, she must have care to guide/ The goods her husba[n]d doth with pain prouide.'[53] But the lock and key were also important as symbols of power and status. By the late sixteenth century, increasingly elaborate locks with decorative casings and complicated internal mechanisms were available to the wealthy; in order to qualify as journeymen, locksmiths' apprentices had to produce 'masterpiece' locks that could take up to an astonishing three thousand hours to make.[54] Coats of arms, personal devices and classical motifs were engraved on casings, while the lock itself might incorporate an extraordinary range of anti-theft devices, including false keyholes, special buttons disguised within the design to activate the lock, coats of arms covering the real lock mechanism – even steel jaws with the power to amputate the thief's fingers, pistols aimed to fire at the thief, or devices designed to shoot a sudden blast of pepper at the unsuspecting intruder. As John Evelyn was to remark, with the 'Improvement of our *Lock-Smiths* work [we] are now come to Produce *Works* as Curious for the *Filing*, and admirable for the Dexterity in *Contriving*, as any we meet with abroad.'[55]

My concern, however, is with the *access* that a lock and key affords; the power and status of entry into particular rooms within the home. Both male and female patrons requested their locksmiths to construct unique devices so that they could ensure maximum security: as early as 1415, for instance, Isabell of Bavaria commissioned a lock which needed five keys to open it (apparently fitted to the doors of the chambers of her ladies-in-waiting to exclude unwelcome male visitors), while Henri II had three separate locks put on the door of his mistress (to deter intruders) which he could operate at one stroke with his own 'master key' (Monk, p. 16). Duplicate keys, though not unknown and frequently depicted in literature for their strategic role in discovering secrets and arranging illicit meetings, were apparently rarely used.[56] As Thomas Tusser explained in *The Points of Housewifery, United to the Comfort of Husbandry* (1580), not only do 'two keys make waste' but 'two keys to one lock in the end is a thief'. As a measure of their importance in the household, Tusser devotes four stanzas to the use of locks and keys in his text on housewifery, advising that 'a door without lock is a bait for a knave' and commanding the housewife to 'Keep keys as thy life'.[57] Without duplicate keys readily available, men and women were sometimes locked out: Anne Clifford, for instance, records that when she and her mother rode to '*Wrest*, my Lord of *Kent's*' in 1603, 'we found the doors shut and none in the house but one servant, who only had the keys of the hall, so that we were forced to lie in the hall all night, till towards morning, at which time came a man and let us into the higher rooms where we slept three or four hours' (pp. 7–8). In the interests of safekeeping, written records were made noting the whereabouts of keys: on 17 February 1615, for instance, Sir George More recorded the delivery to Francis Copp of two papers and 'a litle key, recovered from a cabanet' belonging to the Earl of Somerset, then went to the trouble of having the record witnessed by four men.[58] Household records also listed who held responsibility over which key: useful as an inventory, in emergencies, and perhaps in recriminations over lost keys. Today, such lists of the distribution of household keys can be used to map men and women's access to different rooms within the home.

Symondes' inventory of linen 'as I founde in my House at Cockesden, the laste of February, 1610, after the death of my Wife' is a case in point.[59] Linen, a valuable commodity within an elite household, was commonly kept in chests and trunks for safekeeping; Symondes made a list of who held the keys to which trunks, at the same time noting the condition of the locks and keys in his household. Symondes predictably kept all the keys to the chests in his 'studdy roome' (including 'a fayer desk with his key' and a Cyprus chest 'with a good lock and key'); he also made a note of the 'new lock and key in the dore next adjoyning my studdy, leading into the newe entry, and which William Turner made, and also in the dore a good iron boult'. But even after his wife's death, Symondes did not retain the keys to the chests in her rooms. The key to 'a Wainscott Cheast with a good lock, in the lyttle chamber within my Wifes Chamber' was 'in Frances keeping', while in the 'Garrett over my Wives Chamber' was 'a little black fosser, whereof Besse hath the key'. Symondes apparently continued to observe distinctions of gender in access to personal spaces and objects at Cockesden, keeping strict control over the items in his own study but with women taking responsibility for the chests in his wife's chambers.

Nearly 20 years later, in May 1629, the steward to the Huntingdon estates drew up a schedule of 68 doors with double-plated locks. The keys to prestigious public rooms were kept by high-ranking male servants: the steward held the keys to the great chamber, the door linking the great chamber to the withdrawing chamber, the red bedchamber (probably the prestigious guest or 'best' bedchamber), the Armory door, the chapel door, the great wardrobe, the parlour and, interestingly, the 'gentlewomans dining roome'.[60] The yeoman kept keys to the gallery, the door linking the gallery to the with-drawing chamber, 'the greate chamber dore at the staire hed' and 'the dore of the drawing chamber next my lords chamber'. One William Billaday, probably yeoman of the wardrobe, kept keys to 'my Ladies Wardrope' and 'my Lords Wardrope', while the keys to the banquetting house and 'the little garden dore against the par-ler' were held by Goodman Thorne. Women kept the keys to their personal chambers and, it seems, to the rooms immediately adja-cent to them: the ladies' maids, for instance, held the keys to 'the chamber next where the young Ladies lie', 'the staire hed dore by the young Ladies chamber' and 'the chamber where the maids lie next my Ladies chamber'. This suggests an arrangement of female space in the Huntingdon household: a suite of rooms occupied and controlled by women, to which only they had access with a single key.

The steward's list of double-plated locks reveals how access to ceremonial, public and private space was carefully demarcated within the Huntingdon household according to gender and status. Even if we cannot precisely reconstruct the spatial arrangements of early modern houses, his list is an important reminder both of the differentiations of private space *within* the elite home and of the complexity of social relationships in a large household, whereby different men and women inhabit or take control of different spaces. For gentlewomen this differentiation could allow for the establishment of their own personal space and with it some mea-sure of independence. Certainly in Lady Anne Halkett's diary, the key becomes a way of enacting *control*: when working as a lady-in-waiting to 'Lady H', for instance, Anne relates how:

> there was something of concerne I had to say to her Ladyship, and asked where I might have her alone. Shee told mee shee would come within a litle while to my chamber, where I wentt, and within a litle while shee came there, and I, taking her in my arms, kist her and wellcomed her to my chamber as a great stranger. So locking the doore, wee satte downe.... While wee were att this discourse sir Ch. knockt att the doore. Wee let him in, and hee smiling said, 'I hope you understand one another'.[61]

The women's 'discourse' concerned Sir Charles' apparent (adulter-ous) attraction to Anne and was resolved amicably, but my interest in this passage lies in what it reveals about the etiquette of personal

space in an early modern elite household. Behind the locked door
of Anne's chamber, the two women consider themselves 'alone' – in
private, and in confidence; although master of the house, Sir
Charles has to observe the privacy of the woman's locked door
and respect Anne's personal space (in fact Anne habitually secured
her privacy in the household, as she reveals in her comment that
'after dinner retiring into my chamber as I usually did, the doore
beeing locked and I alone, I was reading a sermon with which I was
very well pleased' [p. 35]).

Alice T. Friedman has persuasively argued that 'while the creation
of the country house helped to place domestic work and family life
directly under women's control, it also opened up the possibility for
an identification of women with the home and for the virtual
exclusion of women from public life' (p. 49). This sense of exclusion
is powerfully voiced by Anne Clifford in her lament while her
husband was 'abroad' in London 'I stayed in the country having
many times a sorrowful and heavy heart...so as I may truly say, I
am like an owl in the desert' (p. 28). But while it is true to say that
'woman was defined as a private rather than a public being' in early
modern England (Ferguson, p. 97), we need to remember the
different ways of being 'private' in early modern England, and
the different distinctions of privacy that were both fashioned and
secured in 'the private domain' of the home. As Jane Rendall, Karen
Offen and Ruth Roach Pierson have argued, the conceptual dualisms public/private, male/female 'contain intrinsic dangers: the first
is that of universalising a particular pattern of experience. The
second is that of essentialising, of implicitly acquiescing in the
separation of spheres in writing the history of women's worlds.'[62]
Not only did many women move beyond 'the private sphere' of the
home in their lives, but 'the private sphere' itself is a complex
domain that we should resist essentialising.

Against the context of the many restrictions imposed upon
women in early modern England, the relative independence and
control that privacy offered – made possible by material objects and
spaces; chambers and closets, chests and cabinets, locks and keys –
was surely of significance to gentlewomen, and should not be
obscured by generalised rubrics of private experience as 'inescapably' public, or 'forever deferred'. Private chambers could offer
women a degree of personal freedom, self-expression and arguably
empowerment which was unavailable to them elsewhere – even
as, in different discourses, privacy was used as an ideological tool

to marginalise women from 'public' life. Thus when Anne Halkett's mother came to punish Anne for her earlier conduct in a clandestine courtship, she did not send her to her room, but deprived Anne of her personal space and privacy: 'my chamber and liberty of lying alone [was] taken from mee, and my sister's woman was to be my guardian, who watched sufficiently so that I had nott the least opertunity either day or night to bee without her' – an instance, perhaps, of *matriarchal* domestic enclosure and surveillance (p. 16). Similarly, Mary Wroth gives voice to the 'liberty' of the woman's private chamber in *The Countesse of Montgomeries Urania* (1620): Pamphilia, for instance, 'went into her bed, but not with hope of rest, but *to get more libertie* to expresse her woe', while Bellamira explains how 'being come to my chamber, and having *liberty by privatenesse* to exercise my sorrow in the absence of all but it selfe, I thus began to mourne' (my emphasis; pp. 51 and 331). As Helen Hackett has observed, in *Urania* private chambers are the places in which women talk, read, and write – powerful and sometimes empowering sites of elite, female subjectivity in an otherwise restrictive world.[63] This should indicate the possibilities for agency that privacy could offer early modern women.

Indeed, this sense of agency is precisely what Brathwaite, Davies, Cranley and Johnson seem to fear. Their accounts of women reading *Venus and Adonis* voice an anxiety about the nature of women's independence within the home and literary marketplace. While the image they fashion of the furtive woman reader of erotic literature may be regarded as conventional rather than historically authentic, we should interrogate the appearance and prevalence of such images in particular periods; in other words, we can question literary and rhetorical conventions in terms of their historical and cultural relevance. The configuration male writers articulate of women's reading, sexuality and space point to important areas of tension in elite culture in the early part of the seventeenth century, particularly perhaps the 1630s: reading and female sexuality; the role of women as consumers in an expanding literary market; the control of private space within the home; the use women made of their privacy. Feminist criticism has often associated women's privacy with their subordination – women's exclusion from the 'public sphere'; the patriarchal 'domestic enclosure' of women – but as Helen Hackett and Lorna Hutson have observed, this axiom can obscure the subtle topographies of gender and space operating in

58 — *Sasha Roberts*

the early modern period.[64] The 'liberty by privatenesse' that women voiced, secured and protected surely indicates the importance of private space to the expression of female subjectivity – the intimate relationship between 'Dwelling' and 'Being' within the home, to use Henry Wotton's words. We do not always need to write early modern women out of their homes in order to discover their opportunities for self-expression and empowerment. Rather, it is only by addressing the complexity and diversity of domestic living arrangements that we will better understand both contemporary practices of female subjectivity and the place of books and reading in women's lives.

NOTES

1.   On the publication history of Venus an*d Adonis*, see Harry Farr, 'Notes on Shakespeare's Printers and Publishers with Special Reference to the Poems and *Hamlet'*, in *The Library*, 4th series, III:4 (March 1923): 225–60, esp. 227–47; and Shakespeare, *The Poems* (Arden Shakespeare) ed. F.T. Prince (London: Routledge, 1988), pp. xi–xx (all references to the text are to this edition).
2.   There are a growing number of studies addressing women's 'domain' in early modern England: Retha Warnicke gives a useful overview of women's private and public lives in 'Private and Public: The Boundaries of Women's Lives', in *Privileging Gender in Early Modern England*, ed. Jean R. Brink (*Sixteenth Century Essays & Studies*, vol. XXIII (1993): 123–40.
3.   *Essays* (London, 1597), ed. Michael Hawkins (London: Everyman).
4.   *House and Household: Wollaton Hall and the Willoughby Family* (London: University of Chicago Press, 1989), p. 8. On the incorporation of private rooms in early modern houses, see Girouard, *Life in the English Country House. A Social and Architectural History* (London: Yale University Press, 1978), pp. 104–8; Lawrence and Jeanne C. Fawtier Stone, *An Open Elite? England 1540–1880* (Oxford: Clarendon, 1984), pp. 340, 343–9, 354–5 and 371–8; and John Summerson, *Architecture in Britain 1530–1830* (London: Penguin, 1953), pp. 44–6.
5.   *Cultural Aesthetics: Renaissance Literature and the Practice of Social Ornament* (London and Chicago: University of Chicago Press, 1991), pp. 76–7.
6.   'A Room Not Their Own: Renaissance Women as Readers and Writers', in *The Comparative Perspective on Literature: Approaches to Theory and Practice*, ed. Clayton Koelb and Susan Noakes (London: Cornell University Press, 1988): 93–116, pp. 96–7.
7.   *The Elements of Architecture* (1624), reprinted in Roland Freart, *A Parallel of the Ancient Architecture With the Modern* (London, 1723), p. xx.

8. 'A British Parnassus: Mythology and the Country House', in *Fashioning and Functioning of the British Country House*, special issue of *Studies in the History of Art*, 25 (1989), p. 231. Withdrawing rooms were to become 'still more feminine in character', Jackson-Stops argues, in the late eighteenth and early nineteenth-centuries (p. 232).

9. *The Diary of Lady Anne Clifford 1590–1676*, ed. Vita Sackville-West (London: William Heinemann, 1923), p. 63.

10. *An Inventory of the household stuffe of the fourth Earl of Huntingdon at Donnington Park, April 1635*, Hasting Inventories Box 11: Huntington Library. On the sixteenth- and seventeenth-century bedchamber, see Girouard, *Life in the English Country House*, pp. 109–10; Summerson, *Architecture*, p. 53; Jackson-Stops, 'A British Parnassus', pp. 232–4; Friedman, *House and Household*, pp. 142 and 147; Peter Thornton, *Seventeenth Century Interior Decoration in England, France and Holland* (London: Yale University Press, 1978), pp. 293–6; and Orest Ranum, 'The Refuges of Intimacy', in *A History of the Private Life. Volume 3: Passions of the Renaissance* ed. Philippe Ariès and Georges Duby (London: Belknap Press, 1989), pp. 218–25. I discuss sexuality and the decoration of elite bedchambers in 'Lying among the Classics: Ritual and Motif in Elite Elizabethan and Jacobean Beds', in *Albion's Classicism: Visual Culture in England 1560–1660*, ed. Lucy Gent (London and New Haven: Yale University Press, 1995): 325–58.

11. 'Inventory of the Goods of the Countess of Leicester, January 1634', reprinted in James O. Halliwell, *Ancient Inventories of Furniture, Pictures, Tapestry, Plate, etc., Illustrative of the Domestic Manners of the English in the 16th and 17th Centuries* (London: privately printed, 1854), p. 1–14; 'An Inventory of household stuffe at Wanstead' (March 1597), Folger Library MS: G.b.4.

12. 'Inventory taken of all the goods and chattels of the late Earle of Essex' (1601), Folger Library MS: G.b.4.

13. 'Inventory taken of all the goods and chattels of the late Earle of Essex' (1601), Folger Library MS: G.b.4; 'Inventory of Goods of Henry Earl of Huntingdon at York' (30 June 1596), Huntington Library MS: Hastings Inventories Box 1 (1). On the use of the study see Ranum, 'Refuges of Intimacy', pp. 225–7; Thornton, *Seventeenth Century Interior Decoration*, pp. 303–4; and Friedman, *House and Household*, p. 146.

14. Arthur Maynwaringe, 'Account of Disbursements at York House since October 10th, 1607', Huntington Library MS: Ellesmere Papers, EL 185. On the closet, see Mark Girouard, *Robert Smythson and the Elizabethan Country House* (London: Yale University Press, 1983), pp. 123–4, 132 and 137; Mark Girouard, *Life in the English Country House*, pp. 47, 56, 122, 129–30, 135, 149, 152, 169–70 and 173–4; Thornton, *Seventeenth Century Interior Decoration*, pp. 290–3; Fumerton, *Cultural Aesthetics*, pp. 125 and 128; and Alan Stewart, 'The Early Modern Closet Discovered', forthcoming in *Representations* (I am grateful to Alan Stewart for showing me the article in typescript).

15. *Knole. Kent* (London: National Trust, 1991), pp. 46–7; 'Inventorie of Earl of Essex's goods at Wanstead (Essex) 1597 by Sir Michael Stanhope', Folger Library MS: G.b.4.

16. 'Inventory of the Goods of the Countess of Leicester, January 1634', reprinted in James O Halliwell, *Ancient Inventories*, p. 5.
17. 'Thomas Hanbury, Inventory of his goods and chattels at Buriton' (August 1611), Folger Library MS: X.d.65.
18. *The Hardwick Hall Inventories of 1601*, ed. Lindsay Boynton (London: The Furniture History Society, 1971), pp. 32–3.
19. 'A Short Commentary on the Hardwick Inventory of 1601', in *The Hardwick Hall Inventories of 1601*: 15–20, p. 16; see also pp. 31–2 of the Inventory.
20. 'The Practical Impact of Writing', in Philippe Ariès and Georges Bejin, eds., *A History of the Private Life*, vol. 3: 111–69, p. 163.
21. *Titus Andronicus*, IV.i.41–64, ed. Eugene M. Waith (Oxford: Oxford University Press, 1992).
22. On being 'confined to the librarie' as a form of punishment practised at Lincoln College Oxford in the early seventeenth century, see Marjorie Plant, *The English Book Trade. An Economic History of the Making and Sale of Books* (London: George Allen and Unwin, 1974), p. 41.
23. *The Diary of Samuel Pepys*, ed. Robert Latham and William Matthews (London: Bell & Sons Ltd, 1976), p. 59.
24. *The Kiss of Lamourette. Reflections in Cultural History* (London: Faber and Faber, 1990, p. 167.
25. Richard Brathwaite, *The English Gentlewoman* (London, 1631), pp. 43 and 47.
26. '"My lady's chamber": Female Space, Female Chastity in Shakespeare', in *Textual Practice*, 4.1 (Spring 1990): 73–90, p. 77; Richard Brathwaite, *The English Gentlewoman* (London, 1631), table of chapters. On women's domestic enclosure, see also Alice T. Friedman, *House and Household*, pp. 46–9.
27. *English Gentlewoman*, p. 131; *A Survey of History: Or, a Nursery for the Gentry* (London, 1638), p. 272.
28. *The Anatomie of the English Nunnery at Lisbon in Portugall* (1623; London, 1662), pp. 16–17.
29. *Venus and Adonis* has attracted little critical attention, but on its portrayal of sexual relations, see William Keach, *Elizabethan Erotic Narratives. Irony and Pathos in the Ovidian Poetry of Shakespeare, Marlowe, and their Contemporaries* (New Brunswick: Rutgers University Press, 1977), pp. 52–84; Coppélia Kahn, *Man's Estate: Masculine Identity in Shakespeare* (Berkeley: University of California Press, 1981): 21–46; Heather Dubrow, *Captive Victors. Shakespeare's Narrative Poems* (London: Cornell University Press, 1987), 15–78; and Jonathan Bate, 'Sexual Perversity in *Venus and Adonis*', in *Yearbook of English Studies*, 23 (1993): 80–92.
30. Golding, *The XV Books of Ovidius Naso* (London, 1593), sig. A.
31. Thomas Freeman, 'To Master W. Shakespeare', in *Runne, and a Great Cast. The Second Bowle*, cited in *The Shakespeare Allusion Book*, vol. I (London: Oxford University Press, 1932), p. 245; *Returne from Parnassus*, cited in *Shakespeare Allusion Book*, vol. I, p. 69.
32. John Davies, *The Scourge of Folly* (c. 1611), cited in *Shakespeare Allusion Book*, vol. I, p. 220; Gabriel Harvey, manuscript note in Speght's *Chaucer*, cited in *Shakespeare Allusion Book*, vol. I, p. 56.

33. Francis Johnson, 'Notes on English Retail Book-Prices, 1550–1640', in *The Library*, 5th series, V:2 (September 1950) 83–112: pp. 92–3. I am grateful to Peter Blayney for discussing Johnson's figures with me; he argues that comprehensive information on book prices is scarce, and it is not always clear whether a particular price quoted by Johnson is for a bound or unbound, new or second-hand copy.

34. Cited in *The Shakespeare Allusion Book*, vol. I, p. 188.

35. *Haec-Vir: or, the Womanish-Man* (London, 1620), sig.Cv.

36. Cited in *The Shakespeare Allusion Book*, vol.1, pp. 67–8.

37. *A Survey of History*, p. 272.

38. It is common in contemporary allusions to Shakespeare's work to refer to the text's leading characters rather than use a standardised notation of the text's title, as in Gabriel Harvey's remark that 'the younger sort take much delight in Shakespeare's Venus and Adonis' (see *Shakespeare Allusion Book*, vol. I, p. 56).

39. Cited in *Shakespeare Allusion Book*, vol. I, p. 189.

40. Cited in *Shakespeare Allusion Book*, vol. I, p. 220.

41. Cited by Alice T. Friedman, *House and Household*, p. 50.

42. ' "Yet tell me some such fiction": Wroth's *Urania* and the "Femininity" of Romance', in *Women, Texts and Histories 1575–1760*, ed. Clare Brant and Diane Purkiss (London: Routledge, 1992): 39–68, p. 40.

43. 'Women Readers in Mary Worth's *Urania*', in *Reading Mary Wroth: Representing Alternatives in Early Modern England*, ed. Naomi J. Miller and Gary Waller (Knoxville: University of Tennessee Press, 1991), pp. 213–14.

44. Cited in Louis B. Wright, *Middle Class Culture in Elizabethan England* (London: Methuen, 1964), p. 132.

45. Lady Anne Southwell, 'To my worthy muse', in *The Commonplace Book of Lady Anne Southwell*, Folger Library MS: V.b.198. For a transcript of the manuscript, see Jean C. Cavanagh, 'Lady Southwell's Defense of Poetry', in *ELR*, 14:3 (Autumn 1984): 281–4.

46. 'A List of my Bookes', in *The Commonplace Book of Lady Anne Southwell*, Folger Library MS: V.b.198.

47. Paul Morgan, 'Frances Wolfreston and "Hor Bouks" ', in *The Library*, 6th series, XI:3 (September 1989): 197–219, p. 200. I am grateful to Mark Thornton Burnett for bringing this article to my attention.

48. I discuss the implications of private ownership of Shakespeare's plays in quarto and a seventeenth-century woman's annotation of the First Folio for notions of textual authority in 'Reading the Shakespearean Text in Early Modern England', in *Critical Survey*, 7:3 (Winter 1995), 299–306.

49. See Morgan, pp. 211, 216 and 218.

50. David Cressy, for instance, describes gentlewomen readers as 'privileged women whose literacy was a social ornament' (*Literacy and the Social Order. Reading and Writing in Tudor and Stuart England* [Cambridge: Cambridge University Press, 1980], p. 128): this generalised description of elite women's reading fails to account for the diversity of women's reading, underestimates the significance of devotional reading for some women, and perpetuates contemporary stereotypes

of women's limited powers of reading. Lorna Weatherill concluded in her research into women's possessions for the period 1675–1725 that household inventories contradict 'the received wisdom that women were much less literate than men', for books were recorded 'in equal proportions in both men's and women's inventories'; similarly, the 'received wisdom' of gentlewomen's limited reading earlier in the period should not be accepted uncritically ('A Possession of One's Own: Women and Consumer Behavior in England, 1660–1740', *Journal of British Studies*, 25 (April 1986): 131–56). Accessing women's reading of Renaissance texts is necessarily problematic given the lack of historical records that have survived – but the field is too important to be ignored. For different approaches to Renaissance women's reading, see Mary Ellen Lamb, *Gender and Authorship in the Sidney Circle* (London: University of Wisconsin Press, 1990), pp. 7–10; idem., 'The Agency of the Split Subject: Lady Anne Clifford and the Uses of Reading', in *ELR*, 22:3 (Autumn 1992): 347–68; Naomi J. Miller and Gary Waller, 'Introduction: Reading as Re-Vision' in *Reading Mary Wroth*: 1–12; Caroline Lucas, *Writing for Women. The Example of Woman as Reader in Elizabethan Romance* (Milton Keynes: Open University Press, 1989), esp. pp. 8, 14 and 27–36; Mary Erler, 'The Books and Lives of Three Tudor Women' in *Privileging Gender in Early Modern England*, ed. Jean Brink, vol. XXIII of *Sixteenth Century Essays and Studies* (1993): 5–17; Louis B. Wright, 'The Reading of Renaissance English Women', in *Studies in Philology* 28 (1931): 139–56, pp. 147–9, 152–3 and 155; and idem., *Middle Class Culture in Elizabethan England* (London: Methuen, 1964). esp. pp. 232–35. On how we may reconstruct a history of reading, see Eugene R. Kintgen, 'Reconstructing Elizabethan Reading' in *SEL*, 30:1 (Winter 1990): 1–18; Roger Chartier, 'Laborers and Voyagers: From the Text to the Reader', in *Diacritics*, 22:2 (Summer 1992): 49–61; idem., 'Texts, Printing, Readings', in *The New Cultural History*, ed. Lynn Hunt (London: University of California Press, 1989): 154–76; Robert Darnton, 'The History of Reading', in *New Perspectives on Historical Writing*, ed. Peter Burke (University Park, PA: Penn State University Press, 1991): 140–67; and idem., *The Kiss of Lamourette. Reflections in Cultural History* (London: Faber and Faber, 1990), pp. 111–87.

51.   Morgan, pp. 208–9.
52.   John Barnard and Maureen Bell, *The Early Seventeenth-Century York Book Trade and John Foster's Inventory of 1616* (Leeds: Leeds Philosophical and Literary Society, 1994), p. 87. There are few studies of the early modern regional book trade, but see *Spreading the Word. The Distribution Networks of Print 1550–1850*, ed. Robin Myers and Michael Harris (Winchester: St Paul's Bibliographies, 1990).
53.   Cited by Ziegler, ' "My lady's chamber" ', p. 76.
54.   See Eric Monk, *Keys: Their History and Collection* (Princes Risborough: Shire Publications, 1974), esp. pp. 13, 16–17 and 22. On early modern locks and keys, see also Vincent J.M. Eras, *Locks and Keys throughout the Ages* (London; Lips' Safe and Lock Manufacturing Co., 1957); Gary Hogg, *Safe Bind, Safe Find: the Story of Locks, Bolts and Bars*

(London: Phoenix, 1961); Albert A. Hopkins, *The Lure of the Lock* (New York, 1928); *Keys and Locks in the Collection of the Cooper-Hewitt Museum* (Washington: Smithsonian Institution, 1987); and Claude Blair, 'The Most Superb of all Royal Locks', in *Apollo*, LXXXXIV (December 1966): 493–4.

55. *An Account of Architects and Architecture*, reprinted in Roland Freart, *A Parallel of the Ancient Architecture with the Modern* (London, 1723), pp. 5–6.

56. I am grateful to A. R. North of the Metalwork Department at the Victoria and Albert Museum for discussing early modern lock and key technolgy with me.

57. Reprinted in *Daughters, Wives and Widows: Writings By Men about Women and Marriage in England, 1500–1640*, ed. Joan Larsen Klein (Chicago: University of Illinois Press, 1992): 205–30, p. 225.

58. Folger Library MS: Loseley Papers, L.b.647.

59. Reprinted in James O. Halliwell, *Ancient Inventories*, pp. 59–86.

60. 'Schedule of doors with double-plated locks' (May 1629), Huntington Library MS: Ellesmere Papers, EL 6478.

61. *Memoirs of Anne, Lady Halkett and Ann, Lady Fanshawe*, ed. John Loftis (Oxford: Clarendon, 1979), pp. 42–4.

62. Jane Rendall, Karen Offen and Ruth Roach Pierson, 'Introduction' to *Writing Women's History: International Perspectives* ed. Rendall *et al.* (London: Macmillan, 1992), p. xxxiii.

63. 'Wroth's *Urania* and the femininity of romance', p. 52.

64. Helen Hackett, this volume; Lorna Hutson, *The Usurer's Daughter.*

3

'A book, and solitariness': Melancholia, Gender and Literary Subjectivity in Mary Wroth's *Urania*

Helen Hackett

Many critics of Mary Wroth's writings have found it useful to read them in terms of topographies of public and private space.[1] It seems especially obvious to do this with her 1621 prose romance, *The Countess of Montgomery's Urania*, since its hero, Amphilanthus, spends most of his time ranging abroad on quests and amorous adventures, while its heroine, Pamphilia, withdraws to her closet or to secluded groves to lament his absence. Specifically, his absence and her consequent withdrawal into private spaces produce female literary activity: in her solitude she habitually writes poetry and reads romances. Pamphilia can seem like a case study in the relationship between private architectural space and the enabling of psychological interiority and subjectivity, ideas explored from other angles in the present volume by James Knowles and Sasha Roberts.

However, seclusion can be a problem for feminist criticism if it is considered not only as an intellectual or aesthetic topography, but also as a topography of domestic politics, in which case it seems to figure women's oppressive confinement to the domestic sphere, or at best a making the best of that socially limiting positioning. Lorna Hutson has shown how a feminist interest in public and private spaces which reads in early modern culture simply an oppressive confinement of women to the home may be mapping back onto the period preoccupations which belong to the twentieth century, and thereby obscuring the precise configurations of gender ideology in the early modern period itself.[2] Another way of historicising the question, at least in relation to the *Urania*, might be by addressing it through Renaissance conventions of melancholia. The Renaissance

melancholic generally voices his or her woes in private, but in so far
as we think of any voicing as public, a bringing out of utterance,
melancholia confuses spatial boundaries.

Wroth makes it abundantly clear that Pamphilia is to be understood as a melancholic. She dresses as a melancholic and shows the
physical signs of wasting which were symptoms of melancholy:

> Dancings and all Court sports were daily in action among
> them, while she sate with much adoe beholding them, but
> her selfe none of the number, shee that before was excelling in
> her apparrell more delicate then any, and none comming
> neere her for daintinesse in that kinde, now wore only black,
> and in wearing that as carelesse, as before extreame curious, her
> hayre that was before, but with greatest care dressed, shee onely
> kept cleane, and neglectiuely wore it, no iewels came about her;
> so as she was a mourner in stead of the most sumptuous habits
> shee was wont to honour the Court withall ... what a miserable
> spectacle was this, to see her, once the comfort of the Court,
> the starre that guided all the sweet delights, now the poore
> testimony of another creature, griefe hauing so decayed her, as
> she seem'd scarce so like her selfe as an ill picture to the life,
> her chamber & her thoughts were only bound to her, or rather
> she to them, and thus did she remaine the sad example of
> forsaken loue.
>
> (*Urania 1*, Bk 3, pp. 392–4)[3]

The emblematic qualities of Wroth's writing are to the fore here:
Pamphilia's dress and demeanour are signifiers of melancholy,
making her like a portrait of melancholy as well as a poor portrait
of her earlier self. Her reading and writing are equally clearly
represented as melancholic pastimes, the fruits of her 'sad-
nesse ... and her solitary retirednesse' (*Urania 1*, Bk 1, p. 76 [num-
bered 66]), conforming with contemporary literary conventions. As
Lawrence Babb puts it in his study of melancholy, in early modern
drama '[m]elancholy men so often come upon the stage reading a
book that reading almost seems to be a conventional dramatic
symptom of melancholy'.[4] And Robert Burton says of melancholics
that 'they delight in floods and waters, desert places, to walk alone
in orchards, gardens, private walks, back lanes; averse from company.'[5] Accordingly, Pamphilia's retreats are not only to her closet,
but also very frequently to such secluded glades.

However, Burton is writing specifically of male melancholics: the examples he gives at this point are Diogenes, Timon and Democritus. The significance of this for the *Urania* is twofold. In the first place, Wroth situates her heroine not merely in her closet, in indoors enclosed spaces, but also in the chosen outdoors far-flung private spaces of the male melancholic, the pastoral spaces of woods and groves. The fact that situating a women in such a locality might have been troubling or challenging is suggested by a passage from Phillip Stubbes where he deplores the licentiousness of the women of Munidol, (that is London), as follows:

> In the Feeldes and Suburbes of the Cities, thei haue Gardens, either palled, or walled round about very high, with their Harbers, and Bowers fit for the purpose. And least thei might bee espied in these open places, they haue their Banquetting houses with Galleries, Turrettes, and what not els therin sumpteously erected: wherein thei maie (and doubtlesse doe) many of them plaie the filthie persons. And for that their Gardens are locked, some of them haue three or fower keyes a peece, whereof one they keepe for themselues, the other their Paramours haue to goe in before them, least happely they should be perceived, for then were all their sport dasht.[6]

Stubbes reprehends these practices as even worse than those of women, who show themselves at the doors of their houses and walk abroad in the city. To display oneself in the city is to be too far out of the house, but the trouble with private gardens is that they are even further outside the house while at the same time not open to view. Their combination of externality with inaccessibility renders them doubly unpoliceable, more threatening than the closet. They are appropriate private spaces for the musing male melancholic, but dangerous areas of potential licence for female seekers after autonomous space.

The second significance of Wroth's explicit representation of Pamphilia as a melancholic is that she affords her the prestigious style of melancholy generally associated with male figures in early modern culture. Historians of melancholy in the period agree that it was viewed in two opposing ways. On the one hand, the Galenic tradition of humoral medicine regarded melancholy as an illness, an excess of black bile which was debilitating and disabling. On the other hand, the Aristotelian tradition, revived by Ficino and his school of Florentine Neoplatonists, regarded melancholy as an attribute of great men, of heroes, and especially of thinkers and men of letters. Jaques in *As You Like It* exemplifies the association of melancholy with verbal giftedness. The Petrarchan figure of the love-melancholic added to this tradition: the melancholy scholar and love-melancholic shared a preference for solitude, frenetic mental activity and the production of writing. The love-melancholic voices the loss or lack of his beloved in verses: the frontispiece of Burton's *Anatomy of Melancholy* depicts several different types of the melancholic, including Inamorato, and the accompanying verses state, 'Some ditty sure he doth indite.'

Both the melancholy scholar and the love-melancholic appear in early modern culture as predominantly masculine types. Women could of course suffer from love-melancholy, but according to Burton this took a rather different form. He has a section headed 'Symptoms of Maids', Nuns', and Widows' Melancholy', a taxonomy which immediately associates female melancholy with lack of sex, placing it on a baser and more physical level than the exquisite and heroic neo-Platonic torment of the Petrarchan lover. Burton begins by describing the tremulousness, despair and solitariness of the female melancholic, which do not differ greatly from the characteristics of her male counterpart. However, he goes on to describe how when in company they may break out in fits of excessive and innappropriate merriment, suggesting a lack of control; and he continues:

> Many of them cannot tell how to express themselves in words, or how it holds them; you cannot understand them, or well tell what to make of their sayings; so far gone sometimes, so stupefied and distracted, they think themselves bewitched, they are in despair.
>
> (pt 1, sec. 3, mem. 2, subs 4, p. 416).

They suffer from various physical symptoms,

> and yet will not, cannot again tell how, where, or what offends them, though they be in great pain, agony, and frequently complain, grieving, sighing, weeping, and discontented.
>
> (ibid.)

According to this account, love-melancholy reduces women to a frenzy of inarticulateness, quite the opposite of the male love-melancholic, who can not only name his grief but puts it into verses for consolation. Burton proposes that male love-melancholics should be persuaded out of their passion by their friends; but for women,

> the best and surest remedy of all, is to see them well placed, and married to good husbands in due time; ... that's the primary cause, and this the ready cure, to give them content to their desires.
>
> (ibid., p. 417)

Their lack is unfruitful and must be closed up by containment in a conjugal union.

Wroth actually includes in the *Urania* a version of the Burtonian female melancholic in Antissia, who in the manuscript sequel to the published *Urania* (which I shall call *Urania* 2) runs mad of her unrequited love for Amphilanthus. We are informed that after Amphilanthus rejected her she retired from society and hired a poet as a tutor. Rosindy relates an encounter with her in which 'she neither sunge, nor spake, nor cried, nor laughed, butt a strange mixture of all thes together, soe discomposed as if pieces of all throwne in to a hatt, and shooke together to bee draune out' (*Urania* 2, Bk 1, f. 11r). She then appears and performs verses with her poet-tutor, which the narrator vilifies: 'schrichoules, hovling dogs, cart wheeles norr any bare tricking on friing pans could be a more detestable sound' (f. 16r). Pamphilia pities her, but is told by Antissius, 'she deserues itt nott'. He says that she is risen to

> such a heigth [*sic*] of poetry which att the best is butt a frency, and yett in Louers itt is a most commendable, and fine qualitie beeing a way most excellent to express their pretious thoughts, in a rare, and couert way.
>
> (f. 13r)

This makes it clear that the out-of-control melancholic Antissia is being included as a foil to Pamphilia: Antissia's poetry is mere raving against which Pamphilia's true high poetry and noble love can be measured. Antissia suffers from melancholy as a malady, whereas Pamphilia's melancholy is of the heroic kind more usually attributed to men.

Not only do some early modern writers like Burton accord higher status to male melancholy; twentieth-century studies of early modern literary melancholia tend to pay little attention to female melancholics.[7] Hamlet is their *locus classicus*, as he is also for Freud, who cites the character in his essay 'Mourning and Melancholia' as an example of how the melancholic can have 'a keener eye for the truth than other people who are not melancholic'.[8] Even Juliana Schiesari, who in her 1992 book, *The Gendering of Melancholia*,[9] introduces a welcome consciousness of gender into this field of study, takes the pessimistic view that the position of gifted melancholic was simply not available to early modern women. Although her purpose is revisionist, she still engages in the ritual discussion of Hamlet, and when she discusses two women writers, Gaspara Stampa and Isabella di Morra, what she finds in their writings is an utterance of their lack of an authorised voice to utter lack.

However, there are enough female melancholics in Shakespeare alone to warrant serious critical attention: Viola, Mariana, Ophelia, Olivia, to mention but a few, their melancholy variously instigated by love or by death, variously controlled or madly uncontrolled in the Burtonian fashion, sometimes even represented as heroic and enabling eloquence. There are also cases of English Renaissance women writers whose work stands in suggestive relation to conventions of melancholy; one example would be Mary Sidney, who presented much of her work as inspired and justified by her role of melancholic mourner for her lost brother.[10] Schiesari seems unaware of her and of Wroth; in a regrettably dismissive footnote she contends that 'the contribution of English women poets during the Renaissance is virtually nonexistent compared with the wealth of the literary production by women in Italy and France' (p. 238, n. 12).

I suggest that it was possible for a writer like Wroth actively to appropriate a discourse of heroic melancholy, and that this was in fact a means of negotiating the problematics of public utterance and published writing by a woman. Thus I am not arguing that gender makes no difference to Pamphilia's posture as a melancholic. I accept with Schiesari that the heroic melancholic was conventionally male, but I do not want to accept her negative position that a woman simply could not lay claim to the position of heroic and eloquent melancholic. Instead, I propose that the established association of melancholy with secrecy and privacy rendered it a legitimating mode for writing by a woman. The combination of femininity and melancholy might seem doubly to intensify constraints of privacy and secrecy; but, as I hope to show, this could be put to strategic use when privacy was announced and laid claim to in writing which was in fact published, and when forms of linguistic restraint or withdrawal were chosen rather than imposed.

This can be illustrated from *Pamphilia to Amphilanthus*, the sonnet sequence appended to the 1621 *Urania*. Like the *Urania* as a whole, the sonnets are marked by an intense self-consciousness of the impropriety of public female utterance, especially when what is uttered is desire. Pamphilia habitually addresses not the absent beloved, but abstract entities or anthropomorphised parts of nature like Love, Grief, Time, Sorrow or Night. In one sonnet, she speaks to 'You blessed shades, which give mee silent rest', and reminds them:

> How oft in you I have laine heere oprest,
> And have my miseries in woefull cries
> Deliver'd forth, mounting up to the skies
> Yett helples back returnd to wound my brest.[11]

She speaks into a void, from which her words return like a dis-embodied echo to pain her with a sense of their own futility. Privacy and introversion here seem to be just about as extreme as they can be, and give the verses almost a stifled or maimed quality. It is important to remember, though, that this is stated in a poem, and a published poem at that. I see Wroth here as announcing the extreme privacy of her own utterance as a means of pre-empting any charge of immodest self-display. The posture of the melancholic, almost the ultra-melancholic which she represents here, enables her to enact this publicising of the virtuous privacy of her own utterance.[12]

Pamphilia/Wroth's virtue as a poet of female desire is thus ensured by assertion of the absence of the male beloved, although this in turn becomes a means to claim the powers of shaping fancy of the Petrarchan love-melancholic. The male lover-poet has the imaginative power to picture his beloved, recreating her in his mind's eye, or enclosing her image in his heart and in his writing.[13] In *Pamphilia to Amphilanthus* the physical absence and indeed the lack of physical description of the male beloved render even more important the female lover-poet's visions of him:

When last I saw thee, I did nott thee see,
  Itt was thine Image, which in my thoughts lay
  Soe lively figur'd, as noe times delay
  Could suffer mee in hart to parted bee;

And sleepe soe favorable is to mee,
  As nott to lett thy lov'd remembrance stray,
  Least that I waking might have cause to say
  There was one minute found to forgett thee;

Then since my faith is such, soe kind my sleepe
  That gladly thee presents into my thought:
  And still true lover like thy face doth keepe
  Soe as some pleasure shadowe-like is wrought.[14]

Where for the male lover-poet the image of his mistress may compensate him for her resistance or for the mortal transience of her beauties, for Pamphilia her vision not only compensates her for the absence of Amphilanthus, but almost seems preferable to him in its reliability and its gestures of affection. She is at least as capable as the male lover-poet of creating an image of the beloved which meets her desires. She practises this in the *Urania* too, where, during Amphilanthus's absence, she retires to the thickest parts of a wood where 'though the sight which she desired, was hid from her, she might yet by the light of her imaginations (as in a picture) behold, and make those lights serue in his absence' (*Urania 1*, Bk 1, p. 73).

Besides such willed and controlled visions, however, the melancholic is also conventionally subject to dreams whose source and authority is less clear. Burton says of the melancholic that 'he... imagineth a thousand chimeras and visions' (pt 1, sec. 3, mem. 1, subs. 2, p. 387), and that 'they see and hear so many phantasms, chimeras, noises, visions, etc.' (pt 1, sec. 3, mem. 3, p. 424). The question, as in *Hamlet*, is what weight or truth should be attached to these apparitions: are they merely chimeras, the fantasies of a disordered brain, or are they prophecies and revelations of truths? For Burton, the visions and forebodings of female melancholics in particular are insignificant, irreligious and mad:

Some think they see visions, confer with spirits and devils, they shall surely be damned, are afraid of some treachery, imminent danger, and the like, they will not speak, make answer to any question, but are almost distracted, mad, or stupid for the time, and by fits.

(pt. 1, sec. 3, mem. 2, subs. 4).

Their condition may be 'by outward objects and perturbations aggravated, solitariness, idleness, etc.' (ibid.).

Against this, Wroth attributes to her melancholic heroine's dreams and visions the weight of profound truth. In Book 4 of *Urania 1* Pamphilia has a haunting dream,

that shee had [Amphilanthus] in her armes, discoursing with him; but hee sad, and not speaking, of a sudden rose, and went to the doore, where shee thought shee saw *Lucenia* calling to him, to whom hee went, and downe the staires with her, then tooke Coach and fled away with her.

(p. 492)

Directly after this, she has a waking vision of Amphilanthus imprisoned in a pit named the Hell of Deceit, flanked by his mistresses Lucenia and Musalina, with the latter about to use a sword to raze the name Pamphilia from his heart (p. 494). Amphilanthus in turn has a vision of Pamphilia as a corpse with his name illuminated inside her breast (p. 554). In one sense these are fantasies and illusions, but they carry the force of allegorical truth as a representation of his inconstancy, their consequent separation, and her constancy and grief. In this Book Amphilanthus will indeed leave Pamphilia for Lucenia and Musalina; her dream is a true prophecy. Wroth, then, makes use of the symbolic potential of the visionary imaginings to which melancholy can give rise.

In *Urania 2* Pamphilia experiences another prophetic dream-vision, and it marks the beginning of some distinct changes in her role as a melancholic and in the intrinsically related matters of her linguistic self-expression and her relationship with Amphilanthus. Up to this point, the lovers have formed a Petrarchan dyad, with the innovation that the female partner is the yearning, verse-writing lover while the male partner is the elusive object of desire. Although there have previously been alternative suitors for Pamphilia, such as Steriamus, they have been conveniently disposed of elsewhere, whereas now Wroth varies the dynamics of the Pamphilia–Amphilanthus pairing by introducing a more serious contender,

Rodomandro, King of Tartaria, a Moor whose eyes shine with love for Pamphilia 'like tow [*sic*] pointed diamounds sett in black foiles' (*Urania* 2, Bk 2, f. 21v). Jealousy of Rodomandro impels Amphilanthus to perform an exchange of vows with Pamphilia. Like much of their interaction – and like the *Urania* itself as a *roman à clef*, like *Pamphilia to Amphilanthus* as a collection of published professions of secret and private feeling – this ceremony occupies an ambiguous position between the public and the private, taking place in front of a select group of the couple's intimate friends. It is described as 'nott as an absolute mariage though as perfect as that', because although it is not a church ceremony it takes place before witnesses and before God (*Urania* 2, Bk. 1, f. 14v).

Shortly after this, Amphilanthus goes by invitation to the court of Candia, where, characteristically, he will eventually become the Queen's lover. Meanwhile Pamphilia goes back to her own country (also called Pamphilia), escorted by Rodomandro but 'sad enough for absence'. What follows marks a distinct turning point in the narrative, and is introduced with a powerful note of foreboding:

> thus so like a sweete, butt weeping euening after the most bright shining day remained the desolate Pamphilia, by this little shadow foreseeinge her longe time of darcker Night, which nowe grew on as the black curtains couering awhile the Seane, wherin the blacker tragidy is to be acted, and the blackest did itt proue, that euer fairest Beautie, ore sweetest fairnes could haue inflicted on.
> (*Urania* 2, Bk 1, f. 38v.)

The theatrical imagery continues a recurrent motif in Wroth's writing,[15] and, combined here with meteorological imagery, alerts the reader to expect a melancholic scene, and a cataclysmic episode. The narrator sustains this note of warning and gloom:

> Absence had wount to bee, and most times was the theame she grounded her sorrows on, butt now she must lament a sadder, and irrecouerable life, and neuer recouering him back againe as her own, butt fettered in bands harder then the Gorgon knott, to bee Cutt onely, nott to be vntied soe knotted is the fate; O poore Pamphilia the treasure of earthly beautie, the richnes of true worthe, now the woefull coffin or hearse of sadnes, and misfortune to inhabitt in, the sepulcher for Joye, and blessings

once inioyed, now buried in, making itt self the monument of itt self, sorrow, and death.

(ibid.)

While she is privately overwhelmed by this sense of impending doom, in public Pamphilia practises the secrecy and self-conceal-ment which Wroth has made integral to her role of melancholic heroine: 'All that day she thus spent, night coming she continued her wounted maner of sadnes, yett came abroad to take away all maner of suspition which might arise in the Tartarian [i.e. Rodoman-dro], her Lords, or great Counselers' (ibid.). As night falls and she retires from the court, 'then came her neerer seruants about her, sorrow, and soe sorrowfull lamenting absence'. These personifica-tions specifically recall the *Pamphilia to Amphilanthus* sonnets, where, for instance, the speaker laments that 'if with griefe I now must coupled bee/Sorrow I'le wed: Dispaire thus governs mee.'[16] As in the poems, here these abstract entities are found more consoling and reliable than the absent beloved. Earlier parts of the *Urania* are also recalled here by the fact that, in her grief, 'yett would she often correct her self' (*Urania 2*, Bk 1, f. 38v). Pamphilia has been consist-ently represented as possessing noble powers of private self-govern-ment which match her public skills of government; in *Urania 1*, during one of Amphilanthus's many absences, we were told that despite her passion and her melancholy 'yet she lost not her selfe; for her gouernment continued iust and braue, like that Lady she was, wherein she shewed her heart was not to be stirr'd, though her priuate fortunes shooke round about her' (Bk 3, p. 411). She now particularly berates herself for her melancholy at this point, imme-diately after their exchange of vows, when she ought to feel most certain of and happy in Amphilanthus's affection. However, her foreboding becomes self-sustaining: 'I must grieue fearing this is profettick to mee to feare in time of assurance' (*Urania 2*, Bk 1, f. 38v).

Thus this moment is marked as the lowest point yet in Pamphi-lia's melancholic history. Consequently, she turns to death as the only adequate remedy:

and soe dy wrech, and brauely in constant dying, bee Victorious ouer Fates, misfortunes, and death, filling the empty sayles of fame with the Constante, swiet, latest breath of purest, chastest, imaculate loue, and soe eternise thy loue in fames highest throne.

(ibid.)

But death does not come; instead, bathetically, 'After a tediousnes of stormes in sadnes', she falls asleep. In her death-wish, introversion has turned to self-annihilation, and an extreme negativity of self has been asserted as heroism, drawing on the discourse of martyrdom. At the same time, though, this is shown as ineffectual and merely rhetorical. Although up to this point Pamphilia's melancholy has empowered her linguistically and thereby enabled self-definition, she now appears to strike a limit to what language can do. Here language is used to wish for an end to selfhood, for a climactic heroic moment after which the rest is silence; but it doesn't happen. Language, especially the language of the melancholic, can define subjectivity as it does for Pamphilia, but it can also have an excessiveness, a redundancy, which is highlighted here.

Pamphilia does not, as she did in earlier introspective scenes of privacy and solitude, write out a poem or take out a poem or a book to read;[17] instead, she undergoes a visionary revelation. The sleep into which she relapses lays to rest her body but not her 'spiritt', and

> in her sleepeless vision I can nott say butt a true, though sorowfull obiect apeer'd, ore better to say her Genius showed her Amphilanthus in a strange Country, amongst a strange fashioned people, honered as hee deserued, and serued by them, in an vnvsuall way, great triumphs, butt hee sad, and leading forthe[18] all in black to bee maried, the whole assembly all in glorious habitts, and triumphant maner, and that as she amasedly stood gazing on them, hee sadly sayd to her, Once my onely Ioye, now my Soules onely torture, Farewell; This was a sorrow, this a hart searing affliction.
>
> (*Urania* 2, Bk 1, ff. 38v–39r)

Pamphilia, as we have seen, has already decided that her grief is prophetic. The next day, however, when she confides in her friend Veralinda regarding her fears of Amphilanthus's inconstancy, Veralinda tells her reassuringly that 'dreames often goe by contraries, and oftner then by truthes' (ibid., f. 40r). Yet this advice in itself creates an uncanny sense of prophecy and fatedness, since Pamphilia in fact hasn't yet told Veralinda of her troubling dream: she remarks, 'Indeed you are an excellent gesser...', for I did butt dreame itt.' And despite this implication that the apparition was 'butt' or *merely* a dream, Pamphilia argues with Veralinda's consolation, protesting that she cannot get the vision out of her head and cannot discount it. In fact, like her earlier dream of Amphilanthus and Lucenia in *Urania 1*, Book 4, it does turn out to be true: later, the Queen of Candia, having tired of Amphilanthus as a lover, plots with his old tutor to persuade him that Pamphilia has married someone else in his absence, such that in his distress he acquiesces in an arranged marriage to the daughter of the King of Slavonia. Pamphilia's dream is, therefore, deeply significant and veracious, not the raving or fantasy of a madwoman, but evidence of heightened prophetic insight, confirming her suspicions, much as Hamlet's vision of his father's ghost causes him to cry out 'O my prophetic soul!'.[19]

This dream marks a significant shift in the co-ordinates of the relationship between Amphilanthus and Pamphilia. Immediately after he has fulfilled Pamphilia's dream by taking part in his actual wedding, Amphilanthus is racked with guilt, and it is his turn to retire to a solitary bed and be tormented by dreams. He sees Pamphilia chastising him, and again, this vision has the force of truth: she is brought 'into his memory, nay into his sight with soe sterne, and furious lookes' (*Urania* 2, Bk 1, f. 50r). After this, Pamphilia increasingly becomes the unattainable one. Previously, Amphilanthus had wandered on adventures while she was left at home to contend with her desires and griefs; now, his conclusive division of himself from her by his marriage forces him to strive for restoration to her favour and even her presence. Amphilanthus had previously indulged in moments of melancholic contemplation, but as he is placed in the position of unrequited yearning, so too his scenes of melancholic behaviour become more frequent and intense. Moreover, where Pamphilia had always been represented as self-controlled in her melancholy, and was able to console her self by treasuring her own constancy, Amphilanthus is frenzied in his despair and tormented by his own blameworthiness. When he attempts to throw himself overboard from a ship on which he is travelling, his female companions deprecate 'his rashnes, that hee who gouerned the world, ore the best part of itt [he is the Emperor], was soe weake in him self...that hee could not ouermaster his passion' (*Urania* 2, Bk 1, f. 61v). He castigates himself for his inconstancy: 'O for euer hated change, O for euer detested change, of all earthly ills, the wurst' (ibid., f. 65r).

Pamphilia and Amphilanthus do not meet again until after a long period of separation. When they do so, there is a marked diference from their earlier encounters. In *Urania 1*, Book 4, at a moment of reunion just before the episode of the Hell of Deceit, Amphilanthus had conducted himself as follows:

> *Amphilanthus* Master of the greatest part of the Westerne World, and once as he assured him selfe, Monarch of [Pamphilia's] heart before shee knew *Asia*, or much more, or scarce so much as her selfe, much lesse her power ouer him, would like a confident man, and commanding louer, neuer shewing as if an account were to be had from him for former faults, vse the time, and take the opportunity offer'd him.
>
> (Urania 1, Book 4, pp. 481–2 [numbered 471])

He passionately embraced Pamphilia, who did not resist – the language and imagery was of swooning and drowning – but the reader may have detected some doubt as to whether Amphilanthus, though irresistible, might not also be arrogant and unworthy.

The reunion in *Urania 2* after his marriage is quite different. Both he and Pamphilia are on journeys, and their boats happen to put in at the same harbour. Tension is built up through their mingled suspicion and doubt of each other's identity, and through an incre-- mental reading of physical signs. Thus, on several different levels, there is a sense of barriers to be overcome.

> Amphilanthus sawe ore hoped hee sawe Pamphilia, she feard, yett would nott bee ouer much troubled if itt wer as she thought Amphilanthus, hee kept his beauer close, and his new shield, and deuise changed, did the better couer him, hee charging his little company to hold him secrett[;] in the other boat was more company, butt all of their owne knowledg, they saluted each other.
>
> (Urania 2, Bk 2, f. 2r)

The fact that the parties accompanying each of the lovers know, recognise and greet each other sets up a contrast with the uncertainty, silence and delay of the central protagonists. Next,

> the Emperour helpt his deerest lady ashoar, though trembling as if hee had bin in the water, and new come out to shake of such vnfreindly coldenesses, she tooke his help, butt trembling to, her

infinite passions beeing such and soe full as she feard the breaking of them, to kindnes she must nott afforde them though his
seruice att that time was deseruing, and timely, yett kindnes must
nott bee, nor appere from her to him.

(ibid.)

The first contact between them is thus in the form of a mutual
trembling, a frisson passed between them, creating a sense of
partial but still obstructed communication. The combination of
mutual desire with self-repression also sets up an intense erotic
charge.

The barriers of doubtful identity and of obscuring items of
armour and clothing are meticulously dismantled through gestures
of partial disrobing, tantalising semi-disclosure and tender physical
contact, sustaining this erotic tension:

hee longed, butt durst nott aduentur to bee certaine itt was she,
his hart, not daring though assuredly hoping itt was she, till she
pulled off her gloue to lift vp a great Vaile she had on, which
beeing thick kept her close and hott.

(ibid.)

Amphilanthus is the first to speak 'with a trembling voice'; he
professes his pleasure in serving the supposedly unknown lady
and asks if he can do any further service.

I pray Sir sayd she, if itt bee nott to vnseemly an office for a
knight to help the dressing of a lady to assiste mee in taking of
this vaile, Madame sayd hee if all vailes were taken away, and
truthe only knowne then should my best blessings shine, soe
pulling off his gantletts, hee soe tenderly, and gently pulled of
her vaile as if hee had bin bred in a lady's chamber, his hande
bare, she was soone assured who itt was, for though the strongest and bravest man breathing, yett hee had hands of that
delicasie for pure whitenes, delicate shape, and softnes, as noe
lady could compare with them.

(ibid.)

Not unlike the passion of an eighteenth-century heroine or indeed
a heroine of twentieth-century romantic fiction, Pamphilia's excessive emotion is expressed physically as a blush: 'she blusht and

looked vpon him with teares in her eyes, and then lookt downe
againe.'

However, it is not our heroine who subsides in a swoon in this
scene, but Amphilanthus:

> hee parceauing this, and finding his fault now more then euer,
> soe as beeing ouerpast with shame, and passion hee sunck to the
> grownde, his healme close she feared might hurt him, who yett
> she could nott butt bee kinde to, quickly vnlaced his healme.
>
> (ibid.)

Pulling off the helmet, Pamphilia sees that his face is pale and he
has fainted. She sends some of their companions for water, and
meanwhile

> washt his face with her teares, teares which were of that efficacie,
> and power as hee beegann to stir, and as she stroaked his pale
> face, and closed eyes which when open were once her cleerest
> skies, hee opend them, weakely looking vp, and taking her hand
> kissed it, speake he was about, butt then fainted againe, she then
> more bold tooke him in her armes layd his head with their help
> who were come with the water in her lap, and then with con-
> tinuall rubbing him, and louingly breathing on him, hee came to
> him self.
>
> (ibid.)

For a while he gazes on her, but cannot speak for passion, and she
covers his eyes with her hand. Where his eyes were once her skies,
now she bends over him, and her tears take on a quality beyond
mere bodily effusion to become almost a medium of divine grace.
One of the many striking features of this highly charged encounter is the failure of speech: emotion is manifested not through
utterance, but through the disabling of utterance, and its supplan-
tation by gesture. In turn, minute gestures carry intense force. To
commit another shameless anachronism, it is tempting to describe
this as a Jamesian moment: as in James's novels, the unspoken, the
finely hinted and intricate codes of movement and dress are what
signify and what give the encounter its electrical quality. This is in
marked contrast to earlier crucial encounters between the lovers
which were distinctively verbal, involving exchanges of personal
narratives and of vows. In particular, at the point when they first

declared their love for each other, Pamphilia admitted Amphilanthus to her closet to read over her private papers with her (*Urania 1*, Bk 2, p. 217); admittance to her erotic favour was thus marked by admittance to intimacy with her literary persona. Her passion for Amphilanthus when unrequited produced a melancholic and authorial persona, whose literary concerns she then in turn shared with him when her passion likewise appeared to arrive at a moment of requital and sharing. By contrast, in the later reunion scene from *Urania 2* we see the failure of linguistic utterance, and, specifically, of male speech. When Amphilanthus revives there is only a short dialogue, a terse exchange of accusations, counter-accusations and self-exonerations, which culminates in Pamphilia taking a vow never to speak to Amphilanthus again (*Urania 2*, Bk 2, f. 2v). Although, paradoxically, her withdrawal from linguistic communication with him is affirmed in the linguistic form of a vow, nevertheless this marks a distinct reversal of those earlier moments when mutual affection was expressed as verbal sharing.

We seem here to move significantly beyond a female appropriation of the verbal giftedness of the male melancholic, to a position where Pamphilia finds power in silence. In a sense, this is an extension of her willed withdrawal into private spaces in *Urania 1*; now she chooses linguistic withdrawal as well. As a complement to this, interest grows in Amphilanthus as a melancholic. As I have said, he has intermittently struck melancholic poses throughout the narrative. However, as Pamphilia cuts him off from dialogue with her he becomes the figure speaking into a void, as she had done to the shades or Night or Grief, as he engages in increasingly lengthy and desperate monologues about his predicament. He becomes the melancholic as a highly articulate, endlessly self-expressive figure, but what is now foregrounded is that his words are unheard and futile. His many long rhetorical laments are purposeless and unattended.

Later, Amphilanthus joins Pamphilia at her father's court in Morea. In her company he is 'wurse then Tantalus who had fruict of the rarest, hanging to his vpper lip, and curious Nectar to his vnder lip yett must famish' (*Urania 2*, Bk 2, f. 17v). The loss of Pamphilia's 'discourse' is presented as an erotic deprivation, regretted more than the loss of her kisses. Communication between them, like many other aspects of Wroth's writing, takes the form of coded messages and veiled meanings: Pamphilia, speaking to her father the King in Amphilanthus's presence, refers to the 'accidents' which have brought her 'greatest torment; the king good man thought noe thing of her speech, and tooke all verbally, nott feelingly, nor vnderstandingly which she was pleased with knowing her words touched in the desired place', that is, they strike home with Amphilanthus (*Urania* 2, Bk 2, f. 18v).

After Amphilanthus leaves the court Pamphilia progresses to writing him letters 'soe full of loue, and affection, as reddy to scorch the paper' (ibid., f. 21r). However, directly after this, she receives a marriage proposal from Rodomandro which, after some persuasion, she decides to accept. To her protest that 'a booke, and solitarines, [are] the onely companions I desire in thes my vnfortunate days', the Tartarian prince rejoins endearingly, 'loue your booke, butt loue mee soe farr as that I may hold itt to you, that while you peruse that, I may joye in beeholding you ... bee solitarie, yett fauour mee soe much as that I may butt attend you, when you waulke in deserts, and woods', where he will guard her from 'serpents, and veminous [*sic*] beasts' (ibid., f. 21v). In fact, Pamphilia's gradual relenting towards Amphilanthus seems to be directly proportionate to her resolution to marry Rodomandro, which she finally decides to do 'against her owne minde, yett nott constrain'd, for non durst attempt that' (ibid., f. 22r). As the marriage puts an official boundary between her and Amphilanthus and publicly announces her inaccessibility to him, so she is increasingly free in admitting him to her private presence, although this does not apparently include dialogue.[20] In the depiction of the wedding, gesture and costume continue to be important. Pamphilia wears 'black, imbroidered with murry, and pearle', recalling her dream of Amphilanthus's wedding and announcing herself to be a melancholic bride; she also wears her hair up, like a married woman or widow, although, as the narrator remarks, 'brides euer vsed to haue ther haire downe' (ibid., f. 22v). After dressing for the ceremony in the presence of the nobles of the court, including Amphilanthus, she solemnly burns 'a lock of haire which she euer till then had worne in her eare' (ibid.).

The day after the wedding, Amphilanthus is found in the conventional pose of the melancholic, 'sitting after his accustumed manner, his hatt ouer his eyes, and his victorious armes in the saddest expressiue maner of sadnes, across' (ibid., f. 23r). Burton records how the melancholic sits in dark corners, 'his hat still in his eyes' (pt. 1, sec. 3, mem. 1, subs. 2, p. 387), and 'Inamorato' on his frontispiece has a large-brimmed hat pulled down over his eyes. In Amphilanthus's case, the word 'victorious' is important, indicating how his prior identity as a martial hero has been taken over by that of the melancholic, which for him is a disablement and disempowerment. Pamphilia in fact, encouraged by his mother and her aunt, the Queen of Naples, allows Amphilanthus to see her privately after the wedding; just as her vow of silence gives her power over him, so her revenge-marriage gives her the power to choose just how far to admit him to her company and her favour. When Amphilanthus and Pamphilia are both amused by the behaviour of one of her ladies, the so-called 'mery Marquess', their eyes meet and they smile; Amphilanthus is able to walk between the Queen of Naples and Pamphilia; and he even, before leaving the court, comes with the merry Marquess to visit her in her bedchamber and 'with deepe groanes stoped her mouth with kisses' (*Urania* 2, Bk 2, f. 25r). None of this, however, apparently compensates for the loss of verbal privileges, rendering ironic that stopping of her mouth which in most scenes of this kind would entail the overwhelming of speech by physical passion.

After this point Amphilanthus travels and indulges in frequent scenes of melancholic self-torment. In Prague, for instance, he tosses on his solitary bed, then goes into a private garden where he repeatedly throws himself on the ground, but each time 'the place liked him not' (*Urania* 2, Bk 2, f. 28r). He spends half the night in 'irresolute waundring', then eventually settles himself sitting with his back to a weeping willow, beside a fountain-statue of a weeping lady.

> O cryde hee howe doth this sadd paseing full Moone, and her watrye shaddow in thes streames, resemble my sorrowes, and as sadly bids farewell in ther slowe softly sliding murmering stream-like pretty small waters seeming loathe to leaue the pretty pebbles, naturally hating change, especiall the sad farewell for euer, neuer to return againe to this sweetnes.
>
> (ibid.)

The greater frequency of such contemplative, private scenes involving Amphilanthus rather than Pamphilia in *Urania* 2 can produce an impression that the sequel is more interested in the hero's interior states. This interest is not necessarily sympathetic, however: a key difference is that earlier scenes of Pamphilia's melancholy consistently stressed her self-control in adversity and its fruits in writing and self-certainty, whereas Amphilanthus is habitually shown as suffering a lack of these qualities.[21]

I have tried to suggest that in *Urania 1*, *Pamphilia to Amphilanthus* and the earliest parts of *Urania 2*, Wroth lays claim to the role of heroic melancholic for her heroine, and that, since Pamphilia is herself a writer, this enables the creation of an intellectually and socially respectable persona for a female writer. In the process her secludedness and withdrawal into privacy is intensified, although this is stated in the highly public medium of a published text and thus serves as a self-protective announcement of virtue and modesty. However, later in *Urania 2*, Pamphilia withdraws even from utterance, at least in the direction of her beloved. Interest increases in Amphilanthus as a melancholic: now he is the speaker of lengthy mournful monologues, but his language is presented as redundant, ineffectual and undisciplined. Male speech becomes a mark of powerlessness, while Pamphilia's chosen silence becomes a site of power.

In the earlier stages, Wroth inverts the gender polarity of the love-melancholic scenario. In her silence, Pamphilia might seem to return to the conventional Petrarchan role of unyielding, unresponsive mistress. However, because we know that she has a gift of eloquence, her willed withholding of language makes her very different from the typical Petrarchan mistress who functions as the object for a male poet's wit and is indeed his textual construction. Pamphilia's *chosen* linguistic reticence and reserve becomes a form of authority because it realises the dominance usually attributed to a mistress merely as compliment. For Pamphilia to lay claim to the verbal giftedness of the male melancholic is one way of formulating female utterance. But having established this at length, to withhold female eloquence reduces the male lover to a state of powerless speechifying and melancholia as malady.

NOTES

1. See, for instance, Jeff Masten, ' "Shall I turne blabb?": Circulation, Gender, and Subjectivity in Mary Wroth's Sonnets', in *Reading Mary Wroth: Representing Alternatives in Early Modern England*, ed. Naomi J. Miller and Gary Waller (Knoxville: University of Tennessee Press,

1991), pp. 67–87; Mary Ellen Lamb, *Gender and Authorship in the Sidney Circle* (Madison: University of Wisconsin Press, 1990), esp. pp. 188–91; Helen Hackett, ' "Yet tell me some such fiction": Lady Mary Wroth's *Urania* and the "Femininity" of Romance', in *Women, Texts and Histories 1575–1760*, ed. Clare Brant and Diane Purkiss (London: Routledge, 1992), pp. 39–68.

2.   Lorna Hutson, *The Usurer's Daughter: Male Friendship and Fictions of Women in Sixteenth-century England* (London: Routledge, 1994), pp. 17–51.

3.   *The Countesse of Mountgomeries Urania* (London, 1621), is referred to in this essay as *Urania 1*. It was a volume of 558 pages divided into four books. It is available in the following modern editions: facs., ed. Josephine A. Roberts (Aldershot: Scolar, 1996); ed. Josephine A. Roberts, *Mediaeval and Renaissance Texts and Studies* (May 1995); Book 1 only, in *An Anthology of Seventeenth-Century Fiction*, ed. Paul Salzman (Oxford: Oxford University Press, 1991).
        There is also a two-book manuscript sequel, now housed in the Newberry Library, Chicago, (call no. Case MS f.Y1565.W95), referred to in this essay as *Urania 2*. An edition is forthcoming, ed. Josephine A. Roberts, *Mediaeval and Renaissance Texts and Studies* (1996).

4.   Lawrence Babb, *The Elizabethan Malady: a Study of Melancholia in English Literature from 1580 to 1642* (East Lansing: Michigan State College Press, 1951), p. 100.

5.   Robert Burton, *The Anatomy of Melancholy*, 6th edn (1641), ed. Holbrook Jackson (London: Dent, 1932), pt. 1, sec. 3, mem. 1, subs. 2, p. 396.

6.   Phillip Stubbes, *The Anatomie of Abuses* (London, 1583), f.48r-v.

7.   E.g. Babb, or Bridget Gellert Lyons, *Voices of Melancholy*, (London: Routledge, 1971).

8.   Sigmund Freud, 'Mourning and Melancholia' (1917 [1915]), in *The Standard Edition of the Complete Psychological Works of Sigmund Freud*, trans. James Strachey *et al.*, vol. 14 (1914–16), *On the History of the Psycho-Analytic Movement, Papers on Metapsychology, and Other Works* (London: Hogarth Press and Institute of Psycho-Analysis, 1957), p. 246.

9.   Juliana Schiesari, *The Gendering of Melancholia: Feminism, Psychoanalysis, and the Symbolics of Loss in Renaissance Literature* (Ithaca, NY: Cornell University Press, 1992).

10.   See Margaret P. Hannay, *Philip's Phoenix: Mary Sidney, Countess of Pembroke* (New York and Oxford: Oxford University Press, 1990).

11.   *The Poems of Lady Mary Wroth*, ed. Josephine A. Roberts (Baton Rouge and London: Louisiana State University Press, 1983), pp. 103–4, poem P34.

12.   See Helen Hackett, ' "In this strang[e] labourinth how shall I turne?": Courtly Writing by Women', in *The Cambridge Companion to Women and Literature 1500–1700*, ed. Helen Wilcox (Cambridge: Cambridge University Press, 1996).

13.   See, for instance, Samuel Daniel, *Delia*, sonnet 34 (1592; facs., Aldershot: Scolar Press, 1969); Sir Philip Sidney, *Astrophil and Stella*, sonnet

38, in *The Oxford Authors: Sir Philip Sidney*, ed. Katherine Duncan-Jones (Oxford: Oxford University Press, 1989).

14.   Wroth, *Poems*, ed. Roberts, p. 99, poem P24.

15.   See Heather L. Weidemann, 'Theatricality and Female Identity in Mary Wroth's *Urania*', in Miller and Waller, pp. 191–209.

16.   Wroth, *Poems*, ed. Roberts, p. 91, poem P10.

17.   See, for instance, *Urania 1*, Bk. 1, pp. 51, 75; Bk. 2, p. 264.

18.   There is a vertical line in the manuscript here which may be read as '1', giving 'leading forthe 1 all in black to bee maried'. In this case it would be the bride rather than Amphilanthus who is dressed in black. However, it is uncharacteristic of Wroth to use numerals in this way, and the point here seems to be the way in which Amphilanthus stands out from the assembly, and his sadness.

19.   William Shakespeare, *Hamlet*, ed. Harold Jenkins (1982; London: Routledge [Arden Shakespeare], 1989), I.v.41.

20.   Pamphilia's vow of silence is sustained for three years (*Urania 2*, Bk. 2, f. 53v).

21.   Eventually, Amphilanthus has another accidental and highly charged reunion with Pamphilia which reprises the scene discussed above (*Urania 2*, Bk. 2, f. 51r). Pamphilia is described as 'his truest wife', and the plot which brought about his other marriage is exposed, such that now, three years on, Pamphilia's vow of silence is formally 'concluded', and they sit 'discoursing one with an other in the old manner' (f. 53v). Although the narrative becomes slightly confused after this, it seems that they spend at least some time living together with Rodomandro as a contented *ménage-à-trois*, followed by Rodomandro's death.

II
Desiring Difference

4

Lyly and Lesbianism: Mysteries of the Closet in *Sappho and Phao*

Michael Pincombe

In a recent essay on 'The (In)Significance of "Lesbian" Desire on the English Renaissance Stage', Valerie Traub worries that in writing on the topic she might be accused of 'creating something quite literally out of nothing'.[1] She continues: 'To this charge I can only answer that I find it inconceivable that within the vast array of erotic choices reported by early modern culture, "feminine" bodies did not meet, touch, and pleasure one another.' The wheel has turned full circle since Queen Victoria refused to believe that there could possibly be such a thing as lesbianism. Now Professor Traub refuses to believe that there could possibly *not* be such a thing as lesbianism. But surely she is right to suppose, despite the paucity of documentary evidence, that at least some women in early modern England gave sexual pleasure to one another; and men no doubt dimly guessed of such a situation.

Indeed, this assumption is confirmed by a play by John Lyly: *Galatea* (written *c.* 1584, printed 1592). This is a pastoral comedy dealing with two young shepherdesses who fall passionately in love with each other, frying in the same flames of sexual desire as conventionally heterosexual lovers do in Elizabethan drama. Galatea tells us of her cross-dressed beloved: 'I had thought the habite agreeable with the Sexe, and so burned in the fire of mine owne fancies.'[2] And Phyllida ruefully concurs: 'I had thought that in the attyre of a boy, there could not haue lodged the body of a Virgine, & so was inflamed with a sweete desire, which now I find a sower deceit.' Actually, both Galatea and Phyllida suspect quite early on in the play that the other may, in fact, be a girl like herself; but they still love each other none the less – and continue to do so even after their diguises have been exposed for what they are. This would seem to make *Galatea* a clear candidate for the first 'lesbian' play on the English stage – although, unaccountably, Professor Traub omits it from her discussion of lesbian desire in English Renaissance drama.

But in this essay, I wish to turn to a less obviously lesbian play by the same author: *Sappho and Phao*, written and performed in 1583/4, just a year before *Galatea*. However, I shall be proposing that the 'lesbian desire' which is enigmatically hinted at in *Sappho and Phao* is not as readily assimilable to modern notions of lesbianism as that so frankly delineated in *Galatea*. Perhaps we should rather describe it as 'Lesbianism'. To make the distinction clear, we need to examine the literary heritage of Lyly's heroine: Sappho.

I

I have said that *Sappho and Phao* is a 'less obviously lesbian play' than *Galatea*; and this may come as a surprise to readers who are familiar with Sappho as the *ur*-lesbian: the great lyric poet who flourished in the early sixth century BC on the Greek island of Lesbos, and celebrated her passionate love for various other women with such style that female same-sex love has come to be called 'lesbianism' after the place where Sappho lived and sang. But this was not the Sappho whom Lyly and the Elizabethans knew. The 'lesbian Sappho', as opposed to what we shall call the 'Lesbian Sappho', only began to emerge at the end of the sixteenth century: John Donne's rather frigid but much-fêted poem 'Sappho to Philaenis', probably written during the 1590s, is the first occasion, as far as I am aware, upon which an English writer imaginatively recreates Sappho as a lover of women.[3] Donne is writing with an annotated copy of Sappho's poems at his side;[4] but most Elizabethan writers seem to have relied rather on the resources of popular mythology and legend, and were more familiar with the Sappho whom they knew as the exorbitantly *heterosexual* lover of Phaon. Their story is told, for example, in the index of Thomas Cooper's *Thesaurus linguae Romanae et Britannicae* (1565):[5]

> *Sappho.* A woman of the yle of Lesbos, a great Poetresse, who made verses called Lyrici: at the laste sh[e] was taken with the loue of a yong man called Phaon, who running awaye from hir, shee not sustayning the anguishe of loue, threwe hir selfe downe from an hill into the sea.

Thomas Peend's note on Sappho in his *Pleasant Fable of Hermaphroditus and Salmacis* (1565) fills in a detail omitted by Cooper:[6]

> *Sapho.* A womā of the Ile *Lesbos*, lerned in Poetrye, beinge forsaken of a yonge man, called *Phaon*, whom she loued: she caste her selfe from the hyll *Leucates*, into the Sea, & so peryshed by loue of hym.

There are numerous other allusions in Tudor and Elizabethan poetry to Sappho as a learned poet or as a suicidally passionate lover – but none of them, as far as I have been able to discover, makes her a lover of other women.[7] *Sappho and Phao* is firmly rooted in this heterosexual tradition; but it has a special place within it, since Lyly is also aware of the lesbian Sappho, even though his own Sappho is not herself a lover of other women. The lesbian character of the ancient poet survives not in Lyly's Sappho, but in her ladies; and to understand why this should be, we must first examine what sort of literary materials he had before him when he sat down to write it.

Not much is known of the historical Sappho; but it seems likely that her poetry was written for a circle of young women – *thiasos* – over whom she had some charge in the sexually segregated society of archaic Lesbos. Her exact relations with these women will never be known; but it is likely that she performed the functions of the male *khorēgos* or chorus-leader: 'Her expression and probable practice of homoerotic love was thus, like that of her male counterparts, a form of *paideia*, not the public expression of a private desire.'[8] This is certainly the opinion of the Greek rhetorician Maximus of Tyre (*c.* AD 125–85), who compares Sappho to the philosopher Socrates: 'What else could one call the love of the Lesbian woman than the Socratic art of love? For they seem to me to have practised love after their own fashion, she the love of women, he of men. For they said they loved many, and were captivated by all things beautiful.'[9] But whatever her sexual orientation may have really been, after her death Sappho acquired a reputation which was eventually to turn her into the passionately heterosexual lover of the beautiful Phaon.

Sappho's poetry was not widely circulated after her death – or even circulated at all.[10] It was only three centuries and more later that Alexandrian scholars rediscovered her work. In the interim, however, she herself had not been entirely forgotten. The Greek comic poets of the fourth century BC had very little information about Sappho, other than that she was a poet who came from Lesbos, and that she was supposed to be very beautiful. They did not know that she loved women. Rather, since she often appeared on pottery in the company of Alcaeus, another poet from Lesbos, the comic writers fabricated an affair between Sappho and her fellow islander; and then added a crowd of rival-poets to make the situation more interesting. Moreover, they seem to have felt that it would be amusing to depict her not as a beauty, but as a small, dark, physically unattractive women. So how did she attract so many lovers? By being good at sex and free with her favours: Sappho became a courtesan with an insatiable sexual appetite; only when she met her husband Kerkylas could that appetite be satisfied – by a man whose name means 'Mr Cock' (Greek: *kerkos*).

But the comic writers did not have it all their own way. We recall that they knew she had been a beautiful poet: no less an authority than Plato (427–347 BC) had ranked 'lovely Sappho' amongst the best poets (*Phaedrus*, 235C); and we have seen that Maximus of Tyre placed Sappho herself within a tradition of Socratic and Platonic *paideia*. Maximus picks up on a potentially embarrassing point: Sappho's poetry reveals that she loved many young women; which could be interpreted as mere promiscuity if her love for them was sexual rather than spiritual. Indeed, it pushes her in the same direction as her comic sister: towards the figure of the courtesan or prostitute. Those who did not wish to see the new or revived *lyric* Sappho contaminated by elements of the old *comic* Sappho had to keep the two figures firmly apart by explaining that they were two entirely different women, both of whom happened to share the same name and place of birth. Here are the words of another Greek rhetorician, Aelian (*c.* AD 170–235) in his *Miscellanies*, as translated by Abraham Fleming in 1578: '*Plato*, the son of *Aristo*, numbreth *Sapho*, the Versifier, and daughter of *Scamandronymus* amonge such as were wise, lerned and skilful. I heare also, that there was another *Sapho* in *Lesbus*: which was a stronge whore, and an arrant strumpet.'[11] Lyly may have owned a copy of Aelian: material from the *Miscellanies* find its way into several of his early works.[12] It certainly seems likely that Lyly used it as source for information concerning Phao – or Phaon, as he is more regularly known in the literature of antiquity. According to Aelian, and other accounts, Phaon was a ferryman of Lesbos who was rewarded by Venus for an act of kindness with an ointment that made him irresistibly attractive to women: 'insomuch that the women of *Mitylen* [on Lesbos] were inflamed with the loue of *Phaon*, his comelynesse did so kindle their affections. To be short, he was taken playing ye leude knaue with a commō whore, and abusing his body in beastly pleasure of the fleash, which sweete meat had sower sawce, for he was slayne and murthered' (12.18; fol. 126r). Actually, the Greek makes no mention of a whore, but merely informs us that Phao was taken in adultery and killed. However, Fleming's translation – or complete rewriting – accidentally touches on a further stage in the progress of the comic Sappho, when the Insatiable Woman meets the Irresistible Man. Phaon, too, ended up as a character in Greek comedy; and it was, of course, not long before the comic Phaon, ranging Lesbos for women to seduce, met the comic Sappho.[13]

However, there was also the 'romantic' version of their encounter we have already noted; and the accounts of Sappho given by Cooper and Peend may be traced back to the entry under 'Sappho' in the late tenth-century dictionary known as *Suda* (or Suidas' *Lexicon*): 'A Lesbian from Mitylene, a lyre-player. This Sappho leapt from the cliff of Leucates and drowned herself for love of Phaon, the Mytilenaean.'[14] This romantic version of the tale is related in the fifteenth epistle of the *Heroides* of Lyly's favourite poet: Ovid (43 BC–AD 17). In fact, 'Sappho to Phaon' was only rediscovered in the fifteenth century;[15] but it was soon added to the other letters, and the whole work was translated by George Turberville in 1567 as *Ovid's Heroical Epistles*. However, Ovid's Sappho – and she is the one which most Elizabethans would have been most familiar with from their schoolrooms – is a hybrid figure: her story is the romantic version related in Suda; but her character is drawn after the lustful Sappho of Greek comedy.

Ovid's Sappho is the most explicitly and excessively lascivious of all his heroines. In a notorious passage where she describes a dream of making love with Phaon, she describes what seems to be a spontaneous orgasm. Here is a modern translation by Florence Verducci: 'I hesitate to say what happens next, but it all happens, there's no choice, just joy, and I'm inundated with it' – a wet dream, then.[16] Ovid has also read Sappho's own lyric poetry, and knows that her songs were addressed to other women; but his own Sappho is less than clear about the kind of love she bestowed upon her girl-friends. She begins her letter by bidding farewell to Anactorie, Cydro, Atthis, and the 'hundreth mo / whome (shame ylaid aside) / I fanside erste' (v. 19; fol. 109v). It might be that the shamefulness of her earlier loves lies not in her having loved women, but so many of them; but the following lines suggest that she loved women in the same way she loved Phaon: 'thou all that loue / from them to thee hast wride'. Ovid's Sappho, then, seems to acknowledge that she has had lesbian affairs in the past, before she met the all-attractive Phaon; but Ovid is really more interested in reworking Sappho in the comic tradition – and it is this Sappho that Lyly also emphasises. By her own admission, Ovid's Sappho is small, dark and extremely lascivious. And though it is nowhere explicitly stated in the text, she also seems to be past her prime; at any rate, she appears to be uncomfortably aware of the difference in age between herself and her lover, who is 'neyther ... a boy, nor a man' (v. 93; fol. 112r). In other words, Phaon is a 'toy-boy' with whom the somewhat older Sappho is infatuated.

Now, critics like to see in Lyly's Sappho a flattering allusion to Elizabeth I;[17] and this adds another dimension to this already heavily over-determined literary figure. Ovid's representation of Sappho, of course, was by no means an obvious model for a figure of Elizabeth. It was too scandalously close to the truth: Elizabeth was 50 when Lyly wrote *Sappho and Phao*; she was no longer as handsome as she had been; and she had a penchant for the company of attractive young men, such as Lyly's master, the Earl of Oxford. On the other hand, the panegyrical figure of the queen emphasised her imperviousness to love and the 'chastity' she had so exquisitely preserved during two decades and more of persistent courtship by her many suitors. As far as I know, Elizabeth's success in fending off these men was never put down to a preference for the company of women; and there is nothing in the play to suggest that Lyly wished to make such a *risqué* suggestion. Indeed, he cleverly manipulates what was, after all, rather unpromising source material into a fairly plausible contribution to Elizabethan panegyric.

Lyly read in Aelian, that Phaon, for his beauty, 'was hidden of *Venus* among long lettisse which sprung vp and grew very rãkly' (12.18; fol. 125v). Lettuce was regarded as an anaphrodisiac; and Venus hid Adonis is a lettuce-bed so that his affections for any other female might be extinguished and she might enjoy him all to herself.[18] In Lyly's play, it is Sappho who is hidden in the herb; as Venus later comes to regret: 'when I noursed thee, Sapho, with lettice, woulde it had turned to hemlocke!' (iv. ii. 10–11). Venus curses Sappho because she herself has fallen in love with Phao, who still dotes on Sappho; but at the beginning of the play, the problem is that the lettuce has killed off *all* sexual affection in Sappho; hence Venus' declaration of war on her former nurseling: 'Sapho shal know, be she neuer so faire, that there is a Venus, which can cōquer, were she neuer so fortunate' (I. i. 33–5). She instructs Cupid to make Sappho fall in love with Phao, which he does – and the result is that Sappho becomes a comic heroine, albeit only temporarily (the play is described as 'The Comedy of Sappho' in the Stationers' Register). In a scene which has always troubled critics who wish to see in Sappho a 'representation' of Elizabeth,[19] we see her tossing and turning in bed in the throes of frustrated passion: 'Oh, which way shall I lye? what shall I doe? Heygh ho! O Mileta, helpe to reare me vp, my bed, my head lyes too lowe. You pester mee with too many clothes. Fie, you keepe the chamber too hotte! – auoide it! it may be I shall steale a nappe when all are gone' (III. iii. 77–81). However, in the soliloquy that follows, in which Sappho reveals her secret but 'impacient disease of loue', her emphasis is less on the extremity of her feelings but on their inappropriate fixation on a humble ferryman. It is left to the love-struck Venus to dilate at large on her burning affections, much in the manner of Ovid's Sappho. In fact, Lyly transfers to Venus all those qualities which were unsuitable for the invention of a pane-gyrical icon of Elizabeth. Venus becomes conscious of her age and of the signs of her age (IV. ii. 14–21):

O Cupid, thy flames with Pysches [*sic*] were but sparks, and my desires with Adonis but dreames, in respecte of these vnac-quainted tormentes. Laugh Iuno! Venus is in loue; but Iuno shall not see with whom, least shee be in loue. Venus belike is become stale. Sapho forsooth because she hath many vertues, therfore she must haue all the fauours. Venus waxeth old: and then she was a pretie wench, when Iuno was a young wife, nowe crowes foote is on her eie, and the blacke oxe hath troad on her foote.

In this remarkable outburst, Venus steps firmly into the role of the old comic Sappho, as transmitted and refined by Ovid. But she also belongs to a 'satiric' tradition in which the goddess of love is travestied as a sex-mad whore – very much like the old comic Sappho, in fact.[20] Indeed, Lyly's Sappho emphasises the distance between herself and her lusty comic and Ovidian ancestress by identifying her adversary Venus as this maniacal figure. Once she has gained control of Cupid and his bow and arrows at the end of the play, Sappho feels confident enough to dismiss Venus in the following suitably priggish terms: 'You are not worthy to be the Ladye of loue, that yeelde so often to the impressions of loue. Immodest Venus, that to satisfie the vnbrideled thoughtes of thy hearte, transgressest so farre from the staye of thine honour!' (v. ii. 58–62).

This is all very ingenious: Lyly has made a passable allusion to Elizabeth from the most unpromising materials, whilst allowing Ovid's Sappho to survive in the person of Venus. But there is no trace of the lesbian Sappho in Lyly's play – or, rather, not in his characterisation of his own leading lady. Sappho herself is not a lover of women: she is impervious to *all* sexual desire; but her ladies are not. Sappho's ladies seem to have nothing but amused scorn for their male suitors. Here is Mileta (I. iv. 34–40):

> It is good sporte to see them want matter: for then fall they to good manners, hauing nothing in their mouthes but 'sweet mistresse,' wearing our hands out with courtly kissings, when their wits faile in courtly discourses. Now rufling their haires, now setting their ruffes, then gazing with their eies, then sighing with a priuie wring by the hand, thinking vs like to be wowed by signes and ceremonies.

Eugenua, however, indicates that perhaps the ladies do really feel some passion: 'Yet we, when we sweare with our mouthes wee are not in loue, then we sigh from the heart and pine in loue'. And Canope complicates matters:

> Wee are madde wenches, if men marke our wordes: for whē I say, I would none cared for loue more then I, what meane I, but I would none loued but I? where we cry 'away,' doe we not presently say, 'go too': & when men striue for kisses, we exclaime, 'let vs alone,' as though we would fall to that our selues.

The ladies are obviously moved by affection, unlike their mistress – but for whom? David Bevington's note in his recent edition of *Sappho and Phao* (1991) on the last twelve words spoken by Canope reads as follows: '(1) Leave us in solitude; (2) Leave that to us, i.e.

trust us to fall to kissing on our own initiative.... *As though* is similarly ambiguous; it can suggest that the women are reluctant or eager to fall a-kissing.' But, surely, we might also read Canope's words in a lesbian context: 'When men strive for kisses, we exclaim: Let us alone! As though we would fall to kissing amongst ourselves once they had left us.' Such a reading might suggest that Lyly dimly conceived Mileta and the other ladies as a *thiasos* with Sappho at its centre; and that it was sexually active – as if Mileta and the rest were to be read as the counterparts of Anactorie and the other Lesbian women mentioned by Ovid in his epistle. We might conclude, then, that these ladies are prototypes of the more obviously lesbian Galatea and Phyllida. But this is not, I think, what Lyly had in mind. Rather, he is hinting that Sappho's ladies indulge in sexual activities which would better be described as 'Lesbian' than 'lesbian'. And here we may usefully turn to a work by an author very similar in spirit and artistic temperament to Lyly: the Greek-Syrian essayist Lucian of Samosata (*c.* AD 115–80).

II

In the fifth of Lucian's *Dialogues of the Courtesans*, Clonarium greets a friend of hers with the following words: 'We've been hearing strange things about you, Laeana. They say that Megilla, the rich Lesbian woman, is in love with you just like a man, that you live with each other, and do goodness knows what together. Hullo! Blushing? Tell me if it's true.'[21] Laeana replies: 'Quite true, Clonarium. But I'm ashamed, for it's unnatural.' But Clonarium insists: 'What does the woman want? What do you do when you are together?' Laeana reluctantly explains that Megilla and another woman, named Demonassa, hired her to provide the music at a drinks party; but that when she had finished playing and was making to leave at the end of the evening, the two women took her to their own bed, and started to make love to her: 'At first they kissed me like men, not simply bringing their lips to mine, but opening their mouths a little, embracing me and squeezing my breasts.' Then, Megilla pulled off her wig to reveal the closely shaven head of a young athlete; and she told Laeana that she was really a man: Megillus. Laeana found this amusing and improbable: 'Then...you have everything that a man has' (291). Megilla explained that she has no need of one: 'You'll find I've a much pleasanter method of my own.' She continued: 'I have a substitute of my own'; and Megilla pleaded with Laeana to let her demonstrate how what *she* has would satisfy the puzzled flute-girl just as much as what any *man* has. Laeana, won over by Megilla's entreaties, and by the gift of a necklace and a pretty dress, finally allowed her employer to do her will: 'I threw my arms around her as though she were a man, and she went to work, kissing me, and panting, and apparently enjoying herself immensely.' And here her story ends. But Clonarium is still in the dark as to what actually went on: 'What did she do? How? That's what I'm most interested to hear.' Laeana replies: 'Don't enquire too closely into the details; they're not very nice; so, by Aphrodite in heaven, I won't tell you!' And there the dialogue itself ends.

Lucian's pornographic vignette is a useful point of departure for an investigation into the secret 'Lesbian' aspect of Lyly's *Sappho and Phao*. We do not know whether Lyly had read any of Lucian's many dialogues between courtesans, gods, sea-gods and the dead. But these short pieces *were* studied (in Latin translation) by the younger boys at Lyly's school: King's, in Canterbury.[22] And we know that Lyly's friend Gabriel Harvey was reading Lucian with Edmund Spenser around 1580 – further circumstantial evidence that Lyly, too, may have known at least something of Lucian's writings.[23] However, I do not wish to claim Lucian as a source for Lyly's play; rather his dialogue may be seen as a general model of the kind of text, written by a man, which both does and does not represent sexual intercourse between women. Lucian's dialogue is remarkably explicit about fore-play: kissing, embracing, fondling; but, as Laeana points out, these are activities which are not unique to what women do when they make love to one another. Megilla and Demonassa act 'like men', and use those organs they share with men: mouths, tongues, hands. But Laeana declines to explain in detail how Megilla made love to her. In other words, the specifically 'lesbian', or woman-to-woman, nature of the sexual intercourse between Megilla and Laeana remains a mystery.

However, this mystery is not impenetrable. When Laeana asks Megilla if she has 'everything that a man has', she employs, in the Greek, a conventional euphemism: *andreion ekeino*, or 'a man's what's-it'. Liddell and Scott explain that the word *ekeino* is used of 'things, of which one cannot remember or must not mention the name' – in this case, *kerkos*. And it's not hard to work out what Megilla's *ti anti tou andreiou*, or 'something instead of a man's what's-it', must be. What she means, but does not explicitly name, is a *baubon* or *olisbos*. Liddell and Scott gloss the latter as *penis coriaceus*: a leather penis, or dildo. The pseudo-Lucian alludes to such a contraption in his *Affairs of the Heart*;[24] and the Greek mimiambist Herodas (*c.* BC 330–250) portrays two women quite frankly discussing the desirability of possessing a leather dildo in his mime called 'Women in a Friendly or Private Situation'.[25] The discovery of this secret device leads me to my final point. Sappho finally bribes Cupid into surrendering unto her the instruments of his power: his bow and the arrows of desire that go with it. Venus is furious that she may no longer direct sexual affection as she pleases; but she can do nothing about it, and storms off swearing revenge. His mother gone, Sappho reassures Cupid that he and his bow and arrows are in safe hands: 'Cupid, feare not, I will direct thine arrowes better. Euery rude asse shall not say he is in loue. It is a toye made for Ladies, and I will keepe it onely for Ladies' (v. ii. 94–6). Cupid's arrows are now not a weapon but a 'toy'; and, moreover, a 'toy made for ladies', which Sappho will keep exclusively for their use – not for the male 'rude ass'. The phallus is still with us, then, in the form of Cupid's phallic arrows, which Sappho's ladies may play with. Is the implication that these ladies – though not Sappho herself – will henceforth have no need to rely on men for sexual satisfaction, because they have *ti anti tou andreiou*: a dildo?

At least one other Elizabethan writer seems to have thought that this is why court ladies use dildos; for Thomas Nashe makes the same imputation in his *Choice of Valentines* (ms. *c.* 1592). Tomalin comes too soon, and Frances has resort to her 'little dilldo'.[26] Tomalin angrily observes of his 'Mistris page' (252, 255–9):

> He wayte's on Courtlie Nimphs, that be so coye,
>   And bids them skorne the blynd-alluring boye.
> He giue's yong guirls their gamesome sustenance,
>   And euerie gaping mouth his full sufficeance.

In other words, these courtly nymphs can reject the company of men, not because they are immune to sexual and, specifically, to vaginal desire, but because they satisfy that desire with a dildo. Their 'chastity', he argues, is therefore a fraud.

Is Lyly hinting at something similar? It is possible that Nashe had Lyly's play in mind when he wrote his poem. At one point, he (or Thomalin) reprimands himself (or the dildo) for betraying the secrets of these young girls and courtly nymphs: 'Thow shalt be whipt with nettles for this geare / If Cicelie shew but of thy knaverie heere' (293–4). McKerrow notes that there may be a reference to Venus' threat to Cupid in the scene we have just discussed: 'you shalbe stript from toppe to toe, and whipt with nettles, not roses....I will handle you for this geare' (*Sappho*, v. ii. 73–6).[27] A variant reading of the relevant lines in Nashe's poem runs: 'If Illian queene knewe of they brauery heere / thou shouldst be whipt wth nettles for this geere'. Nashe is thought to have written his poem around 1592 – the year of the third edition of Lyly's *Sappho and Phao*. And the two men had been associates a couple of years earlier in the late 1580s, when they were both commissioned to write against the antipresbyterian pamphleteer 'Martin Marprelate'. Could it be that Nashe had acquired some 'insider information' as to the bawdy secrets of Lyly's play whilst they were working on their libels? Commentators have been unable to sort out these enigmatic allusions to 'Cicelie' and to the 'Illian queene'. But I wonder if we have here two equally garbled versions of what might originally have read 'Sicilian queen' – namely, the Sappho of Lyly's play. Lyly's Sappho is regularly regarded by the critics as a queen; although she is never so called by characters in the play, where she is described, rather, as 'a Lady heere in Sycily' (II. ii. 3). We are told that Sappho is 'by birth royall' (I. ii. 5–6), but nothing more is said about her parentage. However, the urge to see Sappho as a 'representation of Elizabeth' has promoted her to regal status in the eyes of most commentators. Such is the spell cast by this notion that G. K. Hunter can state that 'Sapho appears in Ovid as the Queen of Lesbos', whereas Ovid's heroine is quite clearly a *bourgeoise*.[28] But this is a mistake also made by Lyly's contemporaries – perhaps as a result of the success of his own redrawing of the ancient legend in *Sappho and Phao*. Robert Greene, for example, one of Lyly's most sedulous imitators, makes the same mistake as Hunter in his *Alcida* (1589), where we learn that '*Sapho* a Queene loued *Phao* a Ferri-man'.[29] The spelling 'Phao' indicates that Greene has Lyly rather than Ovid in mind; and other writers, Nashe amongst them, may have formed the impression that Sappho was a queen. She is a Sicilian queen, rather than a Lesbian one, because it was to Sicily that Phaon removed in the old legend, and because Lyly's Sappho lives in Sicily, too.

Time and space do not permit us to pursue this interesting line of inquiry; and I have only dwelt on Nashe's poem at such length because it is remarkably, indeed uniquely, explicit about the way in which an apparently heterosexual woman might use a dildo for her own pleasure. The lack of such concrete detail makes it difficult for us to talk about the sex women had by themselves without resorting to the critical *ekeino*. We may note the case of Professor Traub's somewhat enigmatic remarks about '"lesbian" desire' with which we began this essay. She does not actually state that *women* 'met, touched, and pleasured one another'. It is only ' "feminine" bodies' that do so – not even female bodies, or, stranger still, not even bodies that are feminine in a way that need not be qualified by those distracting inverted commas. Even more curious is the reluctance critics seem to feel about identifying *Galatea* as a lesbian play. Two recent essays miss the point completely: Phyllis Rackin and Ellen C. Caldwell are both so intent on proving the 'androgynist' credentials of *Galatea* that they ignore its lesbian aspect.[30] But if Nashe's explicit description of the heterosexual Frances's use of the dildo *is* somehow related to Lyly's cryptic hints as to the use of the same instrument among the ladies of Sappho's court, this would confirm the point I wish to make in this essay: Mileta and the rest are *not* necessarily 'lesbian' in our modern sense; but rather 'Lesbian' in the sense relating to the ancient association of Lesbian women with 'obscene' sexual practices: *'Nota est obscoenitas Lesbidum'*, as Fredericus Blaydes comments.[31] True, the two Lesbians of Lucian's dialogue *are* lesbians; and Clonarium reports: 'They say there are women like that in Lesbos, with faces like men, and unwilling to consort with men, but only with women, as though they themselves were men' (289). On the other hand, it appears that the verb *lesbiazo* was used to describe the one sexual activity which women simply cannot practise amongst themselves: fellatio (Liddell and Scott). To make matters even more complicated, the kind of love practised by the arch-Lesbian and arch-lesbian Sappho herself was described by at least one scholar in quite different terms altogether. In the *Epistles* of the Roman poet Horace (65–8 BC) we learn that Sappho was 'mascula' (1.19.28). Porphyrio's gloss on this line reads: ' "Masculine Sappho", either because she is famous for her poetry, in which men more often excel, or because she is maligned as having been a tribade (*tribas*)'.[32] This second explanation refers to a specifically lesbian form of sexual intercourse: tribadism, or mutual clitoral stimulation through vigorous genital contact (*tribade* comes from the Greek word *tribein*: 'to rub'). Indeed, if Elizabethan readers needed to know what a *tribas* was or did, they had only to turn to Guido Morillonus' headnote to Ovid's 'Sappho to Phaon' in Andreas Naugerius's edition of the *Heroides*. Here we learn that this epistle is exceptionally 'lascivious'; and that 'Sappho did not love only men with such abandon, but she was also the tribade of other women; that is, she jumped on top of them and rubbed herself against them; which is why Horace calls her "masculine".'[33] And a copy of this edition was printed in London by Thomas Vautrollier in 1583 – the very year in which Lyly wrote his own piece on the legendary love between Sappho and Phaon. But just what Lyly may have known or read or guessed about the sorts of sexual activities which women may or may not have indulged in amongst themselves is impossible to recover. At the end of the play, Sappho and her ladies retire to a private space unseen by the audience to play with their new toy: 'Come Mileta, shut the doore' (v. ii. 101). Whatever games they play, then, are played within the secret place of the closet.

NOTES

1. Valerie Traub, 'The (In)Significance of "Lesbian" Desire in Early Modern England', in Susan Zimmerman (ed.), *Erotic Politics: Desire on the Renaissance Stage* (London, 1992), pp. 150–69; at p. 164.
2. John Lyly, *Galatea* (1584), in R. Warwick Bond (ed.), *The Complete Works of John Lyly* (Oxford, 1902), vol. 3, v. iii. 117. All quotations from Lyly are taken from this edition.
3. Helen Gardner dates the poem between 1593 and 1596 in her *John Donne: The Elegies and The Songs and Sonnets* (Oxford, 1965), p. xxx.
4. See Stella P. Revard, 'The Sapphic Voice in Donne's "Sapho to Philaenis"', in Claude J. Summers and Ted-Larry Pebworth, (eds.), *Renaissance Discourses of Desire* (Columbia and London, 1993), pp. 63–76.
5. Thomas Cooper, *Thesaurus linguae Romanae et Britannicae* (London, 1565: STC 5226), Index nominum.
6. Thomas Peend, *A Pleasant Fable of Hermaphroditus and Salmacis* (London, 1565: STC 18971), sig. C1v.
7. A few examples of the figure of Sappho in English poetry before *Sappho and Phao* may suffice. As a learned poet, Sappho is mentioned by early Tudor writers such as John Skelton in *Philip Sparrow* (?1505), line 759 (in John Scattergood (ed.), *John Skelton: The Complete English Poems* [Harmondsworth, 1983]); and Thomas Feylde in his *Controversy between a Lover and a Jay* (?1527; 2nd edition ?1532: STC 10839), sig. A1v.

In Elizabeth's reign, Sappho was not infrequently associated with the learned queen, as, for example, in Lodowick Lloyd's *The Pilgrimage of Princes* (?1573: STC 16624), fol. 216r; and in George Puttenham's *Partheniades* (ms. 1581/2: BL Cotton MS Vesp. E.viii), fol. 169r. As a passionate poet, Sappho is mentioned by John Rolland in his *Court of Venus* (Edinburgh, 1575: STC 21258), fol. 36r; and by Humphrey Gifford in his *Posy of Gillyflowers* (London, 1580: STC 11872), fol. 51v. As the passionate lover of Phaon, Sappho is mentioned amongst those who briefly enjoyed love by the author of *La connaissance d'amours* (?1528: STC 5631): 'So had the lady Sapho with Phaon' (sig. D4r); by Peend in his *Pleasant Fable*: 'The learned *Sapho* did some time / to comely *Phaon* sue / For grace' (sig. B3v); by John Burel, writing after *Sappho and Phao*, in his poem addressed *To the Right High Lodowick, Duke of Lennox* (Edinburgh, 1595: stc 4105): 'lykewais Sapho slew hir self I say / Becaus that *Phaon* did her lufe refuse' (sig. H3v). There are many other post-Lylian references in all these categories; and Tudor prose is familiar with Sappho as a heterosexual poet, too. My thanks to Dr Helen Hackett for pointing me towards some of these allusions.

8. Paul Allen Miller, *Lyric Texts and Lyric Consciousness: The Birth of a Genre from Archaic Greece to Augustan Rome* (London and New York, 1994), p. 98.

9. Maximus of Tyre, *Orations [Orationes]*, 18.9; cit. David A. Campbell, trans. *Greek Lyric* (Cambridge, Mass., and London, 1982–92 [LCL]), vol. 1, p. 21.

10. The details concerning Sappho's biography and reputation are taken from Heinrich Dörrie, ed. *P. Ovidius Naso: Der Brief der Sappho an Phaon* (Munich, 1975), pp. 13–29.

11. Aelian, *Miscellanies [Varia historia]*, 12.19; trans. Abraham Fleming as *A Register of Histories* (London, 1578: STC 164), fol. 126r. Fleming is harsher on the 'bad' Sappho than Aelian, who merely notes that she was a courtesan (*hetaira*).

12. Jeff Shulman's note on 'Lyly's Use of Aelian in *Campaspe*' (*N&Q* 227 [1982], pp. 417–18) exaggerates Lyly's debt to the *Miscellanies* in this play; but his general point is well taken.

13. For Phao, see Dörrie, pp. 29–33.

14. *Suda*, Σ. 108; cit. Campbell, *Greek Lyric*, vol. 1, p. 7. For the mythological origins of this 'romantic' legend, see Gregory Nagy, 'Phaethon, Sappho's Phaon, and the White Rock of Leukas: "Reading the Symbols" of Greek Lyric', in his *Greek Mythology and Poetics* (Ithaca and London, 1990), pp. 223–62.

15. The epistle was first rediscovered towards the end of the twelfth century (see Dörrie, p. 51). But it was not until about 1420 that it was put into scholarly circulation.

16. Florence Verducci, *Ovid's Toyshop of the Heart: 'Epistulae heroidum'* (Princeton, 1985), p. 130. In the Latin, the lines run: 'ulteriora pudet narrare, sed omnia fiunt, / et iuvat, et siccae non licet esse mihi'. Latin text from Grant Showerman, trans., *Ovid: Heroides and Amores* (London and New York: 1921 [LCL]), v. 133–4. The words 'et siccae non

licet esse mihi' have always proved awkward to translators. Literally, they read: 'and I may not have dry things'; or 'my things are not allowed to remain dry'. Professor Verducci's fluent version, to my ear, smoothes over the extraordinary roughness of Sappho's description; but it is better than many earlier attempts. Here is George Turberville in *Ovid's Heroical Epistles* (London, 1567: STC 18939.5): 'there is / Naught left vndone that breedes delight' (fol. 113v). We might also note that editors, too, have sometimes found these lines excessively explicit: an alternative reading has *sine te* (without you) for *siccae* (dry things).

17. David Bevington sums up the consensus on the 'identity' of Sappho in his introduction to his recent edition of the play: 'Lyly plainly intended his dramatic portrait of Sappho as a compliment to Queen Elizabeth' (G. K. Hunter and David Bevington (eds.), *John Lyly: 'Campaspe' and 'Sappho and Phao'* [Manchester, 1991], p. 164). The view is endorsed by the single essay devoted exclusively to our play: Theodora A. Jankowski, 'The Subversion of Flattery: The Queen's Body in John Lyly's *Sappho and Phao'* (*MRDE* 5 [1991], pp. 69–86). My own view is that the similarities between Sappho and Elizabeth may easily be overdone.

18. See Dörrie, p. 254.

19. For a list of such critics, see Jankowski, note 7.

20. As, for example, in Thomas Churchyard's 'Show of Chastity', in his *Discourse of the Queen's Majesty's Entertainment in Suffolk and Norfolk* (London, 1578: STC 5226), sigs. C4v–E2r. Lyly knew this text, and imitates it in *Sappho and Phao*. For further details, see the remarks on this play in my study, *The Plays of John Lyly: Eros and Eliza* (Manchester and New York, 1996), pp. 52–78.

21. Lucian, *Dialogues of the Courtesans [Dialogi meretricum]*, 289; in A. M. Harmon *et al.*, trans., *Lucian* (Cambridge, Mass., and London, 1913–67 [LCL]), vol. 7.

22. For the Canterbury curriculum, see T. W. Baldwin, *William Shakspere's Small Latine & Lesse Greeke* (Urbana, 1944), vol. 1, p. 169. Lucian was widely read in Tudor England, as Douglas Duncan has demonstrated in *Ben Jonson and the Lucianic Tradition* (Cambridge and New York, 1979).

23. See Virginia F. Stern, *Gabriel Harvey: A Study of his Life, Marginalia, and Library* (Oxford, 1977), p. 44.

24. See Pseudo-Lucian, *Affairs of the Heart [Amores]*, 28; in Harmon, *Lucian*, vol. 8.

25. Herodas, *Mimes [Mimiambi]*, VI. line 19; in Jeffrey Rusten *et al.*, trans., *Theophrastus: 'Characters'; Herodas: 'Mimes'; The Choliambic Poets* (Cambridge, Mass., and London, 1993 [LCL]). My thanks to Dr Roland Williams for supplying this allusion.

26. Thomas Nashe, *The Choice of Valentines*, in R. B. McKerrow (ed.), *The Works of Thomas Nashe* (1904–10; ed. F. P. Wilson, Oxford, 1957), vol. 3, p. 412, line 239.

27. R. W. Dent's *Proverbial Language in English Drama Exclusive of Shakespeare 1445–1612* (Berkeley, 1984) identifies 'To whip with nettles' as a

proverb (N135.1); but *Sappho and Phao* is the only play in which this so-called proverb seems to occur. It is not attested in any of the plays and poems in the respective Chadwyck-Healey Full-Text Databases; although there are numerous instances of genuinely proverbial collocations of roses and nettles. We must take it, then, that Nashe *had* read his Lyly.

28. G. K. Hunter, *John Lyly: The Humanist as Courtier* (London, 1962), p. 180.

29. Robert Greene, *Alcida* (?1589; London, 1617: STC 12216), sig. C4r.

30. In 'Androgyny, Mimesis, and the Marriage of the Boy Heroine on the English Renaissance Stage' (*PMLA* 102 [1987], pp. 29–41), Phyllis Rackin asserts that *Galatea* 'celebrates androgyny' (p. 34); and goes on to argue that Lyly presents 'sexual difference' as 'arbitrary' and 'endlessly reversible' (p. 37). This is seriously misleading: Venus' decision to change either Phyllida or Galatea into a boy at the end of the play is exceptional; there is no question about the reversibility of the sex of any of the other characters in the play. Professor Rackin would have us believe that the play proposes the 'abolition of sexual difference' (p. 37), but this is clearly mistaken. Venus' decision is only 'arbitrary' in the sense that she makes it without consulting the other gods – *not* in the deconstructively 'free-playing' sense suggested by the phrase 'endlessly reversible'. Moreover, her decision actually *reinstates* sexual difference by insisting that female same-sex love is not a viable alternative to heterosexual love when it comes to lasting relationships such as wedlock. In 'John Lyly's *Gallathea*: A New Rhetoric of Love for the Virgin Queen' (*ELR* 17 [1987], pp. 22–40), Ellen C. Caldwell asserts that the relationship between Phyllida and Galatea is an 'agape of friendship, which matures to an amor blessed by Venus' (p. 38). I am not at all sure what this means; but the essay also ignores – perversely, in my opinion – the lesbianism of the play in favour of androgyny. We have become used to seeing sex sanitised as 'sexuality'; but here it is cleaned up out of existence!

31. Fredericus H. M. Blaydes, ed., *Aristophanis Ranae* (Halle, 1889), note at line 1308.

32. Porphyrio, on Horace, *Epistulae*; cit. Campbell, *Greek Lyric*, vol. 1, p. 19.

33. The Latin reads: 'Nulla autem in epistola mitiores, ac lasciuiores amoris affectus, quam ista expressit Ouidius, eo quod supra muliebrem condicionem in amores arserit Sappho: cum non modo virum, perdite amauerit, sed aliarum quoque mulierum tribas fuerit, id est, insultando illas fricaret, vnde ab Horatio mascula Sappho vocata est' (Andreas Naugerius, ed. *Publii Ovidii Nasonis heroidum epistolae* [London, 1583: STC 18928], p. 124). On the other hand, we learn from Professor Traub of 'the cultural fantasy of the enlarged clitoris' (p. 156); and that it is the use of this organ or a dildo that '*defines* the "sodomite" or "tribade"' in the Renaissance (p. 164). Perhaps; although I have yet to find any evidence of this definitive fantasy in my own explorations of sixteenth-century literature.

REFERENCES

Aelian, *Miscellanies [Varia historia]*. Trans. Abraham Fleming as *A Register of Histories* (London, 1578: STC 164).
Baldwin, T. W., *William Shakspere's Small Latine & Lesse Greeke* (Urbana, 1944).
Bevington, David, and G. K. Hunter (eds.), *John Lyly: 'Campaspe' and 'Sappho and Phao'* (Manchester and New York, 1991).
Blaydes, Fredericus H. M. (ed.), *Aristophanis Ranae* (Halle, 1889).
Burel, John, *To the Right High Lodowick, Duke of Lennox* (Edinburgh, 1595: STC 4105).
Caldwell, Ellen C., 'John Lyly's *Gallathea*: A New Rhetoric of Love for the Virgin Queen', *ELR* 17 (1987), pp. 22–40.
Churchyard, Thomas, *A Discourse of the Queen's Majesty's Entertainment in Suffolk and Norfolk* (London, 1578: STC 5226).
Cooper, Thomas, *Thesaurus linguae Romanae et Britannicae* (London, 1565: STC 5226).
Dent, R. W. *Proverbial Language in English Drama Exclusive of Shakespeare 1445–1612* (Berkeley, 1984).
Dörrie, Heinrich (ed.), *P. Ovidius Naso: Der Brief der Sappho and Phaon* (Munich, 1975).
Duncan, Douglas, *Ben Jonson and the Lucianic Tradition* (Cambridge and New York, 1979).
Feyld, Thomas, *A Controversy between a Lover and a Jay* (?1527; 2nd edn, London, ?1532: STC 10839).
Gardner, Helen (ed.), *John Donne: The Elegies and The Songs and Sonnets* (Oxford, 1965).
Gifford, Humphrey, *A Posy of Gillyflowers* (London, 1580: STC 11872).
Greene, Robert, *Alcida* (?1589; London, 1617: STC 12216).
Herodas, *Mimes [Mimiambi]*. In Jeffrey Rusten *et al.*, trans., *Theophrastus: 'Characters'; Herodas: 'Mimes'; The Choliambic Poets* (Cambridge, Mass., and London, 1993 [LCL]).
Hunter, G. K., *John Lyly: The Humanist as Courtier* (London, 1962).
Jankowski, Theodora, 'The Subversion of Flattery: The Queen's Body in John Lyly's *Sappho and Phao*', *MRDE* 5 (1991), pp. 69–86.
La connaissance d'amours (London, ?1528: STC 5631).
Lloyd, Lodowick, *The Pilgrimage of Princes* (London, ?1573: STC 16624).
Lucian, i.e. pseudo-Lucian, *Affairs of the Heart [Amores]*. In A. M. Harmon *et al.*, trans., *Lucian* (Cambridge, Mass., and London, 1913–67 [LCL]), vol. 8.
Lucian of Samosata, *Dialogues of the Courtesans [Dialogi meretricum]*. In Harmon, *Lucian*, vol. 7.
Lyly, John, *Galatea* (1592). In R. Warwick Bond (ed.), *The Complete Works of John Lyly* (Oxford, 1902), vol. 3.
—— *Sappho and Phao* (1584). In Bond, vol. 3.
Maximus of Tyre, *Orations [Orationes]*. Cit. David A. Campbell, *Greek Lyric* (Cambridge, Mass., and London, 1982–92 [LCL]), vol. 1.
Miller, Paul Allen. *Lyric Texts and Lyric Consciousness: The Birth of a Genre from Archaic Greece to Augustan Rome* (London and New York, 1994).

Morillonus, Guido, Commentary on Ovid's *Heroides* in Andreas Naugerius (ed.), *Publii Ovidii Nasonis heroidum epistolae* (London, 1583: STC 18928).

Nagy, Gregory, 'Phaethon, Sappho's Phaon, and the White Rock of Leukas: "Reading the Symbols" of Greek Lyric'. In his *Greek Mythology and Poetics* (Ithaca and London, 1990), pp. 223–62.

Nashe, Thomas, *The Choice of Valentines* (ms. *c.* 1592). In R. B. McKerrow, ed., *The Works of Thomas Nashe* (1904–10; ed. F. P. Wilson, Oxford, 1957). vol. 3.

Ovid, *Heroides*. In Grant Showerman, trans. *Ovid: Heroides and Amores* (New York and London, 1921 [LCL]).

—— *Heroides*. Trans. George Turberville as *Ovid's Heroical Epistles* (London, 1567: STC 18939.5).

Peend, Thomas, *A Pleasant Fable of Hermaphroditus and Salmacis* (London, 1565: STC 18971).

Porphyrio, Commentary on Horace's *Epistles*; cit. David A. Campbell, *Greek Lyric* (Cambridge, Mass., and London, 1982–92 [LCL]), vol. 1.

Puttenham, George, *Partheniades*. MS. 1581/2. BL Cotton MS Vesp. E. viii.

Rackin, Phyllis, 'Androgyny, Mimesis, and the Marriage of the Boy Heroine on the English Renaissance Stage', *PMLA* 102 (1987), pp. 29–41.

Revard, Stella P., 'The Sapphic Voice in Donne's "Sappho to Philaenis"'. In Claude J. Summers and Ted-Larry Pebworth, eds, *Renaissance Discourses of Desire* (Columbia and London, 1993), pp. 63–76.

Rolland, John, *The Court of Venus* (Edinburgh, 1575: STC 21258).

Shulman, Jeff, 'Lyly's Use of Aelian in *Campaspe*'. *N&Q* 227 (1982), pp. 417–18.

Skelton, John, *Philip Sparrow* (?1505). In John Scattergood (ed.), *John Skelton: The Complete English Poems* (Harmondsworth, 1983).

Stern, Virginia F., *Gabriel Harvey: A Study of his Life, Marginalia, and Library* (Oxford, 1977).

Suda, Cit. David A. Campbell, *Greek Lyric* (Cambridge, Mass., and London, 1982–92 [LCL]), vol. 1.

Traub, Valerie, 'The (In)Significance of "Lesbian" Desire in Early Modern England'. In Susan Zimmermann (ed.), *Erotic Politics: Desire on the Renaissance Stage* (London, 1992), pp. 150–69.

Verducci, Florence, *Ovid's Toyshop of the Heart: 'Epistulae heroidum'* (Princeton: 1985).

ABBREVIATIONS

ELR	*English Literary Renaissance*
LCL	Loeb Classical Library
MRDE	*Medieval and Renaissance Drama in England*
N&Q	*Notes and Queries*
PMLA	*Publications of the Modern Languages Association*
STC	Short Title Catalogue

5

Blackness Yields to Beauty: Desirability and Difference in Early Modern Culture

Kate Chedgzoy

In 1605, a Danish woman, married to a Scotsman, appeared in public before him and an international gathering of his associates, wearing a flimsy, sexually suggestive costume and with black make-up on her arms, hands and face. She was impersonating one of twelve African nymphs, distressed by their ugly blackness, who were seeking the ruler of a country whose name ended with the syllables 'tania', in order to be whitened into beauty – and thereby to demonstrate, by means of the heliocentric symbolism of monarchy, the power of that country. The thematic inspiration for Ben Jonson's *Masque of Blackness* apparently came from Queen Anne of Denmark herself; yet finally, it is her husband, James VI of Scotland and I of England and Wales, who becomes the centre of attention, as his regal light on the African nymphs transfigures them:

> Yield, night, then, to the light,
> As blackness hath to beauty,
> Which was but the same duty.
> It is for beauty that the world was made,
> And where she reigns Love's lights admit no shade.[1]

Masculine royal agency is the focus of interest; but feminine beauty remains its medium, and a performance by female courtiers in one of the few modes of formal public representation open to them the occasion for its display. Responsive as it is to the contemporary academy's concern with issues such as racial difference and women's cultural agency, *The Masque of Blackness* has become the centre of a major critical debate in recent years.[2] Less well known, but remarkably pertinent to that same debate, is a play which was written some two decades later, also to offer a queen the opportunity to perform on stage, and which also includes an intriguing and highly symbolic representation of the 'whitening' of a black woman: Walter Montagu's *The Shepheards Paradise*.[3] Written in 1632–3 to be performed by Henrietta Maria and her ladies, this courtly drama is best known for featuring the first cast list to designate women as performers on an English stage. My present interest in the play, however, centres not on female performance, but on one remarkable embedded moment of what we might – with suitable reservations – call racial performance: a staging of racial and sexual difference which scrutinises the construction of cultural desirability.

The Shepherds Paradise itself is, as its name suggests, a pastoral refuge, to which women apply for admission by describing the sufferings they have endured in the wickedly patriarchal world outside it. Act III apparently stages the attempt of a Moor, Gemella, to gain entry – although the audience, unlike the other characters, is aware that 'Gemella' is in fact the white noblewoman Fidamira in disguise.

Gemella tells a heart-rending tale of her sufferings, and the inhabitants of the Shepherds Paradise duly vote on her admission. Only one vote, that of Moramante,[4] opposes Gemella, and he gives his reasons as follows:

> this unhappy Lady…seems armed with a mind brave enough not to esteem this residence an ease, that shall exclude her from the dignity of queen: which her person we know doth debar her here being a Moor; if she can let her self fall into these prejudices, she shall have my vote, to me more pitied after her admission than before.[5]

Moramante's argument is that to admit Gemella would be inappropriate because her virtues clearly entitle her to the honour of being made Queen of the Shepherds Paradise – a role from which she is nevertheless inevitably debarred by her race. In other words, there is a mismatch between her outward appearance and her inward qualities, which cannot be reconciled within the frame of this hierarchical, aestheticising, self-regarding community. However, Moramante's judgement is promptly and vigorously called into question by Bellesa, the current Queen:

The Contrarieties of nature are
  made for their opposition, not compare;
The Darkeness of the night may be as fair
  for it, as can the day's serenest air
And so this colour of itself may be
  Lovely as ours in its own Degree;
And for the exclusion of her self from hope of being Queen, she
doth no more than all of us, submit to the opinion of the most,
and who knows what one day may be called beauty? since we
see the opinion of it alter every day.[6]

Bellesa invokes cultural relativism and the social construction of
norms of beauty and desirability to justify the admission of Gemella
on an equal footing with the women who already live in the
Shepherds Paradise. Here, the argument seems to depend not on
a reminder to the audience that the Moor Gemella is really the
acceptably white Fidamira, but rather on a belief that, in the right
cultural context, blackness can indeed be defined as beautiful. Later,
however, when Gemella is duly elected Queen, the decision is
challenged by Pantamora, on the grounds that it violates the will
of the Foundress, 'which appoints the Queen to be chosen principally for her beauty'[7] – clearly implying that Gemella, because she is
a Moor, cannot be beautiful enough. It is at this moment that Bellesa
pulls off Gemella's veil, revealing her as Fidamira, whose claim to
the throne is substantiated not only by the 'fairness' thus disclosed,
but by the subsequent revelation that she is in fact the long-lost
princess Miranda. The argument for the desirability of difference is
thus swiftly displaced by the reassertion, on the site of what had
appeared to be that difference, of conventional, high-status feminine beauty.

   In itself, this incident tells us a great deal about the ways in which
the early modern period was beginning to think through issues
about women's cultural status, beauty, and so on, as they might be
inflected by racial difference. But it is particularly significant for my
purposes here because *The Shepheards Paradise* staged its encounter
with difference at the very heart of the British court, in a series of
rehearsals and a performance which engaged the energies of Henrietta Maria and her ladies through the autumn and winter of 1632–
3. The whitening of Gemella – or to describe it another way, the
elimination of disfiguring blackness by means of an encounter with
the courtly values of which the Shepherds Paradise is the seat – is

strongly reminiscent of *The Masque of Blackness*. Two works do not make a trend, of course; but the resemblances between *The Masque of Blackness* and *The Shepheards Paradise*, are no less remarkable because coincidental. Importantly, in neither of these works is there any real encounter with alterity, or interest in blackness for its own sake: it functions, rather, as a trope of difference which, in the case of *The Shepheards Paradise*, interacts with a set of neo-Platonic ideas about beauty and virtue dear to Henrietta Maria's court and thereby enables the representation of whiteness as the embodiment of desirability. The figure of Gemella thus tells us more about the construction of elite white femininity than it does about that difference – which we would now designate as racial – which Gemella is perceived as embodying.

Discussions of emergent notions of racial difference in early modern culture have so far tended to take blackness, otherness, as their object.[8] In the present essay, the story of Gemella/Fidamira serves as prologue to an attempt to make whiteness visible, by considering white women's stake in the construction of racially and sexually marked identities in the early modern period. It is undoubtedly the case that the majority of discussions of the representation of racial difference in early modern texts have so far tended to focus on blackness as an object of scrutiny – often reproducing outrageously racist assumptions – while taking whiteness as an unproblematic, effectively invisible given. This difficulty of making whiteness visible is, in fact, intrinsic to the way it is constructed in Western culture, as Richard Dyer has noted:

> Trying to think about the representation of whiteness as an ethnic category... is difficult, partly because white power secures its dominance by seeming not to be anything in particular, but also because, when whiteness *qua* whiteness does come into focus, it is often revealed as emptiness, absence, denial, or even a kind of death.[9]

It is this process by which white people absent themselves from the construction of racial identities, deny that they are themselves racially marked, which enables the construction of race as a problem of otherness – a burden which is to be borne exclusively by black people. But the position of women is awkward, and troubles this schema: black women because they are often excluded from the category of 'women' in general, which is effectively a white category, and because the category 'black' is often identified exclusively with men. Conversely, white women are both inside and outside the dominant group, included by virtue of their whiteness, excluded by their gender. My aim in this essay is to trace the inscription of these practices of inclusion, exclusion and identification in certain seventeenth century literary texts which I perceive as symptomatic, and to consider how they find a particular focus in the elite white woman's relation to her literary culture.

The dialogic relation between white beauty and black ugliness, which structures both *The Masque of Blackness* and *The Shepheards Paradise*, indicates that whiteness operates as a category which is crucial for the textual construction of female desire and desirability in the Renaissance. As Kim F. Hall notes, pairings of dark and fair women recur in Western cultural tradition, from Pamela and Philoclea in *The Countess of Pembroke's Arcadia* through to the numerous, proliferating instances which could be drawn from modern visual culture – of these, the double-act of Marilyn Monroe and Jane Russell in the film *Gentlemen Prefer Blondes* is perhaps the most blatant example. Hall argues that 'the languages of beauty and colonialism intersect when the ubiquitous "darkness" in these pairings comes to include foreign women who are posed to compete with fair, European women for male attention'; and so in *A Midsummer Night's Dream*, Lysander rejects dark Hermia in favour of the fair Helena with the epithets 'Away, you Ethiope' and 'Out, Tawny Tartar'.[10] We might think too of the way the economy of desire represented in Shakespeare's sonnets turns on the contrast between the 'fair youth' and the 'dark lady', and ask ourselves what would happen if, following Jonathan Crewe's advice, 'instead of always genteelly speaking of Shakespeare's Dark Lady sonnets, we could bring ourselves to call them the Black Woman sonnets'.[11] Teaching the sonnets in Liverpool, I came to understand that students from the local black community had good reasons for arguing that her 'dun breasts' and hair like black wires are not merely rhetorical inversions of the familiar Petrarchan imagery, but do evoke a distinctively African appearance, thereby controverting the European Renaissance's central canons of feminine beauty. And yet, while asserting her ugliness, the speaker of the Sonnets clearly also finds this woman erotically compelling. For the dichotomy between the dark and fair woman is not totally Manichean: Hermia ends up happily paired off, and of course, blackness, beauty, eroticism and desirability are all reunited in the person of Shakespeare's Cleopatra, who is 'with Phoebus' amorous pinches black'.

The historical Cleopatra was not ethnically Egyptian, but of Macedonian descent, although an argument has recently been made, from a black political perspective, for an Afrocentric revision of Egyptian history, which would seek to claim her as part of that heritage. Shakespeare's text departs from previous English works in using terms which seem strongly to indicate that Cleopatra, just as much as Othello or the Prince of Morocco, should be thought of as a black African. Commentators reluctant to concede this point suggest that a phrase like Cleopatra's description of her self as being 'with Phoebus' amorous pinches black' merely implies that she is sunburnt: but given that the notion that Africans were black precisely because of the sun's operations upon their skin still had extensive currency in the early sevententh century, this claim is not wholly persuasive. The *Antony and Cleopatra* performance tradition has typically played on the allure of exoticism, while minimising the signifiers of ethnic difference in order to make Cleopatra conform to more acceptable stereotypes of feminine beauty. I have only once seen the role performed by a black actress, Donna Kroll, in Talawa Theatre Company's all-black production of *Antony and Cleopatra*, which toured Britain in 1991. This production revised conventional attitudes to the play's intertwining of cultural and sexual difference in that it problematised the common critical and theatrical approach which constructs 'Rome' and 'Egypt' as binary oppositions, and in doing so offered a relatively 'Cleopatra-centred' vision of the play.

Founded and directed by Yvonne Brewster, Talawa has fostered work by contemporary black women playwrights, and offered black actresses a rare opportunity to undertake major roles. For example, its most recent production at the time of writing was *Medea in the Mirror*, an updating of the Medea myth by Cuban playwright Jose Triana, staged in Brixton, London in the summer of 1996. In its approach to selecting and staging plays the company has clearly been influenced by feminism, then. Yet in discussing the significance of racial and sexual politics in the company's work, particularly as it affects the choice of plays for the repertoire, Brewster once drew a sharp distinction between Shakespeare, whose works she presumed were available for appropriation by a black company because they are part of a shared culture, and the works of white women writers, typified by Aphra Behn, who for some unspecified reason are perceived as less accessible:

> I know that some women in the past wrote large-scale plays, but I have never found one that would be right for Talawa. The Aphra Behns of this world are beyond my ken. I don't understand what the bloody hell she's on about.[12]

Brewster does not explain what makes Behn so incomprehensible and inaccessible to her; the colloquial phrase 'beyond my ken' may signal either an anxiety that Behn's works are abstruse and élitist in nature, or a sense of their eccentricity to the cultural centrality epitomised by Shakespeare, locating them beyond the margins of culture. In speaking of 'the Aphra Behns of this world', Brewster seems to place Behn as typical of a whole class of women playwrights, endowing her with the burden of representative status which writers outwith the mainstream often have to bear. Indeed, ever since Virginia Woolf adjured 'all women together... to let flowers fall on the tomb of Aphra Behn',[13] she has enjoyed an exemplary, if somewhat problematic, status, as a successful woman writer of the early modern period, and thus in some sense the nearest thing we have to that chimera, a female Shakespeare. Yet Behn's cultural image has also been importantly inflected by her authorship of the novella *Oroonoko* (1688), which in its depiction of the noble slave Oroonoko, his beloved Imoinda, and the social organisation and mores of both their African culture and the Surinam slave society to which they are transported, represents both a foundational text of anti-slavery literature and a key instance of an early modern woman's textual engagement with questions of racial difference. While Yvonne Brewster appears to construct Aphra Behn as both eccentric to mainstream culture and utterly marginal to the concerns of a modern black theatre company, Behn's authorship of *Oroonoko* placed her as a liminal figure: between cultures. Arguably, this ambivalent position is in many ways characteristic of the white woman's location vis-à-vis the intersection of racial and sexual difference.

I want now to elaborate on this point by looking at a particularly celebrated instance – perhaps the most celebrated in our culture – of the dangerous conjunction of race, gender and sexuality in the form of a white woman's desire for a black man. I am referring, of course, to Shakespeare's *Othello*, and especially the scandal – sexual, racial and aesthetic – of Desdemona's desire for Othello. Critical debate on the play has frequently staged racial difference as the point of convergence of anxieties about social and artistic propriety: namely, the fitness of *Othello* for stage representation, and the acceptability of Desdemona's desire for Othello. This mingling of aesthetic and moral/social concerns was initiated by Thomas Rymer's notorious account of *Othello* in *A Short View of Tragedy* (1693). Working to a strict neoclassical schema, Rymer found that the play's impropriety in depicting the active desire of a noble young white woman for a Moor was the effective source of its shocking lack of artistic *bienséance*, as is demonstrated by the obsessive repetitions of his commentary on Iago's attempt to persuade Othello that any desire he engenders in a white woman must be 'foul' and 'unnatural':

> Jago. *I, There's the point: as to be bold with you,*
> *Not to affect many proposed Matches*
> *Of her own clime, complexion, and degree,*
> *Wherein we see, in all things, Nature tends,*
> *Fye, we may smell in such a will most rank,*
> *Foul disproportion, thoughts unnatural*

> [III, iii, 232–7]

The Poet here is certainly in the right, and by consequence the foundation of the Play must be concluded to be Monstrous; And the constitution, all over, to be *most rank/Foul disproportion, thoughts unnatural.*[14]

Concurring with Iago in what the Indian feminist critic Ania Loomba has described as 'a patriarchal view of female waywardness and the necessity of obedience, a racist warning against the rampant sexuality of black men, and a class consciousness which prioritises the submission of women "of Quality"',[15] Rymer detaches Iago's words from their dramatic context and identifies them with both the authorial perspective and his own analysis of what is wrong with the play. It is a curious paradox that the insight into the monstrosity of interracial desire, which is attributed to Shakespeare, also provides the ground for Rymer's condemnation of the play as an aesthetic monstrosity.

Loomba is clearly right to invoke the racist construction of black male sexuality in her comments on Rymer and *Othello*. Undoubtedly, the depiction of the relationship between Othello and Desdemona is informed throughout the play by the cultural attribution to black men, already well established by Shakespeare's time, of an excessive, animalistic sexual appetite, although in so far as it puts the rhetoric of bestiality into the mouths of Othello's enemies, the play does not necessarily endorse these associations.[16] For Iago and Rymer, though, as for many of their successors, the problem lies not in Othello's sexuality, but in Desdemona's: in the fact that she asserts and acts on a desire which transgresses boundaries of race and class. Rymer quotes the attempt made by Giraldi Cinthio, author of Shakespeare's main source for *Othello*, to excuse and explain Desdemona's desire for Othello, only in order to disavow it cynically:[17]

> Cinthio affirms that *She was not overcome by a Womanish Apetite, but by the Vertue of the Moor*. It must be a good-natur'd Reader that takes *Cinthio*'s word in this case, tho' in a Novel. Shakespear... is accountable both to the *Eyes*, and to the *Ears*, And to convince the very heart of an Audience...
>
> (pp. 132–3)

The shock value of the interracial relationship is aggravated for Rymer when the desires of the black man and the white woman are embodied on the stage, and not merely narrated on the page. The italicised phrase is quite a faithful rendering of Cinthio's text, which affirms that the virtuous and beautiful Disdemona (as she is called in the novella), 'tratta non da appetito donnesco, ma dalla virtu del Moro, s'innamoro di lui'.[18] The not insignificant difference is that Rymer conflates the relatively innocuous 'tratta' and 's'innamoro' in the rather more suggestive 'overcome', implicitly eroticising a submission which Cinthio is at pains to mark as 'virtuous'.

Half a century later, Charlotte Lennox's rendering of Cinthio's defence of Disdemona is expressed in more overtly sexual terms which would no doubt have made it even less acceptable to Rymer. Turning up the rhetorical heat, Lennox evokes the uncontrollable waywardness of female sexuality precisely in the act of denying that Disdemona was thus afflicted, declaring that 'not subdued by the irregular Sallies of a female Appetite, but struck with the great Qualities and noble Virtues of the *Moor*, [she] became violently enamoured of him'.[19] Lennox's use of the word 'enamoured' could perhaps be read as an attempt to convey the Italian pun on 'Moro/ s'innamoro', echoing the stigmatised submergence of Desdemona's whiteness in her husband's blackness, which is a recurrent trope in Shakespeare's play.[20] In her commentary, however, she shows more tolerance and sympathy for the heroine's transgression:

> Such Affections are not very common indeed; but a very few Instances of them prove that they are not impossible; and even in *England* we see some very handsome Women married to Blacks, where their Colour is less familiar than at *Venice*; besides the *Italian* Ladies are remarkable for such Sallies of irregular Passions.
>
> (p. 131)

Disdemona's breaching of the boundaries of race and class is to some extent mitigated by her own cultural difference from the English readers whom Lennox addresses, and who are positioned here as complicit with the ideology which sexualises otherness by constructing 'Italian Ladies' as particularly prone to 'irregular Passions'. Lennox's cultural relativism means that unlike Rymer, she does not perceive a relationship between a white woman and a black man as intrinsically shocking because unnatural; what makes it disturbing, in her view, is merely its unfamiliarity. As early as 1694, Charles Gildon had reached the same conclusion, remarking that 'Experience tells us, that there's nothing more common than Matches of this kind, where the Whites, and Blacks cohabit, as in both the Indies'[21] – in other words, in societies where familiarity has diminished the shock value of such relationships. Gildon and Lennox are both prepared to offer a qualified defence of interracial desire, then; but it is not insignificant that they present it as something which is most likely to be found in such safely foreign and distant realms as Italy and the Indies, at the same time as displacing the focus of attention from Shakespeare's play onto its fictional source. In her discussion of *Othello*, Dympna Callaghan argues that 'taking miscegenation seriously (despite the fact that it is the subject of the play) is not conducive to the preservation of Shakespeare as a cultural icon – the purveyor of universal truths' (*Woman and Gender*, p. 36). On the contrary, I would argue on the one hand, that it is precisely Shakespeare's unique cultural position which enabled the recuperation of *Othello* for a legitimating discourse of racism which took miscegenation lethally seriously; and on the other, that much of the controversy which has accompanied *Othello* since the seventeenth century is, at least in part, a function of its relatively sympathetic depiction of the desire of a white woman for a black man.

Works like *Othello, The Shepheards Paradise* and *The Masque of Blackness* participate in a matrix of early modern texts which initiated a crucial set of strategies for constructing and regulating the sexuality of white women and all black people, while obliterating the possibility of recognising the agency of white male sexuality in maintaining the sexist, racist social structures which are ratified by this conjunction. I want now to consider to what extent white women's texts contributed to, or were able to challenge, this process. The fact that in the late seventeenth century a number of white British women began to draw the analogy between slavery and a woman's sexual and economic subjugation in marriage which was to remain a staple of feminist discourse for at least 200 years provides a convenient instance. The anonymous *An Essay in Defence of the Female Sex* (1696), for example, which has been variously attributed to Mary Astell and Judith Drake, offers an account of the origins of oppression which intertwines racial and sexual subjugation:

> By degrees, [men's domination of women] came to that height of Severity, I may say Cruelty, it is now at in all the Eastern parts of the World, where the Women, like our Negroes in our Western Plantations, are born slaves, and live Prisoners all their Lives .... [Even in England] Fetters of Gold are still Fetters, and the softest Lining can never make 'em so easy, as Liberty.[22]

The specificities of the oppression of English women are represented here through multiple layers of racial and cultural differentiation, and in the condemnation of the cruelty with which Eastern women are treated – a condemnation which is presumably to be extended to the negroes on the western plantations – there may be the seeds of an implicit critique of slavery. Nevertheless, enslavement is equated primarily with loss of liberty, and the image of 'Fetters of Gold' marks the discrepancy between the English-woman's representation of her lack of freedom as a form of slavery, and the brutal oppression of actual slaves 'in our Western Plantations', which the writer passes over in silence.

In a text which undoubtedly is by Mary Astell, *Some Reflections Upon Marriage* (1700), she offers an even more forthright representation of marriage as a form of slavery for white women:

> If *all Men are born Free*, how is it that all Women are born Slaves? As they must be, if the being subjected to the *inconstant, uncertain, unknown, arbitrary* Will of Men, be the *perfect condition of Slavery*? ... And why is Slavery so much condemn'd and strove against in one case, and so highly applauded, and held so necessary and so sacred in another?[23]

Astell is being rather optimistic in assuming the widespread condemnation of plantation slavery at this early date, and this points up the problematic ramifications of making feminist use of the analogy between white women and black slaves – an analogy which frequently obscures the fact that slaves, like all black people, come in both genders. In the passage from *An Essay in Defence of the Female Sex* quoted above, for instance, the counterposing of women who are sexually enslaved in eastern harems against plantation negroes fails to take into account the specific sufferings of enslaved African women. Moira Ferguson argues that the failure to recognise the full significance of the use of slavery as a political metaphor by means of which middle- and upper-class white women could interpret their experience 'displayed women's self-perceived cultural impotence alongside the primacy they accorded their own condition. It also betrayed traditional white supremacist attitudes' (*Subject to Others*, p. 23). Ferguson is particularly scathing about the poet Ephelia's apt, if tactless, use of the language of slavery in order to represent the miseries of an unhappy love affair with a slave trader:

> She equates slavery with pain and cruelty, divesting the language of its hideous quotidian reality by reserving it for the sorrows of a free woman, neglected in love.... Ephelia remained heedless of the implication of her language, a myopia common to the age.
>
> (ibid.)

Ferguson does distinguish between her condemnation of Ephelia's solipsistic indulgence in what was, after all, a venerable poetic trope, and its more politically sophisticated deployment in proto-feminist

texts. However, her critique of Ephelia's use of the slavery trope to
depict emotional suffering depends on the post-Romantic assumption, at variance with the practices by which poetry was composed
and publicly circulated in the late seventeenth century, that the
texts under consideration are the work of a female author inscribing
her own experience in the poetic form. Yet there is no firm evidence
that the poems attributed to Ephelia in the 1679 volume *Female
Poems* were all the work of a single author, female or otherwise;
indeed, the question of whether 'Ephelia' ever existed at all was
recently the subject of an intense, if somewhat arcane, academic
controversy.[24]

The feminist literary historian's desire to identify a real female
presence behind the voice of Ephelia's verse, and to posit a woman
writer as the self-conscious user of metaphors of slavery, is clearly
overdetermined. And it is undeniable that whoever 'she' may have
been, Ephelia's poetic use of metaphors of slavery has a particular
resonance for modern investigators of the interwoven histories of
racism and sexism. Ferguson's analysis of Ephelia's poems is
important in that it raises the difficult question of what sorts of
political language and critique are available at different historical
moments. However, feminist critics who seek to find confirmation
of their own political priorities in the literature of the past run the
risk of enacting an anachronistic appropriation of women's texts
and lives which may be both historically questionable and contrary
to their own best interests. It is not particularly helpful either to
blame Ephelia for being politically incorrect, or to claim Aphra Behn
as a heroine because in *Oroonoko* she wrote a text which came, after
her death, to have a paradigmatic function within anti-slavery
discourse. It is all too easy to construct an account in which Ephelia
is guilty of acting as a conduit for the prejudices of her age; while
Behn, in apparently achieving a more progressive understanding of
the mutually interdependent institutions of slavery and racism,
takes some of the heat off less enlightened women writers. But as
Vron Ware says,

> The purpose of exploring the histories of slavery and imperialism
> is not to bring white women to account for past misdeeds, nor to
> search for heroines whose reputations can help to absolve the
> rest from guilt, but to find out how white women negotiated
> questions of race and racism – as well as class and gender.
>
> (*Beyond the Pale*, p. 43)

It is with such issues in mind that the political status of *Oroonoko* has recently been extensively reconsidered by feminist critics. Ros Ballaster has argued that both Aphra Behn's *Oroonoko* and white feminist criticism of it are marked by the

> refusal to employ the black woman as anything other than inappropriable symbol of alterity and incomprehensible suffer-ing.... [T]he figure of the black woman becomes purely iconic, the mute bearer of female suffering onto whom the white female subject can project her own hysteria and be left at liberty to write.[25]

Ballaster further argues that Behn's construction of a self-authoris-ing voice for the anonymous narrator, who has so often been identified with the author herself, is achieved at the expense of the utter social abjection of the black woman, and that as a conse-quence *Oroonoko*'s current popularity among feminist critics can be traced to the text's ability to challenge modern readers to 'consider the ways in which a white "feminist" impulse to win "authority" for the female voice has historically been complicit in forms of racist misogyny' (p. 293). Her analysis thus emphasises a crucial point which has been neglected in many accounts of the early modern construction of discourses of racial difference: namely, that the conditions of possibility for the existence of the subject are recipro-cally constructed in relation with its others. It is not merely the case that the master needs the slave in order to exist as such, but that the slave's identity has to be factored in as a crucial element of what shapes the master's identity. And the representation of black Others in *Oroonoko* has always been one crucial element of Behn's cultural identity, existing in tension with the sexualisation of her image as a writer.

Apart from Virginia Woolf's celebration of her as the first profes-sional woman writer, Behn has traditionally had a very dubious reputation, in which her literary production has often been equated with a form of prostitution. Comparing her with her male contem-poraries, one Dr Doran said:

> No one equalled this woman in downright nastiness save Raven-scroft and Wycherley. ... With Dryden she vied in indecency and was not overcome. ... She was a mere harlot, who danced through uncleanness and dared them to follow. ... [She was] a

wanton hussy [whose] trolloping muse ... wallowed in the mire.[26]

While male authors are censured for the moral imperfections of their text, it is difficult to imagine such condemnation being extended to their identity as sexed and gendered individuals. Indeed, we may assume that Dryden himself would have been less than thrilled by this comparison, since in 1699 he warned the poet Elizabeth Thomas against taking Aphra Behn as a role model, counselling her to avoid 'the Licence which Mrs Behn allowed herself, of writing loosely, and giving (if I may have leave to say so) some Scandal to the Modesty of her Sex.'[27]

For subsequent centuries, Behn's reputation was only partially redeemed by her stirring depiction of the noble savage in *Oroonoko*, her best-known work, and by the novella's status as the inaugural text of the anti-slavery literary tradition. More recently, however, feminist re-evaluations of her writing have found fertile territory in precisely the exploration of sexuality which moralists used to complain about; yet she has been taken to task for the political inadequacy of her representation of racial difference. This is very different from the cultural history of *Othello* – a text with which Behn's *Oroonoko* is not infrequently compared these days – in respect of which critics have been much more eager either to argue that the depiction of blackness is not racist at all, or to defend it in terms of historical relativism. Exceptional female figures like Behn are obliged, it seems, to bear the burden of a certain feminist political desire, from which a canonical author like Shakespeare may be exempt.

Similarly, the early reception of Behn's work found the fact that she wrote so outspokenly about women's experiences and female sexuality problematic, particularly in relation to rumours which suggested that *Oroonoko* might inscribe her own desire for the Other. In *The History of the Life and Memoirs of Mrs. Behn, Written by one of the Fair Sex*, which prefaces Charles Gildon's complete edition of her works, an anonymous woman, who declares herself to be an intimate friend of Aphra Behn, refutes rumours of an improper relationship between the author and the real-life prototype of Oroonoko:

> there was no Affair between that Prince and *Astraea*, but what the whole Plantation were Witnesses of; a generous Value for his

uncommon Virtues, which everyone that but hears 'em, finds in himself, and his Presence gave her no more. Besides, his heart was too violently set on the everlasting Charms of his *Imoinda*, to be shook with those more faint (in his Eye) of a white Beauty. (p. 4)

The authenticity and accuracy of the memoir are highly questionable. For my purposes, however, the question of authorship is of less interest than the energetic demand for authenticity which is still associated with Behn's authorship of *Oroonoko*. Taking a hint from Southerne's claim that Behn 'always told [Oroonoko's] story more feelingly than she writ it',[28] a play based on Behn's *Oroonoko*, broadcast on BBC Radio 3 in 1992, used the framing device of a dinner party hosted by 'Aphra Behn' to motivate her narration of the novella's events, as first-person recollections and in the form of dramatised flashbacks.[29] It seems as if the authors of the play and the memoir were both seeking to aestheticise and monumentalise the textual and remembered traces of Behn's life in order to underwrite the truth value of her text, and to redeem the posthumous reputation of the dead writer from the charges of illicit sexuality which tarnished it in life.[30]

Death, sexuality and female reputation are as closely bound up in the *Life and Memoirs* of Behn as they are in *Othello*, and in the two versions of *Oroonoko* – Behn's novella and Thomas Southerne's subsequent highly successful staging of it. Shakespeare's and Southerne's plays both reach a dramatic climax in staging the murder of a white woman by a black man in the name of sexual propriety, followed by the honourable suicide of the eponymous hero. At the end of *Othello*, no woman is left alive to speak of the events which led to this 'bloody period'; only the intriguingly named courtesan Bianca survives, peripheral as she has been to the play's action, and it is clear that in the world depicted by the play, dominant attitudes to female speech and sexuality characteristic would have made her word count for little. At the end of Southerne's play, Charlotte and Lucy Welldon, the English women who came to seek their marital fortunes in Surinam, are not only still alive, but have succeeded in finding themselves husbands. Yet the limitations placed on their agency in the world of the colony are underlined by the jarring contrast between the comic resolution of Charlotte Welldon's schemes and the tragic conclusion of the other plot, and by the fact that they can only stand silently by while Oroonoko, having just killed Imoinda, turns the knife on himself. However, the significance of this final scene is cast into question when Charlotte returns to speak an Epilogue which plays on the seventeenth century's favourite sexual pun in order to satirise the operatic emotions summoned up by the fate of Imoinda:

> Then bless your stars, you happy London wives,
> Who love at large, each day, yet keep your lives.
> Nor envy poor Imoinda's doting blindness,
> Who thought her husband killed her out of kindness.
> Death with a husband ne'er had shown such charms,
> Had she once died within a lover's arms.

('Epilogue', 11. 21–7)

The clash, in this disconcerting ending, of the different theatrical pleasures afforded by comedy and tragedy serves to unsettle the ideological implications of the play's engagement with questions of race and sexuality; while the insouciance of Charlotte's celebration of female libertinism is hard to take at the end of a play which has suggested that marriage for women may often be little more than a form of voluntary slavery.

It is not my intention to suggest that the survival of the white female narrator at the end of Behn's *Oroonoko* endows that text with greater artistic value or political effectiveness than either *Othello* or Southerne's version of *Oroonoko*. Such issues are surely impossible to resolve, entangled as they are with the very different cultural desires which continue to attach themselves to the figures of Behn and Shakespeare. What I would contend, however, is that both the content and the subsequent history of Behn's fiction reveal with great clarity the painful intricacies of difference which shape the possibilities of cultural agency for figures like Desdemona, Othello, Oroonoko, Imoinda and the anonymous narrator – and, indeed, for their real-life counterparts. Shakespeare and Southerne both afford their tragic hero the dignity of a Roman death; Behn's Oroonoko, enfeebled by 'excess of grief' (p. 95), botches his suicide and is executed in the most grotesque and horrible fashion, while the narrator is absent and her mother and sister are 'not suffer'd to save him' (p. 99). The narrator's lavishly detailed account of Oroo-noko's final tortures is surpassed only by the still more baroque description, constructed from information supplied by Oroonoko himself, of the death of Imoinda:

> he ... gave the fatal stroke, first cutting her throat, and then severing her yet smiling face from that delicate body, pregnant as it was with the fruits of tenderest love.... [H]e laid the body decently on leaves and flowers, of which he made a bed, and conceal'd it under the same cover-lid of nature.
>
> (p. 94)

The 'fatal stroke' is eroticised as a lover's pinch, which hurts and is desired, and Imoinda's death is presented as a merging with an artificially manipulated nature oddly reminiscent of the earlier description of her body adornments, which similarly blur the distinction between nature and artifice. Ros Ballaster argues that the 'fine flowers and birds [carved] all over her body' (p. 68) are a symbol of Imoinda's unrecuperable cultural difference ('New Hystericism', p. 291). But I would also suggest that since within the novella they are primarily perceived as markers of her nobility within the terms of her own culture, and likened to the art, associated with European women, of japanned embroidery, they serve in addition to unsettle the cultural polarities which the narrator's textual strategies have deployed in order to fend off an unwished-for proximity to Imoinda.

At the close of the novella, Imoinda and the narrator achieve a textual intimacy greater than anything they managed during its course, when the narrator concludes her account of Oroonoko's execution with the declaration,

> Thus died this great man, worthy of a better fate, and a more sublime with than mine to write his praise: yet, I hope, the reputation of my pen is considerable enough to make his glorious name to survive to all ages, with that of the brave, the beautiful, and the constant Imoinda.
>
> (p. 99)

Despite this pious wish, it might be more accurate to say that it is Oroonoko's name that has ensured the survival of Behn's reputation. Imoinda, although she quite literally has the last word here, has usually been elbowed out of the simultaneously edifying and titillating encounter between the white woman and the black man –

an exclusion which is a function less of the structure of Behn's narrative, than of the cultural preoccupations which have shaped the variable fortunes of text and writer since the seventeenth century. At an historical moment which is witnessing an energetic revaluation of the role played by factors such as race, sexuality and gender in determining the significance of the writing and reputation of both Shakespeare and Behn, Imoinda's mute and inglorious fate serves as a timely reminder both of the complexity of what is at stake in the representation of difference; and of the way that our own desires as readers may shape our understanding of the past.

NOTES

1. Ben Jonson, *The Masque of Blackness*, in *The Complete Masques*, ed. Stephen Orgel (New Haven: Yale University Press, 1969), 11. 240–4.
2. Kim F. Hall's *Things of Darkness: Economies of Race and Gender in Early Modern England* (Ithaca: Cornell University Press, 1995) offers a through overview of recent scholarship engaging with racial differences in *The Masque of Blackness*, as well as a reading of her own which focuses on the interweaving of race and gender. For an approach which prioritises the place of female cultural agency in the masque, see Clare McManus, 'Defacing the Carcase: Queen Anne and the *The Masque of Blackness'*, in *Refashioning Ben Jonson* (Macmillan, forthcoming), edited by Julie Sanders with Susan Wiseman and Kate Chedgzoy.
3. My attention was drawn to Montagu's play, and its relevance to the current essay, by 'Notorious Whores', a paper given by Sarah Poynting at the Northern Renaissance Seminar/Women and Dramatic Production 1570–1670 meeting at Bretton Hall College in November 1994. A version of *The Shepheards Paradise* was published in 1659, but it omits the scene I discuss here. I am therefore extremely grateful to Sarah Poynting for her generosity in providing me with transcripts of various versions of this scene from several different manuscripts, and for pointing out to me that the unusual textual complexity of this scene may well reflect concerns with its content (private communication, February 1995).
4. I am tempted to see in this name a pun on 'Moor-lover', although this seems rather odd given Moramante's opposition to Gemella's admission.
5. Folger ms. Vb 203, fol.26r. I have modernised the spelling.
6. Ibid., fol.26v.
7. I quote here from the published version of *The Shepheards Paradise* (London, 1659), p. 167.

8. For an overview of such work, see Kim F. Hall, 'Reading What Isn't There: "Black" Studies in Early Modern England?', *Stanford Humanities Review*, 3, 1 (1993), 23–33.

9. 'White', *Screen* 29 (1988), 44–64 (44).

10. ' "I Rather Would Wish to be a Black-moor" ': Beauty, Race and Rank in Lady Mary Wroth's *Urania'*, in Margo Hendricks and Patricia Parker (eds.), *Women, 'Race' and Writing in the Early Modern Period* (London: Routledge, 1994), pp. 178–94 (p. 181).

11. Jonathan Crewe, *Trials of Authorship: Anterior Form and Poetic Reconstruction from Wyatt to Shakespeare* (Berkeley: University of California Press, 1990), p. 120.

12. Quoted in Lizbeth Goodman, *Contemporary Feminist Theatres: To Each Her Own* (London: Routledge, 1993), p. 159.

13. *A Room of One's Own* (1929) (London: Grafton, 1985), p. 63.

14. *A Short View of Tragedy*, in *The Critical Works of Thomas Rymer*, ed. Curt Zimansky (New Haven: Yale University Press, 1956), pp. 82–175 (p. 150); italics original.

15. *Gender, Race, Renaissance Drama* (Manchester: Manchester University Press, 1989), pp. 40–1.

16. See for example Iago's words to Brabantio in I.i: 'an old black ram / Is tupping your white ewe' (88–9), 'you'll have your daugher cover'd with a Barbary horse' (110), 'Your daughter and the Moor are now making the beast with two backs' (115–16). Among the many recent discussions of this subject, see for example Anthony Gerard Barthelemy, *Black Face Maligned Race: The Representation of Blacks in English Drama from Shakespeare to Southerne* (Baton Rouge: Louisiana State University Press, 1987); Jack D'Amico, *The Moor in English Renaissance Drama* (Tampa: University of South Florida Press, 1991); and Elliott H. Tokson, *The Popular Image of the Black Man in English Drama, 1550–1688* (Boston, Mass.: G.K. Hall and Co., 1982).

17. Cinthio's tale is the seventh story in the third decade of the *Hecatommithi* (Venice, 1566). The earliest known English translation was not published until 1753 (see below, fn. 16); there is no consensus on whether Shakespeare would have read the original Italian, or the French translation of 1584, or even a now-lost English version. On the possible influence of the French translation, see E.A.J. Honigmann, '*Othello*, Chappuys and Cinthio', *Notes and Queries* 211 (1966), 136–7.

18. Quoted in H.H. Furness (ed.), *A New Variorum Edition of Shakespeare's 'Othello'* (London, 1886), p. 377. A fairly literal rendering into a contemporary idiom might be '[Disdemona], not moved by female desire, but by the Moor's virtue, fell in love with him'.

19. *Shakespear Illustrated* (1753), 2 vols (New York: AMS Press, 1973), I, 101. The book represents the first substantial source study of Shakespeare's plays: Lennox reprints (in translation where appropriate) all the major sources then recognised, with extensive critical commentaries.

20. See for example, 'thou black weed' (IV.iii.69), or Desdemona's self-identification, in the same scene, with her mother's dead maid

Barbary, whose name recalls the designation of Othello as a 'Barbary horse'.

21. 'Some Reflections on Mr. Rymer's Short View of Tragedy', *Miscellaneous Letters and Essays* (1694), (New York: Garland Facsimile, 1973), pp. 64–118 (p. 99). By 1710, however, he was endorsing Rymer's point of view, asserting that 'Nature – or what is all one in this case, Custom' made the marriage intolerable. See 'Remarks on the Plays of Shakespeare', in Brian Vickers (ed.), *Shakespeare: The Critical Heritage*, 5 vols (London: Routledge Kegan Paul, 1974–81), II (1974), *1693–1733*, 226–62 (259).

22. I quote here from Margaret Ezell, *The Patriarch's Wife: Literary Evidence and the History of the Family* (Chapel Hill: University of North Carolina Press, 1987), pp. 116–7.

23. Quoted in Moira Ferguson, *Subject to Others: British Women Writers and Colonial Slavery, 1670–1834* (London: Routledge, 1993), p. 25.

24. Maureen Mulvihill's *Poems by Ephelia, c. 1679: The Premiere Facsimile Edition* (Delmar, NY: Scholars Facsimiles and Reprints, 1993) treats the works associated with 'Ephelia' as the literary production of a single, historically identifiable woman – assumptions which are rejected in Germaine Greer's review of the book, 'How to Invent a Poet', *Times Literary Supplement*, 25 June 1993, 7–8. Mulvihill defends herself in a letter to the *TLS*, 3 September 1993, 15.

25. 'New Hystericism. Aphra Behn's *Oroonoko*: The Body, the Text, and the Feminist Critic', in Isobel Armstrong (ed.), *New Feminist Discourses: Critical Essays on Theories and Texts* (London: Routledge, 1992), pp. 283–95 (pp. 292, 293–4).

26. Quoted by Montague Summers, 'A Memoir of Mrs. Behn', in *The Works of Aphra Behn*, 6 vols (London: William Heinemann, 1915), I, xxix–xxx.

27. Quoted in Margaret J.M. Ezell, *Writing Women's Literary History* (Baltimore: Johns Hopkins University Press, 1993), p. 72.

28. 'Dedicatory Epistle', in *Oroonoko*, ed. Novak and Rodes, pp. 3–5 (p. 4).

29. I would like to thank Debby Bruns for bringing the existence of this production to my attention; I have so far been unable to find out any details about its authorship.

30. My thinking here is indebted to the theoretical constructs proposed in Elisabeth Bronfen's *Over Her Dead Body: Death, Femininity and the Aesthetic* (Manchester: Manchester University Press, 1992), although I am at odds with Bronfen's claim that the conjunction of death, femininity and the aesthetic she theorises is only inaugurated in the Romantic period.

6

A Rose for Emilia:
Collaborative Relations in
The Two Noble Kinsmen

Gordon McMullan

I

There is an odd moment early on in Shakespeare and Fletcher's *Henry VIII*, when Norfolk describes the meeting of Henry of England and François of France at the Field of the Cloth of Gold. He tells Buckingham that he

> saw them salute on horseback,
> Beheld them when they lighted, how they clung
> In their embracement, as they grew together,
> Which had they, what four throned ones could have weighed
> Such a compounded one?[1]

This emphasis on a kind of organic, compound royalty – two kings merged into one worth more than four separate kings – echoes Renaissance descriptions of the hermaphrodite, the figure of perfect sexual union, projected in Plato's *Symposium* and embodied in, for instance, the longed-for encounter of Amoret and Scudamore at the close of Book Three of the 1590 *Faerie Queene* or in the strange portrait of François I *'en travesti'*, in which the King is dressed half in women's and half in men's clothing. What is distinctive about Shakespeare and Fletcher's hermaphroditic vision, though, is that the perfect figure is created from the conjunction of two beings of the *same sex*.

There is a similar moment in the playwrights' last collaboration, *The Two Noble Kinsmen*, which occurs at the tensest point of the contest between Palamon and Arcite, the play's inseparable protagonists. The object of their dispute, the Amazon Emilia, has still (despite unyielding pressure from a patriarchal culture embodied in the imperious duke, Theseus) not made up her mind which of them she will marry. As a result of her indecision, the kinsmen are obliged by Theseus literally to enter a tug-of-war for her, and as the struggle gets under way, she cries out in despair:

> Were they metamorphosed
> Both into one! – O why? There were no woman
> Worth so composed a man

> (5.5.84–6)

If only, she appears to hope, rather than the one killing the other, these two men, undifferentiated in their nobility, could merge into one ideal being; but then, she fears, the resulting superhero would no longer desire her. Yet, in the dark, politically astute world of the Shakespeare/Fletcher collaborations, the projection or expression of such perfection seems guaranteed to betray itself. In *Henry VIII*, the union of the Kings at the Field of the Cloth of Gold turns out to be no more than an empty, glittering display for political advantage; here in the *Kinsmen*, the homoerotic expression serves not so much to suggest Emilia's desire for the kinsmen as to reveal her sexual orientation. In fact, in view of her development in the course of the play, it is possible (somewhat mischievously, perhaps) to read in these lines Emilia's hope that this metamorphosis might take place precisely *because* the 'composed' kinsman would no longer want to marry her, and that she naturally frames her will as an image of same-sex union because she prefers to resist heterosexual desire and remain within the Amazonian sexual world into which she had been born. In other words, she transfers onto the kinsmen (with some justification) her own experience of and preference for same-sex mutuality and love.

But 'composition' is also a *textual* act, and these lines do much more than reveal Emilia's desire to evade the heterosexual union expected of her. For anyone working on this or other collaborative playtexts – particularly in view of the tenor of recent theories of collaboration – her words invoke several centuries of editorial and critical evasion of the problems of authority raised by collaborative drama. How, exactly, do we deal with texts which appear to have been written by more than one author? How do we determine and interpret the signs of collaboration? Should we differentiate between co-authors? Or treat them as one for the sake of an aesthetics of coherence? How do we figure the relationship between the authors? If as careful and conservative a commentator as G. E. Bentley can acknowledge that 'as many as half of the plays by professional dramatists [on the Jacobean and Caroline stage] incorporated the writing...of more than one man', it would seem essential for anyone working on the drama of this period to come to terms with the question of collaboration.[2] Yet it is only in very recent years that critics have begun to acknowledge the importance of this issue as a prerequisite to an adequate understanding of the operations of the theatre. Contemporary approaches to the subject have polarised, though, tending either to presume the autonomy of the individual author, to dismiss as irrelevant or unscholarly any attempt to connect issues of textuality and sexuality, and to proceed to 'disintegrate' the text on the basis of linguistic 'evidence'; or else, while provocatively opening up for discussion the relationship of the sexual and the textual, to collapse the possibility of agency into a general celebration of the social text and the homosocial economy.[3] Neither attitude seems to me yet to have proved itself in fruitful interpretation of the play or plays in question, or indeed – and this is my principal contention in this essay – to have achieved the sophistication offered by *The Two Noble Kinsmen* as a model for analysing the ramifications of collaboration in Renaissance drama as a whole.

I do not wish to suggest here that Shakespeare and Fletcher sat down to write a metadrama of collaboration, nor do I wish to offer an (admittedly tempting) allegorical reading in which the kinsmen and their prize would mirror the collaborators and their play, since each of these interpretations would presume the very issues of intentionality and agency that the play, I would argue, puts under scrutiny; but I do wish to suggest that *The Two Noble Kinsmen* offers an alternative model for collaborative endeavour which provides for the necessarily complex relations both between the two collaborators and between the collaborators and the object of their joint labour, which examines the connection between collaboration and sexuality, and which monitors bleakly the struggle between ideology and agency that is enacted in collaborative production. For the purposes of this essay, I will focus particularly on the relations of sexuality and agency by way of a close reading of the language and actions of Emilia, the object of the collaborative struggle played out between the eponymous kinsmen.

II

Emilia's desire to see two men 'composed' of (or metamorphosed into) one looks forward to a critical tradition which has done its best both to deny the close collaborative construction of this and other doubly or multiply authored plays (and especially of those in which Shakespeare was involved), and at the same time to find ways to contain those writers who persist, by working collaboratively, in questioning in a very practical way the boundaries of authorship. One notable critical strategy has been the creation of a kind of hermaphrodite out of the two most notorious collaborators in Jacobean drama, Francis Beaumont and John Fletcher – the same John Fletcher, that is, who, after Beaumont's early retirement, worked for a year or two with Shakespeare. This merging or uniting process begins with the earliest commentaries on this collaborative canon, the dedicatory verses to Humphrey Moseley's propagandistic 'Beaumont and Fletcher' Folio of 1647, which reveal how much emphasis was already being placed at that time on the impossibility of separating the work of the two writers. For George Lisle, their collaborative facility was such that 'the world ne'er knew / [Whether] 'twas Francis Fletcher or John Beaumont writ.'[4] Jasper Maine devotes his entire verse to this issue, addressing the playwrights as:

> Great pair of authors, whom one equal star
> Begot so like in genius, that you are
> In fame, as well as writings, both so knit,
> That no man knows where to divide your wit,
> Much less your praise.

> (d1^r)

Intimate collaboration of this kind is seen to have a miraculously undifferentiating effect, which goes far beyond the mere blurring of boundaries between individual authors. John Denham, writing about the blend of nature and art in the plays, echoes the collaborative indistinction noted by Maine:

> [N]one
> Can say, here nature ends and art begins,
> But mixt, like th'elements, and born like twins;

So interweav'd, so like, so much the same,
None this mere nature, that mere art can name.

(b1ᵛ)

The 'twinning' image is taken up by John Webb, in another dedicatory verse, who calls Beaumont and Fletcher's plays '[t]he rich
conceptions of ... twin-like brains',

> Whose chiming Muses never fail'd to sing
> A soul-affecting music, ravishing
> Both ear and intellect; while you do each
> Contend with other, who shall highest reach
> In rare invention; conflicts that beget
> New strange delight.

(C2ᵛ)

Webb thus represents collaboration and competition as two sides of
the same coin, locating the collaborative process within the framework of a game in which two competitors work to narrow rules,
competing for brilliance of expression. But he also writes of the
'ravishing of the ear', and the undercurrent allusion to the myth of
the nightingale in his poem implies an uncomfortable relationship
between collaboration and rape.

Webb's connection of collaboration with competition and with
sexual violence has clear resonances for *The Two Noble Kinsmen*. We
see a prime example of cooperative competition as the inseparable
cousins struggle for the hand of Emilia, and the nightingale allusion
echoes a particularly awkward moment towards the end of the play
when Theseus gleefully describes the contest between the kinsmen
as being like that of 'two emulous Philomels' (5.5.124) trying to out-
sing each other. By this stage of the play, the social and cultural
pressure embodied in the duke has forced the kinsmen, even as
they compete for sexual rights over Emilia, to share with her the
role of victim; and in the shared metaphor, collaboration is seen in
an intimate relationship both with competition and with sexuality.

The play's sexual/textual economy is made bluntly clear by the
Prologue, uttering the first line of the play – 'New plays and
maidenheads are near akin' – an assertion that is explained thus:
'Much followed both, for both much money gi'en,/If they stand

sound and well' (Prologue 1–3). This locates the play firmly (and
tastelessly) within a market economy and a framework of commodity exchange into which familial ties are dissolved and the stageplay
and the woman as object of sexual transaction are seen to be, like
the play's protagonists, 'near akin'. In the wake of this, the Prologue demonstrates an anxiety about authorship which he resolves
by invoking the value of collaboration in a broad sense. Acknowledging the play's source in Chaucer, he admits to his nervousness
about this inheritance – 'it were an endless thing,/And too ambitious, to aspire to him,/Weak as we are' (22–4) – and (via a nautical
metaphor) seeks the very tangible assistance of the audience to
make it work: 'Do but you hold out/Your helping hands, and we
shall tack about/And something do to save us' (25–7). As Jeffrey
Masten notes, these applauding hands are 'also the hands that
pay to see the play, the handshaking that seals the bargain,
the collaborating hands of exchange and commerce' (Masten, 340).
Collaboration – in its broadest sense encompassing both audience
response and the authors' negotiation of source-materials – is both
the source and the solution of the play's anxieties about textual
authority.

It is perhaps worth considering at this point two assertions
which Wayne Koestenbaum makes in his spectacular but
often problematic book *Double Talk: The Erotics of Male Literary
Collaboration*, which seem to me (though they are specifically
made in respect of texts written between 1885 and 1920) to have
tremendous resonance for early modern collaborative plays in general and for *The Two Noble Kinsmen* in particular. The first is that
'[b]ooks with two authors are specimens of a relation, and show
writing to be a quality of motion and exchange, not a fixed thing';
the second that '[m]en who collaborate engage in a metaphorical
sexual intercourse, and the text they balance between them is alternately the child of their sexual union, and a shared woman.'[5] This
latter observation, despite its deliberate attempt to shock, is oddly
familiar to students of Fletcher because of Aubrey's notorious anecdote, written at the end of the seventeenth century, about Beaumont and Fletcher:

> They lived together on the Banke side, not far from the Play-
> house, both batchelors; lay together...; had one wench in the
> house between them, which they did so admire; the same
> cloathes and cloake, &c., between them.[6]

The two 'between them's here ensure that the reader acknowledges that the wench is shared in a manner similar to the clothes; at the same time, the doubling of 'lived together' and 'lay together' emphasises the sexual possibilities of the latter – 'With her, on her, what you will', as Iago glosses his 'lie' in *Othello* (4.1.33) – but this time with homosexual insinuation. Aubrey's anecdote, like Koestenbaum's theory, oscillates uneasily between poles of heterosexuality and homosexuality; in neither case does the 'wench' or the 'shared woman' have any active role in the situation.

Koestenbaum draws his model for collaborative reading from the work of Luce Irigaray and Eve Kosofsky Sedgwick on the homosocial basis of patriarchy, and it is worth noting the reservations that these writers have about their own theories, in particular their concern that a theory of culture based on transactions between men will tend either to obliterate, or at the very least to limit, the woman who is the traffic of those transactions. Sedgwick announces early on in *Between Men* that 'the isolation, not to mention the absolute subordination, of women in th[is] structural paradigm...is a distortion that necessarily fails to do justice to women's own powers, bonds, and struggles.'[7] Irigaray outlines the role of woman within patriarchy – at least for as long as she remains a virgin – as 'pure exchange value', claiming that, as a result, '[w]oman is never anything but the locus of a more or less competitive exchange between two men.' She goes on to ask a related question: 'How can this object of transaction claim a right to pleasure without removing her/itself from established commerce...without provoking the consumer's anxiety over the disappearance of his nurturing ground?'[8] It is precisely this question that is, I would claim, broached by *The Two Noble Kinsmen*, as Emilia's resistance to the exchange-economy within which Theseus expects her to operate provokes considerable anxiety both in the kinsmen and in Theseus himself.

III

The impossibility of differentiating clearly between the two kinsmen is apparent from early on in the play. When Theseus first sees them in battle, he makes no attempt at all to individuate them, seeing them simply as '[l]ike to a pair of lions' (1.4.18). Shortly afterwards, the Jailer and his Daughter (who has already fallen in love with Palamon) differ over which is which. The Daughter seems sure that the taller one is Palamon, not Arcite, yet her suggestion that her father 'may perceive a part of him' (2.1.51–2) is ambiguous, implying either that the Jailer sees only Arcite's arm or leg or else that, in seeing Palamon, he sees a part of Arcite. In this second reading, the two kinsmen are already partially 'metamorphosed into one', and, in view of their identity, the Daughter's wistful contrast between her Wooer and the kinsmen – 'Lord, the differ-ence of men!' (2.1.55–6) – comically demonstrates the tendency to the highly subjective which will eventually lead her into madness.

   The kinsmen, too, see themselves as exact counterparts. As they languish in their prison cell, Palamon describes them as 'twins of honour' (2.2.18), considering it 'a main goodness' that their 'for-tunes/Were twinned together' (a belief he will be forced to shed by the end of the play), and acknowledging the claim that 'two souls/ Put in two noble bodies, let 'em suffer the gall of hazard, so they grow together,/Will never sink' (2.2.63–7). The nature of this 'twin-ning' is seen as both collaborative and homoerotic in their exchange. Arcite does discuss marriage, but largely in terms of sexual gratification (the 'sweet embraces of a loving wife,/Loaden with kisses') and of the production of sons, described tellingly as 'figures of ourselves' (2.2.30–1, 33) and, in his long speech of con-solation, he figures imprisonment as a defence against the corrupt-ing influence of women:

> We are young and yet desire the ways of honour,
> That liberty and common conversation,
> The poison of pure spirits, might, like women,
> Woo us to wander from. What worthy blessing
> Can be, but our imaginations
> May make it ours? And here being thus together,
> We are an endless mine to one another:
> We are one another's wife, ever begetting
> New births of love; we are father, friends, acquaintance;
> We are in one another, families –
> I am your heir, and you are mine; this place
> Is our inheritance...
>   Were we at liberty,
> A wife might part us lawfully, or business
>
> (2.2.73–84, 88–9)

Palamon agrees, asking 'Is there record of any two that loved/Better than we do, Arcite?' and adding 'I do not think it possible our friendship/Should ever leave us' (2.2.112–13, 114–15). It is at this moment, the moment of the pledging of eternal, self-reflecting love, that Palamon sees Emilia in the garden below, picking (what else?) narcissi, and falls instantly in love with her. And it is at this same moment that the interchangeability of the kinsmen leads them for the first time towards tragedy.

Arcite looks and, of course, since he shares everything with his friend, falls in love, too. Palamon, not realising the inevitability of this, wants Arcite to agree that Emilia is profoundly beautiful, asking 'Might not a man well lose himself and love her?' (2.2.156), which is, of course, precisely the tragic bargain required of him by the close of the play. And when Arcite does announce his desire for Emilia, he seems surprised that Palamon should have expected anything else. 'Am not I/Part of your blood, part of your soul?' he asks, adding

> You have told me
> That I was Palamon, and you were Arcite.
> . . . Am not I liable to those affections,
> Those joys, griefs, angers, fears, my friend shall suffer?
> . . . Why then would you deal so cunningly,
> So strangely, so unlike a noble kinsman,
> To love alone?

> (2.2.189–95)

This (whether staged as naïve or as ironic) is the inescapable logic of their self-reflecting love, and the introduction of heterosexual desire tears apart the illusion of their courtly mutuality. From this moment on, they are competitors, implacable and ferocious, and Emilia becomes 'the prize and garland/To crown the question's title', as Theseus phrases it – the excuse for, and reward of, a struggle between men.[9] At the same time, the origins of the struggle in mutual regard are never forgotten, and the collaborative and the competitive are revealed as two sides of the same coin – most obviously in the scene in which, disarmingly, the kinsmen help arm each other for their fight – and Emilia finds herself the unwilling object of a competition which is also a homosocial transaction. Unwilling she might be, particularly as the struggle between the kinsmen is manipulated by Theseus to ensure that she does not remain unmarried, but it is essential to note that she is by no means the passive object of that struggle: she in fact sustains a remarkable belief in her own agency which is only finally shattered by the external forces embodied in the oracle in Act 5.

Emilia's interest in the narcissus as, beyond their prison window, the kinsmen first swear undying love to each other, and then declare war over her, serves several purposes. Not only does it mockingly underline the homoeroticism of Palamon and Arcite's friendship, it also marks the moment at which difference enters their world for the first time. Emilia, even before she sees them, has prefigured their attitudes as suitors, focusing now on the rose rather than the narcissus. It is, she claims, the 'best of flowers', and she explains why:

> It is the very emblem of a maid;
> For when the west wind courts her gently,
> How modestly she blows, and paints the sun
> With her chaste blushes! When the north comes near her,
> Rude and impatient, then, like chastity,
> She locks her beauties in the bud again,
> And leaves him to base briers.

(2.2.137–43)

The rose here figures the virgin's agency, her ability to choose or refuse. And as the play progresses, it appears that the west, a lover of gentle restraint and feminine care, is figured in Palamon, and the north, an impatient, blunt and masculine lover, in Arcite. These associations merge with the kinsmen's preference for Venus and Mars respectively as their divine patrons, and Palamon and Arcite, initially undifferentiated, begin gradually to develop the distinctions (*generic* distinctions, I would argue, not 'personal') that Emilia later wishes could be metamorphosed into another, ideal union.

This passage, with its emphasis on chastity, prefigures Emilia's resistance to her suitors' advances, and, in conjunction with her wish to have a gown patterned with narcissi, reminds us both of her Amazonian origins and of her apparent same-sex orientation. We are made aware of her sense of solidarity with women in general early in the play when she refers to one of the grief-stricken queens who come to Theseus for assistance as 'a natural sister of

our sex' and kneels in their support.[10] Theseus is eventually only
persuaded to avenge the queens (and therefore to delay the marriage for which he is impatient) by Emilia's assertion that, if he does
not, she will henceforth 'not dare/To ask [him] any thing, nor' – in a
splendid partial non-sequitur – 'be so hardy/Ever to take a husband' (1.1.202–4). Emilia wins in the short term, but, from this
moment on, Theseus is constantly seeking ways to manoeuvre
her into the marriage she does not desire.

Theseus's determination to see Emilia married is given a curious
gloss in 1.3, in which the Amazonian sisters discuss the depth of
feeling between Theseus and his old friend and fighting-compa-
nion Pirithous, and Hippolyta acknowledges that it is unclear
whom Theseus loves the most, her or his old friend: 'I think,' she
says, 'Theseus cannot be umpire to himself,/Cleaving his conscience
in twain, and doing/Each side like justice, which he loves best'
(1.3.44–7). The language she uses to describe the relationship
between the friends is curiously sexual – 'Their knot of love,/Tied,
weaved, entangled, with so true, so long,/And with a finger of so
deep a cunning,/May be outworn, never undone' (1.3.41–4) – and
her observations prompt a reminiscence from Emilia which seems
both to equate her with Theseus in the intensity of their same-sex
emotion and to suggest a reason for Theseus's determination to see
her safely married.

Emilia's model for relationships is her childhood friendship with
a girl called Flavina, who died ('took leave o' th' moon,' as Emilia
puts it, mindful as ever of the influence of Diana) when both were
just eleven. The loss of this friend (a Shakespearean interpolation
entirely absent from the Chaucerian source) was clearly deeply
traumatic for Emilia. The friendship she describes was emulative,
focused on similarity rather than difference – 'What she liked/Was
then of me approved; what not, condemned – / No more arraignment' (1.3.64–6) – and this emphasis on 'like' is sustained until she
concludes with her firmly held belief that 'the true love 'tween
maid and maid may be/More than in sex dividual' (1.3.81–2). Her
sister Hippolyta, recently conquered by, and married to, Theseus, is
not surprisingly a little taken aback, and she attempts to remon-
strate. Emilia replies with a simple yet remarkable assertion of
sexual relativity: 'I am not/Against your faith, yet I continue mine'
(1.3.97–8). In this scene, Emilia both voices an emotional and sexual
ethos of her own and comes very near to establishing a pattern
which Theseus cannot acknowledge because it mirrors so very

closely his own experience of same-sex friendship. Moreover, she tries to posit a mutual understanding between same-sex and opposite-sex desire that the society of the play cannot tolerate.

Her passionate assertion that 'the true love 'tween maid and maid may be/More than in sex dividual' raises fascinating questions not only about Shakespearean sexuality but also about textual authority. As Peter Stallybrass has recently pointed out, the phrase 'sex dividual' is not the reading in the earliest printed text of *The Two Noble Kinsmen* – the 1634 Quarto – but is rather the product of eighteenth-century emendation: the 1634 text has the phrase sex *in*dividual'.[11] Stallybrass sets out to demonstrate the inadequacy of our understanding of the word 'individual' for analysing its function in early modern England, and one possible reading he offers for 'sex individual' refers to the figure of the hermaphrodite. As he suggests, the gender of the two women in Emilia's assertion would be 'of central import, since it would be that which defined them as superior to the intermixing of genders in an androgyne often imagined in the Renaissance as defining the ideal of love' (606). In other words, Emilia considers same-sex love between women to be superior not only to male–female love, but even to the idealised male–female love exemplified in the hermaphrodite. In this light, her later desire for composition of the kinsmen into a kind of same-sex hermaphrodite can be read as a projection of a still higher and purer expression of mutuality and love – purer because undisturbed by difference – which argues for a kind of collaborative agency transcending societal and cultural demands.

IV

The unique form of tragicomedy – a simultaneous death and marriage – which is created at the close of the play, however, provides a generic rejection of Emilia's dreams. Arguably the bleakest moment of the play (at least as bleak in its dismissal of human agency as the final scene) is the oracle scene in Act 5, in which Arcite, Palamon and Emilia arrive to make offerings to their respective patron god or goddess and each receives an equivocal sign.[12] Arcite sacrifices to the male god Mars, associating himself (the abrupt north wind of Emilia's prefiguring) with the tragic mode, with blood, war and violence. Palamon sacrifices to the female god Venus, associating himself (Emilia's gentle west wind) with the comic experiences of

love and sex. This deliberate strategic differentiation suggests
that the choice Emilia has to make is, in a certain way, a *generic*
choice, a choice between tangibly different generic modes, a choice
which she neither wants nor is, finally, allowed to make. This is
the supreme moment of competition in the play, the moment at
which the kinsmen differentiate themselves most clearly. Yet, paradoxically, the scene effects a structural equivalence not only
between the two kinsmen, but between the two kinsmen *and*
Emilia, since it follows steadily the parallel religious rituals undertaken by each of the three protagonists and the equally ambivalent
(or, perhaps better, equally deceptive) signs they receive from
the gods.

At the altar, each kinsman is given a sign which can be favourably
interpreted, though (unlike in the Chaucerian source) we are
denied access to the gods' plans; and then it is Emilia's turn.
Dressed in white, she prays once more to Diana, pale virgin-hun-
tress, goddess of the moon. Her wish for chastity is repeated, as is
her rejection of sex, figured as blood. As her prayer continues, its
sexual charge grows: she characterises Diana insistently as a virgin
and she makes a curious equation, reminiscent of Webb's dedicatory poem for the 1647 Folio, between the vagina and the ear, 'into
whose port/Ne'er entered wanton sound' (5.3.11–12). She is, she
says, 'bride-habited/But maiden-hearted', asking Diana either to
choose for her the better of the two kinsmen or (and this is clearly
her preference) to 'grant', as she puts it, 'The file and quality I hold I
may/Continue in thy band' (5.3.24–6). We then witness the first of
two signs from the goddess which are no less equivocal than
Emilia's prayer. Emilia arrived bringing a '*silver hind, in which*
[was] conveyed incense and sweet odours' (5.3.0.4–5), a gesture which,
as Eugene Waith has pointed out, evokes the myth of Iphigenia (the
setting for which, Aulis, is mentioned in the first scene).[13] Emilia is
thus consciously associating herself with the virgin of the myth as
yet another mute plea to be let off the hook by Diana. This is,
however, a vain hope.

The first sign from the goddess involves both the hind and one of
the two flowers with which Emilia was earlier associated, the rose,
equivocal symbol of virginity and desire, and, in this context, of
agency: '*Here the hind vanishes under the altar, and in the place ascends a*
rose tree, having one rose upon it' (5.3.26.1–2). Emilia's response is
extraordinary, both for its deliberate misinterpretation and for its
metaphoric intensity:

> See what our general of ebbs and flows
> Out from the bowels of her holy altar
> With sacred act advances – but one rose!
> If well inspired, this battle shall confound
> Both these brave knights, and I, a virgin flower,
> Must grow alone, unplucked.

(5.3.27–32)

Wilfully, Emilia rejects the obvious implication that where Diana once substituted a hind for the virgin Iphigenia, here it is the hind that is removed, leaving only the virgin Emilia to be sacrificed; and she misreads the – now overtly phallic – rose-tree as a sign of her continued virginity. Moreover, she gives away her true feelings towards Palamon and Arcite: that 'this battle shall confound/*Both* these brave knights' (5.3.30–1). Yet her doubts about this interpretation can be traced easily enough in her phrasing: 'If well inspired' has echoes of a subject beyond the contest, implying either that she is doubtful about her own inspiration or else that she suspects that Diana is capable of misleading her; and the 'but' in 'but one rose!' suggests a fear of disappointment which is instantly confirmed in the second part of the sign:

> *Here is heard a sudden twang of instruments*
> *and the rose falls from the tree*
> The flower is fall'n, the tree descends. O mistress,
> Thou here dischargest me – I shall be gathered.
> I think so, but I know not thine own will.
> Unclasp thy mystery. (*To her women*) I hope she's pleased;
> Her signs were gracious

(5.3.32.1–37)

Her confusion is now intense. She recognises that the message is over; she also recognises a 'discharge', a dismissal. Her language becomes staccato with uncertainty, and she fades from public utterance into private in a nervous aside: 'I hope she's pleased.'

Louis Adrian Montrose has suggested (in an essay on *A Midsummer Night's Dream*, the early Shakespearean play to which *The Two Noble Kinsmen* is indebted) that '[a]n awareness that the commonest Elizabethan term for [the blood of menstruation] was "flowers" adds a peculiar resonance to certain occurrences of flower imagery in Renaissance texts.'[14] He examines specifically the moment in *A Midsummer Night's Dream* at which Oberon recalls seeing Cupid shoot an arrow '[a]t a fair vestal' (2.1.158) only to have the 'fiery shaft/Quench'd in the chaste beams of the watery moon' (2.1.161–2), allowing the vestal to pass on '[i]n maiden meditation'. The arrow meanwhile falls upon 'a little western flower', which '[b]efore milk-white', becomes 'purple with love's wound' (2.1.166–7). Montrose analyses this as a moment of 'erotic violence', and points to a double effect, arguing that the 'change suffered by the flower may have suggested not only the blood of defloration but also the blood of menstruation' (62). This dual signification for 'flower' seems to me to operate in the oracle scene of the *Kinsmen*, too. Diana, goddess of the moon, is described as a 'general of ebbs and flows'; the noun 'flows' then doubles as a verb to compete with 'advances' for control of the directional phrase 'out from the bowels' and is echoed in the word 'dischargest'. This menstrual framework – within Montrose's reading particularly of a blood-red flower such as the rose as menstrual blood – augments the phallic effect of the rising and falling rose tree such that the rose becomes a symbolic palimpsest: at once a symbol of virginity, menstruation and defloration, and thus a sign of the heterosexual path a woman is obliged to tread if she is to mature in Theseus' Athens.

The verb 'discharge', which can obviously denote a flowing out or loss of fluid, extends this moment of oracular menstruation, and has further – violent – potential as the blast of a gun, and the association here of the phallus and death, taken in conjunction with the biblical sense of 'fall'n' as the sexual knowledge that leads to destruction, opens up the religious connotations of 'gathered', a term which thus serves not only as the opposite of 'unplucked' (Emilia as virgin flower cropped or deflowered by a husband) but also as yet another image of death, the patriarchal idea of being 'gathered to one's fathers'. Sexual maturity is thus forced upon an unwilling Emilia by a hostile environment intent on breaking her resolve. Her agency is equated with a refusal to grow up, with a preference for her own sex which is read as childishness, and she is left bewildered and unprotected by a goddess who builds hopes only to crush them. To this point, she has been consistent in her resistance to the sexual and societal pressure voiced by Theseus, but from here on her language becomes weaker and

more confused, and by the end of the play she succumbs in an
Isabella-like silence to marriage to the eventual victor of the tug-
of-war.

V

Yet who is the victor? And what of the kinsmen for whom Emilia's
agency has been compromised? Arcite, as the devotee of Mars, wins
the warlike competition, yet within half a scene he has died violently and arbitrarily, ironically fulfilling his own evocation of the
tragic mode. Palamon, the devotee of Venus, is given the opportunity to taste the fruits of marriage, thereby in turn fulfilling his own
self-appointment as the personification of the comic mode. Yet this
is hardly victory: indeed, Palamon has moved further and further
towards Emilia's own experience as a victim within the contestatory
environment of the play. The metaphors used to describe him
increasingly draw upon the feminine, and he has been forced
against his will and all his strength to touch the phallic obelisk
which was the object of the tug-of-war in a movement which,
though unseen because off-stage, rehearses the eventual forcing
of the reluctant Emilia. This transfer of violence and violation
from Emilia to the two kinsmen is, as we have already seen, underlined by Theseus's exultant reference to earlier, mythical
metamorphosis in his description of the fighting kinsmen as 'two
emulous Philomels' trying to out-sing each other. Authority is
channelled through Theseus by harsh divine intervention which,
expressing as it does the need for resolution, is also generic and
theatrical obligation; environment overwhelms agency; and, at the
altar, the kinsmen, who have been at once collaborators and competitors, are given equivocal signs which lead one to death and the
other to irreparable loss.

To assert that the relationship demonstrated in the play between
collaboration and sexuality is a conscious one – the 'theme', if you
like, of the play – would be, as I have suggested, to presume the
kind of clear, univocal intentionality that collaborative analysis precludes, or at least heavily compromises. But it is, I think, possible to
argue that the homosocial economy of the play – its particular
involvement in processes of exchange, reciprocity and competition
between men; its association of the virgin and the stageplay as
objects of negotiation and trade; and its refusal of agency to the

woman who is the object of exchange – foregrounds a series of equivalences between the sexual transactions that are the subject of Jacobean theatre in general and of this play in particular and the processes of collaborative production that sustained that theatre. At the same time, the play's unique tragicomic structure provides a counterweight to theories such as Koestenbaum's which privilege the collaborators as autonomous agents 'balancing' the text between them. Palamon and Arcite have, finally, no more agency in this play than the virgin Emilia over whom they struggle: their roles are assigned by generic and ideological forces beyond their control and of which they understand remarkably little.

The closing (and controlling) paradox of the play – Palamon's heartfelt cry, 'That we should things desire which do cost us/Loss of our desire! That naught could buy/Dear love but loss of dear love' (5.6.110–12)[15] – not only gives expression to an irreconcilable gulf between opposite-sex and same-sex desire (noting, as it does, the necessity of Arcite's death to make way for Palamon's marriage to Emilia) but also conveys the basic interpretive problem presented by collaboration: that the quest *either* to merge together *or* to differentiate between collaborators is inevitably a destructive one. Just as the kinsmen are difficult to differentiate, sometimes contrasting, sometimes merging together, and are projected by Emilia as an impossible perfection if metamorphosed into one (an impossible perfection, moreover, which would be above mere sexual transactions), so, in the study of collaborative texts, the collaborating playwrights both demand and defy individuation, seeming at times tangibly different, at others inseparably merged. We do learn, to a certain extent, to differentiate between them. They do have different sets of defining characteristics. At the same time, we learn that generic and theatrical obligations are in constant conflict with assertions of agency, and we learn, too (painfully), that either to separate or to merge – to attempt to extract the individual from the relations of difference that provide the illusion of individuality – is both to limit and to destroy.

NOTES

1.   William Shakespeare and John Fletcher, *Henry VIII*, 1.1.7–11. This and all subsequent quotations from the plays and collaborations of

Shakespeare are drawn from Stanley Wells and Gary Taylor (gen. eds.), *William Shakespeare: The Complete Works* (Oxford: Clarendon Press, 1986). Wells and Taylor give *Henry VIII* its alternative Jacobean title, *All is True*. I would like to note my gratitude to Lorna Hutson for helpful and productive discussions as I was revising this essay, and also to Helen Cooper and Peter Stallybrass for helpful suggestions.

2.   G. E. Bentley, *The Profession of Dramatist in Shakespeare's Time* (Princeton: Princeton University Press, 1971), 199.

3.   See, *inter alia*, Bentley, *Profession*; Cyrus Hoy, 'The Shares of Fletcher and his Collaborators in the Beaumont and Fletcher Canon, 1–7,' *Studies in Bibliography* 7–9, 11–15 (1956–62); Jonathan Hope, *The Authorship of Shakespeare's Plays* (Cambridge: Cambridge University Press, 1994); Jeffrey Masten, 'Beaumont and/or Fletcher: Collaboration and the Interpretation of Renaissance Drama', *ELH* 59 (1992), 337–56. Masten's article is an effective critique of the work of Hoy and the other 'disintegrators', drawing on the work of Michel Foucault in particular for its theoretical base. The term 'disintegration' comes from E. K. Chambers, 'The Disintegration of Shakespeare', Annual Shakespeare Lecture, 1924, in *Proceedings of the British Academy, 1924–1925* (London: Oxford University Press, 1925), 89–108. For extended commentary on collaboration and the Jacobean stage, see chapter 4 of my book, *The Politics of Unease in the Plays of John Fletcher* (Amherst: University of Massachusetts Press, 1994), with which I am here, to a certain extent, taking issue. See also my essay, '"Our Whole Life is Like a Play": Collaboration and the Problem of Editing', *Textus* 9 (1996), 371–94.

4.   Francis Beaumont and John Fletcher, *Comedies and Tragedies* (London, 1647), b1^r.

5.   Wayne Koestenbaum, *Double Talk: The Erotics of Male Literary Collaboration* (New York: Routledge, 1989), 2–3.

6.   John Aubrey, *Brief Lives, chiefly of Contemporaries*, ed. Andrew Clark (Oxford: Clarendon Press, 1898), I: 95–6.

7.   Eve Kosofsky Sedgwick, *Between Men: English Literature and Male Homosocial Desire* (New York: Columbia University Press, 1985), 18.

8.   Luce Irigaray, *This Sex Which Is Not One*, trans. Catherine Porter with Carolyn Burke (Ithaca: Cornell University Press, 1985), 186, 31–2.

9.   Theseus's description comes at 5.5.16–17, as he orders Emilia to watch the contest: her refusal to do so is her last assertion of independence. Wells and Taylor follow the first quarto (1634) in reading 'price'; modern-spelling 'prize' seems a more appropriate pairing for 'garland'.

10.   1.1.125. In context, the 'natural' queen is contrasted to a painted representation, but I think Shakespeare chooses his wording with care in order also to emphasise Emilia's solidarity with women.

11.   Peter Stallybrass, 'Shakespeare, the Individual, and the Text', in Lawrence Grossberg, Cary Nelson and Paula A. Treichler (eds.), *Cultural Studies* (New York: Routledge, 1992), 593–610.

12.   Wells and Taylor split this scene into three (5.1–3).

13. William Shakespeare and John Fletcher, *The Two Noble Kinsmen*, ed.
     Eugene M. Waith (Oxford: Clarendon Press, 1989), 191.
14. Louis Adrian Montrose, ' "Shaping Fantasies": Figurations of Gender
     and Power in Elizabethan Culture', 62, in Stephen J. Greenblatt (ed.),
     Representing the English Renaissance (Berkeley and Los Angeles: Uni-
     versity of California Press, 1988), 31–64.
15. Cf. [William Rowley], *The Birth of Merlin*, ed. Joanna Udall (London:
     MHRA, 1991), 1.1.94–5: 'It is a desperate Game indeed this Marriage,/
     Where there's no winning without loss to either.'

III
Naming/Locating

7

Space for the Self: Place, Persona and Self-Projection in *The Comedy of Errors* and *Pericles*

Amanda Piesse

In the system of production that we know, including that of sexual production, men are distanced from their bodies. They have relied upon their sex, their language and their technology to go on and on building a world further and further removed from their relation to the corporeal. But they are corporeal. They therefore need to reassure themselves that someone really is looking after the body for them. Their women or wives are guardians of their corporeal unity... a body-object which is there, which does not move, that he can go back to whenever he likes ...

Luce Irigaray[1]

In Plato's account of the the propriety and desirability of male and female homoeroticism, Aristophanes relates in charming detail the events which led up to the establishment of the three sexes, male, female and androgyne: 'In the first place ... each human being was a whole with its back and flanks rounded to form a circle' with 'four hands and an equal number of legs and two identically similar faces upon a circular neck ... four ears and two organs of generation'. He goes on to relate how 'when they wanted to run quickly they turned rapidly over and over in a circle'. This composite being is swift, happy and strong. The gods being jealous of such perfection, Zeus decides to bisect the creature (with the threat that should they behave in a wanton or lascivious manner, they will be bisected again and have to hop around on one leg each), and when this work of initial bisection is complete, 'each half yearned for the half from which it had been severed … in their longing to grow together they perished of hunger and their general neglect of their concerns, because they would not do anything apart.'[2]

It is the reunited body, that which is the perfect consummation of the male and female parts, which is signalled as the ideal state. It is easy to see how the rhetoric of the divided self, of doubleness and of yearning for some kind of spiritual completion, is assimilated into the rhetoric of the Renaissance from the classics. In moving from the private and epitomised divided self or divided family to the public and macrocosmic domain of the divided kingdom, the motif of the divided or lost self as representing the divided or as yet undiscovered territory – be it sociological or geographical – frequently reappears.

The construction of identity, and especially female identity, in the Shakespearean drama is regularly to be seen operating through a dislocation between what is said and what is seen, through a dislocation between expectation and experience both for the female characters and for the male characters who observe and interact with them. *The Comedy of Errors* and *Pericles* are both preoccupied with identity and with regaining what has been lost through both a physical and an experiential voyage of discovery. For Syracusan Antipholus and Pericles, loss of a significant other and the journey into unfamiliar territory necessary to regain the other are the main motifs of dislocation and uneasiness over identity. For Adriana and Marina, preservation of self and presentation of self is repeatedly challenged both by dialogue with the onstage audience and by the pressures of a more interiorised, domestic changing location.

While the plays have this much in common, the political hegemonies which reign over their inceptions are quite different. That the process of self-discovery which is apparent in each play is quite different one from the other is as evident as is the difference between the end-gains. By looking at the differences between the means and the ends of both Elizabethan and Jacobean regal self-presentation, it is possible to align a historicised reading alongside a gendered one. It seems to me that where an Elizabethan notion of the acceptance of the diffracted self is necessary to Adriana's self-recognition in *The Comedy of Errors*, the influence of the Jamesian[3] rhetoric of unification and the projection of self as a unified whole can be clearly seen in the restitution brought about in *Pericles*. I would further assert that the difference between the Elizabethan and the Jacobean hegemony is a gendered one, that the

Elizabethan notion of the diffuse, diverse and diffracted self is one which is essentially the outward form of a female hegemony.[4]

When James VI of Scotland came to the English throne in 1603, his political rhetoric at once assimilated and superseded the refracted images promulgated by the Queen. She was Queen of historical revision and reversion, as past fashioned present through the assimilation of classical learning into English, as Spenser refashioned popular history through his overwhelmingly popular account of the Tudor myth, through Polydore Vergil's rather more sober but no less influential account of Tudor history. She was Queen of ambivalence and assimilation, as princess jostled with priestess, and matriarch with Marianism. That Elizabeth consciously projected various images of self at various stages of her reign is an argument much demonstrated and debated.[5] What concerns me here is not the specific icons, but the very fact of the variety of selves, the refracted images, which appear throughout her reign. The bifurcation of the princely self is upheld by law[6] but the images are myriad.

When James became King in 1603, his explicit desire was to gather together the refracted and confused images into a unified and unifying image of stability and consistency. Within this basic framework of unification, multiplicity may be allowed to exist in a controlled fashion.[7] Where Elizabeth had responded to disquiet about her situation as a non-reproducing female head of state by allowing herself to be perceived as androgynous, sexless or even occasionally masculine,[8] James had rather to contend with disquiet about his arrival from a foreign nation perceived as inferior and unruly, and set about portraying himself as unifier, peacemaker (his emblem was *beati pacifici*) and stressing his natural, lawful and conciliatory inheritance of the Tudor mantle through his physical descent from Henry VII in his early speeches before parliament.[9] He stressed his role as both inheritor and reformer of the Elizabethan hegemony by assimilating some of Elizabeth's symbolism,[10] whilst asserting his re-establishment of the hierarchical norm with a male head of state providing a line of heirs for the greater stability of the kingdom, both by regularly using the rhetoric of familial and paternal relationship and by assimilating Elizabeth's iconography into figures of unity and fruitfulness,[11] at once associating himself with the divine justice paraded by Elizabeth and dissociating himself from her barrenness. Where Elizabeth is painted as dominating the New World, her feet upon the maps of the places newly

colonised by her explorers, James asserts his connections with the
united kingdom by aligning his family tree – the map of his family
– with the charts drawn up of his newly acquired kingdom.

Where Elizabeth strove to establish herself as wedded to the
nation ('I have long since made choice of a husband, the kingdom
of England...charge me not with want of children, forasmuch as
every one of you are my children...').[12] James turns a similar
rhetoric to a hardly subtle re-establishment of proper order, com-
miserating with his new subjects that the nation has been 'so long
disordered and distracted',[13] and assuring it of the 'perfection of all
things',[14] unity, now that he is present as husband ('What God hath
conjoined let no man separate')[15] and as father ('By the law of
nature the King becomes a naturall father to all his lieges...bound
to care for the nourishing, education and vertuous government of
his children').[16] It would appear that where Elizabeth is multiplicity
and diffraction, James is unity and singularity of purpose. The
publication in England of James' *Basilicon Doron*[17] coincides almost
to the day with the death of Elizabeth I. This gentle, thoughtful text
sets out plainly James' view of the relationship between monarch
and people, and the ways in which a king's private and public
personae might be expected to complement and interact one with
the other. Viewed in the framework of Irigarayan theory, it is easy
to see that the self-representation favoured by Elizabeth is a feminine one, multiple, open to interpretation, flexible, undefined,
whilst the control and release principle which informs the Jacobean
hegemony is masculine.[18]

If the Renaissance sense of self was determined by political and
cultural hegemony, so too was the Renaissance sense of place and
space. A steady output of maps and charts by the Flemish carto-
graphers Mercator and Ortelius demonstrate the degree to which
sense of place might differ according to the medium in which the
chart is produced. Whilst Mercator produced essentially useful
maps, shipping charts, and so forth, Ortelius produced works of
art, illustrated impressions of the land which while startlingly accurate in their representation of land masses, intended to interpret the
meaning of newly discovered areas and reinterpret the beholder's
sense of the familiar place. *The Comedy of Errors* and *Pericles* are not
unique in that they involve specific travel to specific places as a
macrocosmic representation of the search for self, but in these two
plays in particular, the journeying by the male characters seems
particularly apposite. The chief female characters of Adriana in *The*

Comedy and Marina in *Pericles* are allowed by the playwright to appear to construct themselves through their speech in opposition to the familiar, reacting against the stereotypes provided by the male characters in the drama. The sense of self and presentation of self in these two plays change in accordance with both the onstage audience and the persona of the character suggested by changing location.

When Shakespeare prepared his *Comedy of Errors* for the stage in the late 1580s, he was at once imitating and refashioning, offering an alternative version of two melded originals.[19] Plautus' *Menaechmi,* on which the Shakespearean text is loosely based, has a set of twins who are not aware of each others' presence and even unsure about each others' existence, being separated from each other and from the arbiter of identity, the mother, at birth. One of them arrives, in defiance of a national exclusion order, in the town where the other has grown up and wed, and massive confusion inevitably ensues as each is taken for the other by wife and courtesan alike. Shakespeare takes on this scheme but doubles, diffuses voraciously. Each twin now has a servant, each of whom is twin to the other. The confusion is compounded by the fact that both masters are called Antipholus and both servants Dromio. Further, the servants become involved in a confusion over a kitchen wench, where one is engaged to her but the other recoils from her greasy advances in less than gallant distaste. So in a loose sense there is also the doubling of the main plot and the subplot, a certain degree of twinning in the action itself. Shakespeare works up his own version of the play to make the notion of alternative versions of self its most prominent feature. The development of the role for Adriana is all part of this. She continually questions herself, tries to identify a role for herself which allows her to synchronise her view of herself with the view that others project onto her. In dialogue with Luciana, a confidante invented entirely by Shakespeare, she interrogates the whole notion of selfhood and asks for alternative perspectives on her life. She is the one figure in the play who consciously and consistently seeks a consonant point of view, aware of the multiple personae imposed upon her by the different protagonists, and seeks resolution actively, articulately and assertively. This desperate seeking after secure identity is a domestic and quotidian version of the universal serious note in the play. When Adriana is disowned by the man she believes to be her husband, she expresses her hurt in terms of a dissolution of identity:

Ay, ay, Antipholus, look strange and frown,
Some other mistress hath thy sweet aspects;
I am not Adriana, nor thy wife.
The time was once when thou unurg'd wouldst vow
That never words were music to thine ear,
That never object pleasing in thine eye,
That never touch well welcome to thy hand,
That never meat sweet-savour'd in thy taste,
Unless I spake, or look'd, or touch'd, or carv'd to thee.
How comes it now, my husband, O, how comes it
That thou art then estranged from thyself?-
Thyself I call it, being strange to me
That undividable, incorporate,
Am better than thy dear self's better part.
Ah, do not tear away thyself from me;
For know, my love, as easy may'st thou fall
A drop of water in the breaking gulf,
And take unmingled thence that drop again
Without addition or diminishing,
As take from me thyself,and not me too.
How dearly would it touch thee to the quick,
Shouldst thou but hear I were licentious?
And that this body, consecrate to thee
By ruffian lust should be contaminate?
Wouldst thou not spit at me, and spurn at me
And hurl the name of husband in my face,
And tear the stain'd skin off my harlot brow,
And from my false hand cut the wedding-ring,
And break it with a deep divorcing vow?
I know thou canst; and therefore, see thou do it!
I am possess'd with an adulterate blot,
My blood is mingled with the crime of lust;
For if we two be one, and thou play false,
I do digest the poison of thy flesh,
Being strumpeted by thy contagion.

(II.ii.110–43)

She constructs herself as she imagines that she appears to him, lost
because her identity as a wife depends on his recognition of her as
such. Her experience of loss of identity is expressed therefore as a

series of negatives (ll.114–16) and complains that in rejecting her he rejects himself (l.120). She uses the Protean language of fluid identity that Syracusan Antipholus used about himself at the beginning of the play ('I to the world am like a drop of water that in the ocean seeks another drop' [I.ii.35–6]) and, most importantly, asserts self by hurling questions at him, a form which demands response, a verbal, aural, assayable response, demanding an acknowledgement of her existence through interaction. The ambivalence here is that as husband and wife they are at once different and the same. Her insistence on her identity as separate from but dependent on his is a serious version of the comic double vision brought on by the presentation of the two sets of identical twins. Antipholus' reponse, or lack of it, is all the more alarming for Adriana since it takes place in the home, at table, the locus which should be the safe haven of domestic hierarchy and conjugal identity, the place where her function, as much as anything, defines her identity. The person who defines her denies her in the very place whence her conjugal identity takes its meaning. The moment is fraught with emotional tension, and, in an effort to assert her mistress's authority over the lesser orders at least, Luciana turns on Dromio, urging obedience from him which will at least preserve Adriana's role as mistress over the servants in her own house:

> Why pratest thou to thyself and answerest not
> Dromio, thou snail, thou slug, thou sot

> (II.ii. 193–4)

to which he replies, bemused and bewildered by such an onslaught from a complete stranger,

> I am transformed master, am I not?

> (II.ii.195)

The text hovers on the margins of seriousness and here Shakespeare insists on the double text, on the possibility of an alternative reading which Adriana has so strongly invoked. The transformations, the decisions about whether you are what you think you are or whether you are what someone else thinks you are, are here heavily underscored by the fact that the serious matter in hand is communicated in the burlesque language of cheerful insult. Antipholus' dazed inability to make the switch from Adriana's impassioned outpouring to Luciana's virulent berating signals his difficulty in understanding the ambivalence of communication.

Adriana does not simply demand definition from her perceived husband. Touchingly, she relies on Luciana for an alternative point of view, continually questioning her own perceptions and struggling for a proper referent by which to judge them. For example, when Luciana confesses that Syracusan Antipholus, whom they think is Ephesian Antipholus, tried to make love to her, Adriana wants every last detail, trusting Luciana even in this situation:

> Ah, Luciana, did he tempt thee so?
> Might'st thou perceive austerely in his eye
> That he did plead in earnest, yea or no?
> Look'd he or red or pale, or sad or merrily?
> What observation mad'st thou in this case
> Of his heart's meteors tilting in his face?

(IV.ii.1–6)

When Luciana confesses that (as they suppose) her sister's husband 'did praise my beauty, then my speech' (IV.ii.15) Adriana launches into blistering invective:

> I cannot, nor I will not hold me still
> My tongue, though not my heart, shall have his will.
> He is deformed, crooked, old and sere,
> Illfac'd, worse bodied, shapeless everywhere;
> Vicious, ungentle, foolish, blunt, unkind,
> Stigmatical in making, worse in mind.

(IV.ii.17–22)

causing Luciana to enquire (quite reasonably after all that),

> Who would be jealous then of such a one?

(IV.ii.23)

which in turn elicits the response,

> Ah, but I think him better than I say

(IV.ii.25)

Adriana, in a number of ways, acknowledges the inadequacy of a single way of seeing, of a single mode of perception, of a single way of being. What matters is the interrogation of the view held, of the continual testing of the self who is doing the seeing, the possibility of a positive ambivalence or a proper duality of perception.

What I have just said offers an internalised, individualised, unified version of the speech. But like so much else in the play, the speech itself is ambivalent. It also means that Antipholus' treatment of her has disoriented her to the point that it has finally divided her perception; she doesn't know who she is or what she thinks any more. She is a deeply serious version of what Syracusan Dromio expresses at III. ii when, having been rejected by lookalike masters all morning, on finding a version of his master whose general perception of things at last seems at least to resemble his own he cries, in almost tearful relief,

> Do you know me, sir? Am I Dromio? Am I your man?

and, in sudden final hope,

> Am I myself?

(III.ii.72–3)

As Dromio claims an external recognition of an essential self from his master, so Adriana voluntarily accepts one from a spiritual mistress. In seeking the truth about her husband she leaves her own realm of authority and goes to the abbey, the site of a higher authority vested in a woman whose role as spiritual mother gives her conjoint authority over man and woman alike. The apparently lunatic Antipholus has claimed sanctuary in the abbey, and in order to reclaim her husband from his status as persecuted refugee and draw him back into her medium, that of the domestic environment, Adriana must face up to the fact that no matter how unreasonable his behaviour, hers was not fitting for the character that is called wife. The abbess accuses:

> The venom clamours of a jealous woman
> Poisons more deadly than a mad dog's tooth...
> Sweet recreation barr'd, what doth ensue
> But moody and dull melancholy...
> The consequence is then, thy jealous fits
> Hath scar'd thy husband from the use of wits.

> (V.i.69–70, 78–9, 85–6)

Luciana, having facilitated Adriana's attempts at self-definition throughout, appeals to her to protest;

> Why bear you these rebukes and answer not?

> (V.i.89)

but Adriana replies that the abbess has shown her a picture of herself which fits her own perception

> She did betray me to my own reproof

> (V.i.90)

In mending the marriage, the abbess facilitates the mending of the perception.

Male difficulty with identity in the play concerns itself with externals rather than introspection. Syracusan Antipholus, for example, fears that the dislocation he experiences is due to externalised rather than internalised feelings;

> They say this town is full of cozenage,
> As nimble jugglers that deceive the eye,
> Dark-working sorcerers that change the mind,
> Soul-killing witches that deform the body,
> Disguised cheaters, prating mountebanks...

> (I.ii.97–101)

he says at the end of Act I, and, in a moment which borders on recognition of the division of the self at the centre of the play,

> There's none but witches do inhabit here,
> And therefore 'tis high time that I were hence;
> She that doth call me husband, even my soul
> Doth for a wife abhor. But her fair sister,
> Possess'd with such a gentle sov'reign grace,
> Of such enchanting presence and discourse,
> Hath almost made me traitor to myself; ...

> (III.ii.155–61)

He is afraid of witches but cannot leave because positively enchanted, both by outward appearance and the speech which creates the self Luciana presents to him. His dilemma more importantly is that he is either traitor to himself (by accepting Adriana's demand that he acquit himself as her husband, thus betraying Luciana and his own desire), or, he is unwitting traitor to the other half of self, his twin, by the very same action. Or perhaps it is simply that in turning aside from his search for his brother in pursuit of his own happiness, he is traitor to his own higher calling. The line itself offers a divided definition, and the only way resolution is to be found is through an arbitrary decision by Antipholus as to whethter he will play the role Adriana insists is his, or the role he knows is appropriate to his own view of himself.

There is a similar moment for Ephesian Antipholus. When in Act V he is trying to prove that he is telling the truth whilst his wife is lying, he uses increasingly insistent physical detail to verify his presence at a scene. He must prove himself in terms of externals, the very thing the play continually urges us to mistrust.

> By th'way we met
> My wife, her sister, and a rabble more
> Of vile confederates; along with them
> They brought one Pinch, a hungry lean-fac'd villain;
> A mere anatomy, a mountebank,
> A thread-bare juggeler and a fortune-teller,
> A needy-hollow-ey'd-sharp-looking wretch; ...

> (V.i.235–41)

Amanda Piesse

The description gets more and more detailed, the text pointing out the hyperbole of the physical description by the compounded hyphenated figure. Ephesian Antipholus is desperate to establish his presence at the scene; this is the 'I must have been there, I saw it with my own two eyes' approach. Yet Shakespeare makes Antipholus admit that this is 'a mere anatomy', that he perceives the truth only of the outward and visible sign. A verbal version of this kind of self-assertion takes place earlier in the play, as again Antipholus urges the truth of his story, and Dromio corroborates it by close verbal echoing which resolve into physical proof;

Dromio:	Sir, sooth to say, you did not dine at home
Antipholus:	Were not my doors lock'd up and I shut out
Dromio:	Perdiy, your doors were lock'd, and you shut out.
Antipholus:	And did she not herself revile me there?
Dromio:	Sans fable, she herself revil'd you there
Antipholus:	Did not her kitchen maid rail, taunt and scorn me?
Dromio:	Certes she did, the kitchen vestal scorn'd you
Antipholus:	And did not I in rage depart from thence?
Dromio:	In verity you did: my bones bear witness
	That since have felt the vigour of his rage.

(IV.iv.67–76)

The faultless adherence to the iambic line and the absolute replication of Antipholus' story powerfully conveys the indignation that the aggrieved Antipholus feels. But the verbal replication means nothing, since they could simply be corroborating an agreed fabrication, and besides, the question and response formula (a mock-version, perhaps, of Adriana's assertion of self above) is only self-corroborating. This perverse kind of twinning of language eventually gives way to the physical evidence: time and place cannot be insisted upon merely by language, but must have hard physical evidence to prove it. Shakespeare intimates that the men in the play are still insistent on a single sense of self, and of the same self in any given place or time at any given moment. Unlike the women, they are not ready to acknowledge the possibility of coexisting alternative versions of self.

The play itself enacts this notion of selective viewing. It is easy to forget, amidst the hurly-burly of burlesque, that the play has an extremely serious matter in hand. Egeon's life is at stake throughout. He is condemned to die, since Syracusans are banned from Ephesus on pain of death. He risked his life to come to Ephesus in search of

his son, the living pattern of his own future; he risks his present self
in an Aristophanic seeking after another part of self, in an attempt to
ensure the existence of his projected image into the future. Egeon,
reappearing in the final scene, almost loses his identity and his life
because of his sons' failure to recognise him. Sequestered in prison,
and virtually absent from the audience's consciousness throughout
the busy toings and froings of the play, he bewails how the passing
of time has changed him almost beyond recognition

> Not know my voice? O time's extremity,
> Hast thou so crack'd and splitted my poor tongue
> In seven short years, that here my only son
> Knows not my feeble key of untun'd cares?
> Though now this grained face of mine be hid
> In sap-consuming winter's drizzled snow,
> Yet hath my night of life some memory...
>
> (V.i.307–14)

Changed beyond recognition, his identity is at this moment dependent on outward appearance. It is once again the abbess who becomes
the redeemer, her spiritual status allowing her a degree of recognition which goes beyond physical representation, her role as wife
allowing her a special recognition of him who is her other half:

> Speak old Egeon, if thou be'st the man
> That hadst a wife once call'd Emilia,
> That bore thee at a burden two fair sons?
>
> (V.i.341–3)

At the end of the play, the questioning woman is defined as the
explicit arbiter of identity. From Emilia's recognition springs restitution and resolution. It is the wife who acknowledges the husband,
the mother who recognises the sons. As the duke struggles to recognise that each half of the two sets of twins is valid in its own right,

> One of these men is *genius* to the other;
> And so of these, which is the natural man,
> And which the spirit? Who deciphers them?
>
> (V.i.332–4)

the notion of supernatural intervention, one figure working as a perfect Platonic image of an earthly imperfection, is swept away. The working of the play ultimately accepts, even valorises, the workings of multiple identity as a means of arriving at the truth of being. Different selves are appropriate to different places and different situations; as we have seen in the cases of Adriana and the Abbess, the playing of different roles in different places with different places yields up the ultimate truth of the situation again and again.

The search for the other half of self and for the lost child take a very different form in *Pericles*, but the quest is ultimately the same. Time, place and sense of self in the wider context of family relationship and hierarchical relationship interrelate with the explicit siting of the individual in relation to family, society and history. The figure of Gower as commentator immediately invites the audience to locate and identify the play in a historical and in a literary paradigm. Gower is the locus of familiarity against which the tale of Pericles more starkly appears as 'other', dislocated in time and in actual location from the place where the chorus or the narrator stands. Consciously drawing the audience's attention to the fact that it is watching and assessing the play, the chorus figure can then go on selfconsciously to manipulate different methods of showing and telling to increase the audience's sense of difference from the hegemony within which the play operates. In detachment, then, the playwright can examine physical places and domestic spaces and situations. The use of the chorus invites the audience to interpret the play as a series of signs to be read. There is a sense here in which the characters are subordinate to the schemata which drive the play.

Physical dislocation in the play is used to figure moral and amoral exploration. The vocabulary used to articulate Pericles' experiences in Antioch is that of the fall. Where he comes seeking perfection, marriage, fruitfulness, desiring to 'taste the fruit of yon celestial tree' (I.i.22) he finds empty show, incest, stultification. Sailing east in search of paradise, he finds a postlapsarian existence in a state of advanced disintegration. Physical reproduction is stifled by what he finds; the impossibilty of responding to the conundrum stifles verbal productivity too, and the theme of silence in the face of evil strangely attaches to the male protagonist in this play. Where Pericles' experience in Antioch provides the anti-type of family, so the thematic mainframe of the play provides the inversion of the moral norm, the father seeking salvation through silence and the daughter preserving her virtue through speech.

When Pericles ventures out in love again, he is clad in the patriarchal protection lent him by his father's armour. The protection has almost been lost, and is retrieved from the sea in a state which renders it virtually useless. But it affirms Pericles' place in a paradigm of existence where the proper values of family existence are apparently in grave danger, and it allows him the proper disguise for the emblematic procession which will lead him before Thaisa. The armour shows him to be his father's son, and also to be of the same order as those who gain approval in the proper patriarchal hierarchy of Pentapolis which operates in direct contrast to Antioch. Here there is no danger attached to open articulation of the truth; on the contrary we see the process of narration embodied in the dialogue as we see the procession, have it articulated by Thaisa and its significance explained by her father. Here is the proper hierarchical order where true meaning resides with the patriarch, whose great pleasure is to gloss his daughter's empirical discovery. For Pericles, it is important that where in Antioch he interpreted and responded to the verbal and visual signifiers, here in Pentapolis he provides the symbol of himself, creating himself anew in the image in which he would have her behold him. His outward show is rusty, past its best; since he is underneath it not a copy but the renewed image of his father, it is apparent to the audience, as it strains to read these signs, that Pericles is here emblematically the very opposite of Antiochus' daughter.

It is in this redeemed location and situation that the deaths of Antiochus and his daughter are reported. They have become a myth, a story to be told and shuddered at, once the reality of Simonides and Thaisa are present to replace them. They have suffered an unnatural death as befits their unnatural practice. The vocabulary of fruitlessness retrospectively becomes one of unnaturalness, and the audience sees how right and how lucky Pericles has been to dislocate himself physically and morally from such unnatural behaviour. His journey by sea, his symbolic immersion in it and his subsequent arrival at the court of Simonides once he has put on the whole armour of his father symbolises a safe passage from potential damnation into the presence of proper order.

That the court of Simonides has become the locus of fruitfulness in the play is underscored by the manipulation of various forms of articulation in this episode. True presentation of self through one's utterances is foregrounded as being of the utmost importance within the action of the play itself, and the use of Gower as chorus works throughout to underpin this valorisation of the spoken word. It is for this reason that Pericles' grief-stricken silence at the loss of his daughter is so powerful, and the casting in gold of an epitaph for a child not dead is so heinous a crime.

The loss of Thaisa and the subsequent necessary estrangement of Marina interrupt the movement towards attainment and fruitfulness. Where the sea gave up Pericles to Thaisa, it now robs him of her. The medium of baptism has apparently become the place of death. In this topsy-turvy environment, Pericles chooses to leave his daughter, for her better nourishment, in the place the audience symbolically associates with famine. Conversely, Thaisa having been rescued and awakened by the inarticulate discourse of music, elects for herself a positive form of fruitlessness and becomes a votaress of Diana. The symbolisms of physical and spiritual nurture and nourishment are closely bound up with place and with the validation of language as a medium of truth in the play.

Language, like family relationship, is to be redeemed in this play. At the beginning of Act IV, Marina, like Perdita in *A Winter's Tale*, enters as an emblem of pastoral innocence, bearing flowers, discoursing on her own birth out of the jaws of death. Constructing her own birth from the sea, she asserts her own sense of self both consciously in relation to her father and, unwittingly, in relationship to her mother.

Marina:	When I was born, the wind was north…
	My father, as nurse says, did never fear,
	But cried, 'Good seamen!' to the sailors, galling
	His kingly hands, haling ropes;
	And, clasping to the mast, endur'd a sea
	That almost burst the deck.
Leonine:	When was this?
Marina:	When I was born

(IV.i.51–8)

She can articulate her own history and subsequently has an unshakeable notion of self, despite the several social and physical dislocations she encounters. Leonine, equally unwitting, develops the affinity further, urging 'Come, say your prayers'. Marina locates herself firmly in her own history: Shakespeare consolidates the affirmation by locating her by analogy in the wider scheme of things. Marina's death, like her mother's is notional, a matter of conjecture and report rather than actual. The representation of her which remains in Tarsus is an outward and visible sign of the means she uses to preserve herself in her dislocated state in the brothel – shining words. The point here is that the audience is shown in a series of emblematic and linguistic signs that Marina's sense of self is rooted in an innate history, and it does not change, no matter what cultural, social or historical space she is inhabiting.

But for Marina to preserve herself by speech is an inversion of the moral norm. Where silence normally betokens chatity, Marina's constant assertion of an unreconstructed self is made manifest in her shining words. Her abduction results in her arrival at the brothel in Mytilene, where the Bawd and the Pander, who are what they are to such a degree that they need no further naming, plan to sell her virginity to the highest bidder.

She refuses to respond to their attempted construction of her or to that of her potential clients as her verbal intercourse with Lysimachus demonstrates:

Lysimachus: Now, pretty one, how long have you been at this trade?
Marina: What trade, sir?
Lysimachus: Why, I cannot name't but I shall offend.
Marina: I cannot be offended with my trade. Please you to name it.
Lysimachus: How long have you been of this profession?
Marina: E'er since I can remember
Lysimachus: Did you go to't so young? Were you a gamester at five or seven?
Marina: Earlier too sir, if now I be one.
Lysimachus: Why, the house you dwell in proclaims you to be a creature of sale.
Marina: Do you know this house to be a place of such resort, and will come into't?

(IV.vi.65–79)

Refusing to be constructed by place or language, Marina gently shows Lysimachus that he is ashamed to articulate the construction he places on her and therefore makes him ashamed both of the linguistic construction and the act he was to perform to recreate her physically as a whore. By preventing such a construction of self through language she prevents the physical construction. The role of creator becomes hers as it prevents an act of perverted creation. The playwright bestows her with a kind of linguistic motherhood as here she becomes arbiter of her own identity. The visible sign of purity (we remember her emblematic entrance in IV.i) and the language of purity are consonant. Where outward appearance and inner self have been dislocated – with serious consequences in the case of Antiochus' daughter and as a gentle trial in the case of Simonides and of Pericles himself – here the two become consonant in the figure of Marina to redeem both the time and the place. Instead of the brothel recreating and transforming Marina into a nameless icon like Pander and Bawd, instead of transforming her into an empty nameless thing to provide a soulless function, she transforms the place. Shakespeare demonstrates how the working out of the meaning of things, at a local level in the dialogue between Marina and Lysimachus but at a cosmic level in terms of the way the play demands the interpretation of its many emblems, results in the rebirth of the images being constructed.

The ultimate outcome of the interpretation of signs is Pericles' recognition of the daughter through her singing – the linguistic sign – and through her physical resemblance to her mother – the iconographic sign. Showing and telling become consonant, the sign and the signified are one. In the final hierarchical inversion, the daughter symbolically gives birth to the father as she restores the literary symbol of life and fruitfulness, language.

Where Adriana's sense of place, persona and self-projection embraced the notion of different selves for different places and different people, Marina insists on a single construction of her identity despite her continual spatial and social dislocation. She constructs her identity through her knowledge of herself, her father and her mother, creating herself out of her own history. It is that stability which allows the reunification of the family through recognition of each other. I would contend that where the Elizabethan play allows diffraction and multiple personae, the Jacobean play works towards fixity and restitution. Both plays however demonstrate in different ways the Irigarayan notion of female openness and multiplicity. The traits are obvious throughout *The Comedy of Errors*, and I do not propose to reiterate them here. Marina, while remaining stable in her own identity, is able to respond and react in different situations to reassert her own sense of being. Pericles cannot regain himself until he regains the stabilising influence of the female arbiter of identity.

Where working from an Elizabethan or a Jacobean set of ideals renders up disparate readings, a twentieth-century feminist perspective – specifically an Irigarayan one – suggests that Shakespeare's construction of female identity has a resonance beyond that of cultural expression. The faithful representation of womankind necessitates the allowance of mutiplicity and flexibility, whatever the cultural hegemony dictates.

NOTES

1. *The Irigaray Reader*, ed. Margaret Whitford (Oxford: Basil Blackwell, 1991), 48–9.
2. See Plato, *The Symposium: A New Translation*, trans. W. Hamilton, Penguin Classics (Penguin, 1951), 59–61.
3. I use 'Jamesian' to mean pertaining to the King in particular and 'Jacobean' to mean pertaining to the cultural hegemony.
4. 'Now woman is neither closed nor open. Indefinite, unfinished/infinite, *form is never complete in her*...This incompleteness of her form, of her morphology, allows her to become something else at any moment, which is not to say that she is (n)ever unambiguously anything...For woman cannot mean herself...and besides does not want for herself the power of expressing...that would assign her to some concept...She cannot relate herself to any being, subject or whole that can be simply designated....Man's autoeroticism presupposes an individualisation of the subject, of the object...if only for an instant, the moment of substitution' (ed. Margaret Whitford, *The Irigaray Reader* [Oxford: Blackwell, 1991], 55–6.
5. See Philippa Berry, *Of Chastity and Power: Elizabethan Literature and the Unmarried Queen* (London: Routledge, 1989), 63.
6. On the subject of the Queen's two bodies, see Marie Axton, *The Queen's Two Bodies*, (London: London Royal Historical Society, 1977). The legislation supporting the doctrine is set out at 12.
7. See Christopher Durston, *James I*, Lancaster Pamphlets (London: Routledge, 1993), chapter 6 for the degree of religious freedom James was prepared to tolerate.
8. There is a large body of literature connected with the projected personae of Elizabeth I, and more recent publications are beginning to query both the apparent masculinity of some of the projections previously accepted, but more importantly to deny the notion of 'a coherent 'base' ideology of the cult of Elizabeth, arguing that 'it rather was comprised of a loose collection of discourses, which accorded different weight to various ideas of Elizabeth and which defined the

female monarch in relation to different subjects' (Berry, 63). Early
accounts of a 'base ideology' include E.C. Wilson, *England's Eliza*
(1939: London: F. Cass and Company, 1966); Frances Yates, *Astraea:
the Imperial Theme in the 16th Century* (London, etc.: Routledge and
Kegan Paul, 1975); more recently, Leah Marcus, *Puzzling Shakespeare:
Local Reading and its Discontents* (Berkeley: University of California
Press, 1988), Berry and eds. S.P. Cerasano and Marion Wynne-Davies,
Gloriana's Face (London, etc.: Harvester Wheatsheaf, 1992) are
amongst those deconstructing the previously held views.

9.   ' ... by my descent lineally out of the loynes of *Henry* the seuenth is
      reunited and confirmed in mee the Vnion of the two Princely Roses
      of the two Houses of *Lancaster* and *Yorke*' (King James VI and I,
      Political Writings, ed. Johann P. Sommerville, Cambridge Texts in the
      History of Political Thought [Cambridge: Cambridge University
      Press, 1994] 137).

10.   Jonson and Dekker's entertainment for the King designed in 1604
      shows the King directly descended from Brutus, ushering in a time
      of peace, the figure of Astraea standing on the summit of two arches
      which illustrate the fortunate isles of Great Britian and the cedar,
      which signified fertility.

11.   'How much greater reason haue wee to expect a happie issue of this
      greater Vnion, [that of England and Scotland] which is only fastened
      and bound vp by the wedding ring of *Astraea* (Sommerville, 137). For
      an account of the transferring of iconography between the two
      monarchs and a picture of the arch constructed for James' entry
      into London, see Graham Parry, *The Seventeenth Century: the Intellec-
      tual and Cultural Context of English Literature 1603–1700*, Longman
      Literature in English Series (London: Longman, 1989), 12–14 and
      also plate 2.

12.   See Berry, 66.

13.   See Sommerville, 63.

14.   See Sommerville, 63.

15.   See Parry, 11.

16.   See Sommerville, 65.

17.   For the full text, see Sommerville, 1–61.

18.   See note 4 above.

19.   It is generally accepted that Shakespeare uses two Plautine plays,
      Menaechmi and *Amphitruo* as source material for *The Comedy of Errors*;
      see Geoffrey Bullough, *Narrative and Dramatic Sources in Shakespeare*,
      Vol. I (London: Routledge and Kegan Paul, 1957) or the introduction
      to the Arden Shakespeare, ed. R.A. Foakes, xxiv–xxxiv.

8

Calling 'things by their right names': Troping Prostitution, Politics and *The Dutch Courtesan*

Mark Thornton Burnett

I INTRODUCTION

Marston's *The Dutch Courtesan*, written in 1604–5, delineates a crumbling, phantasmagoric world of bewildering transformations in which stable points of reference are unavailable and in which persons are subject to violent alterations of manner and appearance. The opening scene stages a grotesque spectacle of distortion and disease, the characters being metaphorically reduced to the level of animals: grubs, sharks and cockles. Mulligrub is perceived as a 'Shark' (I.i.1), advancing his 'snout' (I.ii.2) to discover the theft of irrecoverable goblets; they will be 'hammer'd out' (I.i.5) into another form, Freevill tells him, their metal recast so as to be unrecognisable.[1] Or the play's concern with metamorphosis shows itself in reflections upon the body corrupting, reifying and turning into an inanimate object. Every species of illness afflicts bodies in *The Dutch Courtesan*, which are plagued with decay and caught up in a self-destructive process. Teeth ache (II.ii.65); jaws syphilitically drop (I.i.39); and coughs announce the inescapability of the grave (IV.iv.18–26). It is a fantastic vision of living and non-living materials resolving themselves into the elements of which they are constituted.

These startling transfigurations are accompanied by suggestions that the characters themselves may convert to objects at any moment. When Cocledemoy escapes from Mulligrub's tavern with Mary Faugh, his 'movable chattel, his instrument of fornication' (I.i.14), the blind harper is left playing to dishes and candles as his audience. Medicinal objects circulate as the emblematic signs of the decomposing subject: Mary Faugh is likened to a 'glister-pipe' (I.ii.12), and Cocledemoy describes Mulligrub as a mixture with which he will 'gargalize' (III.ii.31) his throat. But these changes are in thrall to a larger system which makes even institutions fragile. The chaste household may be contaminated and revert to a brothel, Freevill fears (I.i.62), and it is in the play's representation (or 'troping') of prostitution and the prostitute that its political implications reside.[2]

II FIGURING PROSTITUTES

Linked to the dizzying insecurities is an urge to fix, to locate meaning and to sort out uncertainties into neatly packaged categories: by defining what appears to be unreliable, characters seek to establish for themselves a sense of order and stability. The occupation of the prostitute exercises Freevill and Malheureux, who endeavour to explain the ways in which it serves social functions. For Freevill, frequenting brothels is 'recreation' (I.ii.64), although his supposed defence of the profession only manages to underline the oppression of the prostitute by a market economy which the male client controls (I.i.92–127). 'Are strumpets, then, such things so delicate?' (I.ii.129) asks Malheureux, struggling to find a correlation between his recent experience and the patriarchal assumptions which govern his sexual conduct.

A will to interpret the prostitute goes hand-in-hand with acts of naming and calling, attempts to declare an unshakeable identity in the face of disorder and collapse. It is 'not in fashion to call/things by their right names' (I.ii.99–100) states Freevill, while Mary Faugh attacks Cocledemoy who will 'Call a woman the most ungodly/names!' (I.ii.15–16). Malheureux worries that 'the world/Calls lust a crime' (II.i.127–8), and is terrified lest he commit 'Some deed whose very name is hideous' (IV.ii.15). At critical points in the action of *The Dutch Courtesan*, names are used to reassure, to restore an illusion of continuity, to allow the enjoyment of a moment of authority. At the same time as they manifest a need to understand the unpredictability of the social order and to halt a flow of ceaseless exchanges, they betray a fascination with the unnameable, with deviant sexual practices, with that which cannot easily be determined.[3]

In particular, anxieties about social upheaval and decline focus upon Franceschina, the prostitute. The strategies enlisted to describe or 'trope' her point to a desire to regulate what is seen to be a dangerously unbridled sexuality. Dismemberment and reduction mark the ways in which she is figured. Being Dutch, she is illicitly enticing and unknown, but her nationality also dictates that she be contained and placed at a distance. She is, according to Freevill, his 'creature' (I.i.140), in other words, a construction of his own invention. The diminutives associated with her – 'Dutch Tanakin' (I.i.141), for example – imply belittlement, as does the supposed softness and therefore pliability of her disposition. 'She's none/of your ramping cannibals that devour man's flesh, nor any/of your Curtian gulfs that will never be satisfied' (I.ii.86–8) declares Freevill, confident of the passivity of the woman he has created and colonised, even as his words rebound upon themselves and imply a secret wish to be consumed by an alien and voracious prostitute. Each appearance of Franceschina is characterised by fragmented objects indicating her presence rather than extended descriptions. Her 'short-heels' (I.ii.92), 'voice' (I.ii.104) and 'breast' (I.ii.106) are her insignia, parts which fail to cohere into a whole. Finally, she is imagined by Freevill as a 'a statue, a body without a/ soul, a carcass three months dead' (II.i.133–4), an artifact upon which Malheureux projects necrophilic fantasies. Simultaneously, however, these efforts to mould her meet with only partial success; Franceschina continues to exercise an influence and, despite the categorising to which she is subjected, cannot be clearly identified or named: Franceschina, Frank Frailty and Frank of Frank Hall, she attracts these and other titles.

Many of the fears which Franceschina arouses are matched by her capricious behaviour, although she is obliged by circumstances to swing wildly between fidelity, outrage and the pursuit of revenge. Furious at the treatment she has been accorded, she contemplates a dramatic conversion which testifies to the shifting energies with which she is associated: 'Mine body/must turn Turk for twopence' (II.ii.39–40). Taking on the persona of a lusty male lover in one of her songs, she excites additional worries, embracing inconstancy and blurring the boundaries that conventionally keep male and female distinct (II.ii.54–60).

Purity and saintliness are the hallmarks of Beatrice, Franceschina's apparent opposite. The language of Spenserian abstraction and excess enlisted to address her – Beatrice's 'chaste eyes' (II.i.3) purge

Freevill of the 'base affections of unfruitful heats' (II.i.7) – confirms
her place as the powerless recipient of her suitor's extravagant
encomiums. On the other hand, behind the panegyric lurks the
possibility that Beatrice, too, wields captivating, threatening abil-
ities:

> Your eyes shall be my joys, my wine that still
> Shall drown my often cares. Your only voice
> Shall cast a slumber on my list'ning sense.
> You with soft lip shall only ope mine eyes
> And suck their lips asunder. Only you
> Shall make me wish to live, and not fear death,
> So on your cheeks I might yield latest breath.
> Oh, he that thus may live and thus shall die
> May well be envied of a deity!
>
> (II.i.40–8)

These impassioned hyperboles point to a nervous realisation that
Beatrice is the controller who is capable of making Freevill drunk,
casting a slumber on him and paralysing him, as did the sirens who
hypnotised Ulysses' sailors by appealing to their 'list'ning sense'.
Demonically, like Faustus' Helen, she will suck open his eyes (metaphorically dispossessing him of his soul), dictating when he wakes
and sleeps; created by Beatrice, Freevill runs the risk of becoming a
love-struck, mechanical manikin. If Beatrice is an enchantress, then
she is equally a goddess who has power over Freevill's mortality:
the terms employed are confusedly interchangeable. Things are not
what they seem in *The Dutch Courtesan*; forces combine to encour-
age an intense preoccupation with problems of definition and the
potential loss of identity, and Franceschina functions as a scapegoat:
the abusive treatment of the prostitute permits a range of anxieties
to be conveniently discharged. But the shadowy Beatrice is no less a
victim of a society in which a terror of disempowerment dominates.

III POLITICAL CONTEXTS

When James I ascended the English throne in 1603, he was faced
with the difficulty of establishing himself as a monarch separate
from yet complementary to Elizabeth I, his predecessor.[4] Above all

it was necessary for him to define his role as husband, father and sovereign in relation to his immediate family and subjects. Only recently nominated by Elizabeth, he was now required to make known the character that would distinguish his reign, a recurrent theme in his early parliamentary pronouncements. Apart from surviving a rash of conspiracies in the first years, James also stressed his creative capacities, the territorial usefulness of being able to unite two kingdoms, and the power that he enjoyed as a patriarchal ruler whose future royal line was guaranteed. It is with these considerations in mind that I want to turn to *The Dutch Courtesan* and to its political unconscious.

The political embeddedness of *The Dutch Courtesan* has been recognised before, although comment has tended to concentrate upon direct satirical allusions rather than the more diffuse meanings which a drama can generate. Jonathan Goldberg has noted that the play, performed before James several times, owes some of its humour to satirical remarks about the Scottish dialect, patron saint and customary rapacity, concluding that it 'pleased the king for... the same reasons that Jonson's antimasques succeeded. James countenanced what he would not have tolerated behind his back.'[5] When Cocledemoy, for instance, disguised as Andrew Shark, a 'cheating Scotsman', claims to have been shaving (cheating) the English for two years (II.iii.21), Marston is launching an attack on those Scots who came south with James at his 1603 accession. It has also been suggested that the play may have appealed as the Family of Love, represented in *The Dutch Courtesan* by Mary Faugh and Mistress Mulligrub, was one of James' particular annoyances; certainly, he roundly condemned the movement in *Basilikon Doron*, first printed in 1599, in which he states: '*as to the name of Puritanes, I am not ignorant that the style thereof doeth properly belong onely to that vile sect amongst the Anabaptists, called the Family of loue.*'[6] Under Elizabeth, members of the Family of Love had been persecuted as it was believed that they participated in seditious, Catholic activity directed against the Crown, and the situation did not improve when, in 1604, elders of the sect presented James with a unpopular petition distinguishing themselves from Puritans and promising to be faithful and dutiful subjects.[7]

But the political ramifications of *The Dutch Courtesan* stretch further than these observations, and it is possible to locate points of Jacobean interest which operate more covertly and subversively. Mistress Mulligrub's complaint as she lays the dining-table that the room stinks of smoke – 'perfume! This parlor does so smell of profane tobacco' (III.iii.47) – may have raised a laugh from a royal spectator who had written about precisely this problem in *A Counterblaste to Tobacco* (1604): 'is it not...great..vncleanesse that at the table...men should not be ashamed, to sit...puffing of the smoke of Tobacco...making the filthy smoke and stinke thereof, to... infect the aire[?].'[8] There also seems to be a connection between James' contempt in *Daemonologie* (1597) for 'reuenging' witches who are taught by the devil how to use 'vncouthe poysons' and the devilish, witch-like and poisoning Franceschina: 'Me would puisson' (V.i.14), she remarks, 'for know de deepest hell/As a revenging woman's naught so fell' (V.i.14–15).[9] Nor may it be coincidental that, in *Basilikon Doron*, James urgently instructed his son to avoid the company of courtesans, 'which are nothing else, but *irritamenta libidinis*'.[10]

Looming large among the worries which vexed James in 1603 was how to commemorate the execution of his mother, Mary Stuart, 16 years before. At the time of the events leading to her trial, Mary had been widely vilified in English and Scottish propaganda as a witch and a whore; in the words of one contemporary, she was 'the very plague & calamity of our countrie, the very groundworke & chiefe impulsiue cause of all these treasons and conspiracies'.[11] Wrote William Kempe in 1587 to the conspirators: 'what *Circes* charme, thy wicked mind bewicht[?]' and 'Yet you bewitched wretched wights, her *Siren* songes did hear'.[12] Labelled an adulteress, murderess and mermaid (or prostitute), a Clytemnestra and a Circe in virulently anti-Catholic writings and prints, Mary was singled out as fomenting discontent, plotting against the English crown and endangering international relations.[13] Criticism of Mary was toned down in the period following the execution, but there could still be a case such as that involving William Leonard, a 'gentleman in the law', who came before the authorities in 1595 for having claimed that 'Bothwell went commonly to bed with her; that the late Queen was a whore, and that he could show a book in his study which proved it.'[14] The early years of James' reign witnessed a major rehabilitation programme: a pall was sent to cover Mary's tomb, and in 1612 her body was moved from Peterborough Cathedral to Westminster Abbey where it rested opposite a monument to Elizabeth. Finally the Scottish Queen had been placed among her royal relatives and her transgressions neatly exorcised.[15]

The Dutch Courtesan does not clearly communicate its political undercurrents. Whenever the play broaches a Jacobean issue, it does so obliquely, guardedly, in coded languages. Those concerns which intrigued James enter the play obscurely, always under the cover of diverting entertainment. Marston treads carefully. Nevertheless, it is striking that the drama rehearses the same tropes that underscored the campaign against Mary Stuart, as if it draws some of its energy from what must have been in 1603 residual discourses. In an enigmatic remark, Cocledemoy accuses Franceschina of being 'as false, as prostituted and adulterate, as some translated/manuscript' (IV.iii.7–8), a statement which recalls Catholic propaganda, carried across the Channel. More obviously, Franceschina sees herself as a stricken nightingale (I.ii.111–18), and in contemporary bestiaries, sirens were thought to be not mermaids but nightingales.[16] Identified as a 'siren' on two occasions (I.ii.104 and I.ii.110), Franceschina is at the same time a succubus who will scratch out Beatrice's eyes (II.ii.81–2) and stage-manage her suitor's murder; not surprisingly, she is warned by Freevill not to 'turn witch before thy time' (II.ii.95). But her witch-like qualities are repeatedly emphasised. 'O Divla, life o' mine art!' (II.ii.40), Franceschina exclaims, 'Ten tousant devla! Dere sall be … no spirit but divla in me' (IV.iii.40, 43). Transformed into an embodiment of the deity she has consistently invoked, Franceschina is eventually portrayed as 'this fair devil/In shape of woman' (V.iii.44–5). In 1603 it may have been thought that Mary Stuart had been put to rest, but *The Dutch Courtesan* revives memories of a Protestant polemic against entrapment, witchcraft and assassination attempts, hinting at the resurrection of James' ghostly predecessors.

In sharp contrast to Franceschina is Beatrice whose name recalls Dante's mistress and the numerous titles – Diana, Laura or Idea, Cynthia, Gloriana and Belphoebe – with which Elizabeth was identified. There are several points at which the representation of Beatrice intersects with the cult of Elizabeth.[17] A chaste virgin, Beatrice, thinking that her lover is dead, mercifully forgives Franceschina who has engineered his downfall: 'gentle minds will pity though they cannot love' (IV.iv.60), she argues. Her selfless behaviour stimulates the concealed Freevill to cry, 'to have such a wife/Is happiness to breed pale envy in the saints' (IV.iv.79–80), but when he reveals himself, Beatrice is overcome and falls into a faint, only to be revived soon afterwards. To the end Beatrice is true to her name: Beatrice, from 'Beatrix', meant she who blesses. Any obvious

Elizabethan associations are understated, however, in *The Dutch Courtesan*, a play that works at the level of verbal nuance rather than boldly drawn parallels. A scandal had already erupted in 1596 over Spenser's depiction of a merciful, forgiving Elizabeth in Book V of *The Faerie Queene*. In canto ix, Duessa, a transparently disguised Mary, Queen of Scots, is placed on trial, and judged by Mercilla, a version of Elizabeth; James, in the words of a contemporary, 'conceaued great offence', and threatened Spenser with the severest punishments.[18] *The Dutch Courtesan* proceeds more hesitantly, muffling its Elizabethan echoes or hiding its allusions behind the farcical complications of the interweaving plots. Marston does not make Spenser's mistake.

The furore aroused by *The Faerie Queene* never resulted in Spenser being brought to trial to receive judgement for his ill-advised poetic exercises. Other writings of the later Elizabethan period, however, demonstrated a fascinated inquisitiveness about the dispensation of justice in exegetical treatises upon the apocalypse. Theologians such as Giacopo Brocado, Heinrich Bullinger, John Foxe and George Gifford produced pages unravelling the significances of the bizarre creatures and events of *Revelation* and, if their works were unavailable in English, they quickly made their way into translated pamphlets.[19] The typical argument maintained that the woman clothed with the sun and standing on the moon, blessed with marriage to Christ, represented the true church (also symbolised by a dove); her antithesis was the scarlet, bejewelled whore of Babylon who rode upon the waters with a cup of abominations in her hand and astride a seven-headed beast with a long, curling and serpentine tail. The reformers commenting upon the spectacle agreed that the whore connoted the Catholic Church, and the beast of revelation the Antichrist, the triumph of the papacy and the last days of Protestant ascendancy.[20] In the early years of her reign, it had been hoped that Elizabeth would herald a new era of purity within the Church and, to this end, millenarians saw the Catholic powers as monsters to be routed if there were to be a conclusive victory; as Carol Z. Wiener states: 'almost all ... took it for granted that their battle was not simply a struggle between two political entities but was a fight of universal significance between the forces of good and evil.'[21]

Usually it is accepted that the structure and philosophy of *The Dutch Courtesan* are most informed by Marston's intimate acquaintance with Montaigne's essays. My own sense is that apocalyptical thought exerted an equally powerful pressure: the birds, beasts and creatures that engulf Marston's play have their counterparts in the protean animal forms that inhabit *Revelation*, and both play and scripture are filled with devils, spirits, jewels, rings and cups. Cocledemoy teases Mulligrub with the story of 'twenty-four huge, horrible, monstrous, fearful, devouring ... Serpents' (II.iii.44–5, 47) emerging from the holes of the conduit, 'which no sooner were beheld but they turn'd to/mastiffs ... cocks ... bears .. . which bears are at this hour to be yet/seen in Paris Garden, living upon nothing but toasted cheese/and green onions' (II.iii.47–52). It is hardly surprising that the vintner should declare that the serpents' extraordinary appearance 'portends something' (II.iii.54). Beyond the jest may be glimpsed the locusts with snake-like tails which plague the world, the lion-horses or the beast of the bottomless pit haunting the revelation of John the divine.[22] Bantering with Tysefew, her suitor, Crispinella jokes about unnatural prodigies born after a gestation of ten months, and monsters with hunched backs and twisted features (IV.i.42–4, 69–71). 'Monstrous' is indeed a recurrent term in the play (V.i.45, 100) which is linked to reflections upon eclipses (V.iii.1) and the 'beast of man' (V.iii.66), lust. 'What news from Babylon?' (III.i.209) inquires Freevill, while Cocledemoy, anticipating the success of his intrigues, states: 'Tomorrow is the day of/judgment' (IV.v.123–4). Taking up his redemptive role in the final scene, Cocledemoy criticizes Mulligrub for his dishonest business practices:

> But brother, brother, you must think of your sins and iniquities. You have been a broacher of profane vessels; you have made us drink of the juice of the whore of Babylon. For whereas good ale, perrys, braggets, ciders, and metheglins was the true ancient British and Troyan drinks, you ha' brought in Popish wines, Spanish wines, French wines, *tam Marti quam Mercurio*, both muscatine and malmsey, to the subversion, staggering, and sometimes overthrow of many a good Christian. You ha' been a great jumbler.
>
> (V.iii.102–10)

The comic admonition couples direct allusion to the cup of abominations and the sacred vials of *Revelation* with reflections upon the mythic founding of Britain as a new Troy by Brutus (like James, a kind of exile) and threats about the overthrow of worthy Protestant beverages by adulterated Catholic spirits: Mulligrub's dealings tip the playworld towards terrifying and apocalyptic confusions.

Passages such as these form an alliance with broader, more urgent political questions, the situation of a new monarch pursuing fresh foreign policies and attempting to adjudicate between Protestant demands and his own Catholic sympathies. The local meanings stirred up by *The Dutch Courtesan* bring to mind, too, earlier iconographic traditions and images. They hark back to representations of Elizabeth as the chaste moon of reformed religious truth or as a soldier crushing the apocalyptic beast beneath her feet.[23] Taking these conventions into account, it is tempting to reconsider Beatrice, the 'dove-like virgin' (IV.v.81) who first appears in a night scene as the moon is waning and the sun is rising (II.i.1–62), and who is associated with illumination and light. The identification of Franceschina with the whore of Babylon is implied but not clarified. Already in anti-Catholic invective Mary Stuart had been branded as the Antichrist, and in Book I of *The Faerie Queene*, Duessa is linked to the great whore in the potent phrase, 'false sorceresse'.[24]

What grants a radical potential to the biblical subtexts of *The Dutch Courtesan* is that *Revelation* was one of the books James, in his writings, highlighted and revered as particularly important. In *Ane fruitfull meditatioun*, printed in Edinburgh in 1588, he dwells upon 'ye woman cled with scarlet' and 'ane beast out of ye sea, ye bloodie Romane impyre'; his heroic poem, 'Lepanto', released as part of *Poeticall Exercises at Vacant Houres* in 1591, celebrates the victory of the Christian over the infidel in rhetoric borrowed from *Revelation*; and *A Premonition to all Most Mightie Monarches, Kings, Free Princes, and States of Christendome*, published in 1609, constitutes a frantic and extended effort to predict the exact date when the Antichrist will reign: '*Babylon* ... doth clearely and vndenyably declare that *Rome* is, or shalbe the Seat of that Antichrist,' he pronounces.[25] Half-mocking but inscrutable, Marston approaches royal obsessions with levity in *The Dutch Courtesan*, which casts a sly glance at the fears which fuelled a millenarian's nightmare.

IV THEATRICAL PERFORMANCES

In assessing Marston's political contexts, the question of his immediate social and theatrical provenance inevitably arises. *The*

Dutch Courtesan derives much of its valency from the state of London in 1604, a city afflicted by disease, a continuing war with Spain, the treason trials and executions at Winchester associated with the conspiracies of Raleigh and others, and a decline in trade.[26] More generally, however, as I shall suggest, it can be seen as a response to and a shaping force behind the dramatic form known as the 'disguised ruler play'.

Plays involving disguised rulers proliferated in the early Jacobean period, and concerned the actions of a monarch who deploys his statecraft in hiding, banishing corruption and reforming abuses, only to reveal himself in the closing stages. A determining element in their popularity is an investment in political questions, and many work in such a way as to suggest parallels with James's own interests and preoccupations. Shakespeare's *Measure for Measure* (1604) builds in references to the king's elevation of principles of temperance and justice, his predilection for disguise, his dislike of parading himself in public, and his uncompromising views on calumny and slanders.[27] Although uneven in its effects, Middleton's *The Phoenix* (1603–4), a play which is comparably positive in its representation of the monarch, constitutes an essay in didacticism, and a lesson in royal duties and responsibilities.[28] Marston himself is somewhat at odds with strategies of laudatory affirmation and instructive example. A satiric objectivity and critical scrutiny are the hallmarks of his dramatic perspective. The inept Gonzago in *The Fawn* (1604) may be a version of James, the 'wisest fool in Christendom', while *The Malcontent* (1604) blends barbed comment on the flattering practices of favourites with disparaging remarks about Scottish barnacles, boots and gallants, concerns of immediate relevance to the early Jacobean court.[29] In this respect, Marston participates in a wider cultural matrix, a mood of political dissent which stamped a number of contemporary plays with subversive meanings. Dramatists linked to the Children of the Queen's Revels seem to have been particularly susceptible. The 1605 collaboration, *Eastward Ho*, led to Chapman and Jonson being imprisoned for mocking lines supposedly composed by Marston against James's Scottish retinue, and similarly unpalatable material in Day's *The Isle of Gulls* (1606) resulted in 'sundry' being 'committed to Bridewell'.[30] Wherever one looks in the private performance spaces of early Jacobean London, there are shared assumptions and repeated complaints, linked through personal connections and common patronage networks.

In such a climate of hostile opinion, *The Dutch Courtesan* occupied a central position. That the play could be enlisted to mount a political critique is suggested in the number of disguise plays which bear the imprint of its influence. *The London Prodigal* (1604) shows Luce dressing as 'Tanikin', a *'Dutch Frow'* to plead for her husband's virtue, and it is joined by Dekker's *The Honest Whore, Part II* (1604–5) in which Hippolito's enslavement to lust invites comparison with Malheureux's desire for a prostitute.[31] The process of imitative adaptation is most sharply illustrated, however, by two slightly later productions. Indebted to *The Dutch Courtesan* in several areas (Franceschina's name, the pursuit of a fish, and the doubling of the plot), Beaumont and Fletcher's *The Woman Hater* (1606) lampoons a host of Jacobean practices, including reckless expenditure and whimsical promotion procedures, and its vision is encapsulated in the Duke of Milan's claim that he gives 'to be thought liberall' rather than 'to reward any particular desert'.[32] Cut from the same cloth is Sharpham's *The Fleire* (1605–6): closely modelled on Marston's play, it anatomises (in the wake of the Gunpowder Plot) a kingdom spiralling towards moral bankruptcy, rocked by the sale of knighthoods, the attentions of favourites, the effects of tobacco and the cheating ways of Scottish upstarts.[33] When we consider the interests that dictated dramatic production, moreover, further parallels emerge. It is clear that Beaumont and Marston (and possibly Sharpham) knew each other from the Inns of Court (their fathers were prominent lawyers), and both had access to or a part in the composition of the 'Ashby Entertainment', the 1607 masque presented at the Leicestershire seat of the Hastings family.[34] Cultivating the patronage of the Hastings family, indeed, may have been one of the means whereby Beaumont, Fletcher and Marston were able to pursue and develop a mutually held political agenda.

The Dutch Courtesan dovetails with these theatrical traditions in a number of ways. True to his name, Cocledemoy zig-zags his way through the drama, flattering and correcting, putting on the roles of French pedlar and Scottish barber, operating forcibly as an example of the confusion of categories and conjunction of opposites that Marston explores. For much of the play, Cocledemoy is an English gallant impersonating a foreigner, which recalls the position of the new monarch acclimatising himself to an unfamiliar London culture. In addition, James may well have applauded the actions of Cocledemoy, who brings members of the Family of Love to account through confession and penance. Where Marston is particularly distinctive, however, is in his simultaneous reinforcement of and opposition to a contemporary theatrical convention. For Cocledemoy is no prince in disguise, but a roguish figure who restores only a parodic form of normality. *The Dutch Courtesan* is singularly lacking in forces of constituted authority, and part of the play's destabilising impact must surely reside with its promotion into leading positions of Cocledemoy, a Proteus, and Freevill, a libertine.

In this connection, the circumstances of the play's first performances are an important element in interpreting the covert nature of its political inflections. It has recently been argued that *The Dutch Courtesan* was staged in 1606 as part of the entertainments accompanying the visit to England of James' brother-in-law, Christian IV of Denmark.[35] Despite the place accorded to the play during these celebrations, its success with audiences is less easy to determine.[36] In 1606, Anthony Nixon stated in *The blacke yeare* that 'other mens works...are sacrificed for bringing in *The Dutch Courtezan* to corrupt English conditions, and sent away *Westward* for carping both at Court, Cittie and countrie'.[37] There are several ways of contextualising Nixon's enigmatic remark. Following the play's performance, censorship may have been visited upon a number of contemporary dramatists but not Marston himself. Alternatively, *The Dutch Courtesan* may have provoked such offence that the playwright chose to withdraw from the theatre altogether at this time, and not in 1608, as has sometimes been thought.[38] In alluding to *Westward Ho* (1604), the observation also suggests either that Marston fled when an uproar over his drama had subsided, or that he was sent to (but did not spend time at) the Fleet prison in Newgate, located to the west of the city walls. In any event, Nixon's pamphlet affords a rare contemporary insight into the disputes and controversies that work such as *The Dutch Courtesan* may have attracted.

V CONCLUSIONS

To the readings I am proposing here there can be many objections. A saintly figure Beatrice might be, but she is also branded a prostitute by her enemies (II.ii.91). The Dutch nationality of Franceschina poses difficulties as the Netherlands had joined Protestant military forces against Spanish insurgences.[39] It is not so much mimetic correspondences which attract me, however; I am more

interested in discursive relations and want to draw attention to
Leonard Tennenhouse's recommendations in a discussion of *Measure for Measure*: 'To avoid the problem of reading these plays as if
they were historical allegories, let us assume that certain modes and
genres gain preference at a given moment because they elaborate
some collective fantasy about the origins and limits of power.'[40] *The
Dutch Courtesan* can be read along similar lines: by attending to its
multiple contexts, we can begin to understand its shared systems of
signification, its common discourses and its interlocking codes. The
prostitute functions as an instance of what has been termed 'the
coercive logic of narrative, the conflation of identity and destiny'
and, in 1603, the narrative of England was being rewritten and
speculation was rife about the future courses the nation would
take.[41] Troping Franceschina dispels the destabilising and disinteg-
rative threat she poses to masculine mastery. Broken into pieces,
she becomes an assembly of bits to be put back together by a
controlling designer. The somatic fragments of Franceschina affirm
male wholeness and completeness.[42] In the plague-ridden years of
the earlier part of James's reign, these fantasies carried a powerful
political charge for a monarch who prided himself on his virtue and
who was anxious to restore health to the body politic, to secure the
patrilineal descent of his family, to unite his disparate kingdoms,
and to legitimate the foundations of his rule. Foucault has described
the brothel as a heterotopia, a counter-site 'in which the real sites,
all the other real sites that can be found within the culture, are
simultaneously represented, contested, and inverted'.[43] *The Dutch
Courtesan* produces something like this effect, appealing to and
criticising the King, flirting with onomastic issues of identity and
name, and representing two women, a virgin and a whore,
between whom Freevill must make his choice. A comparison suggests itself with James: only when he had defined himself in relation to his biological mother, Mary, and his political mother,
Elizabeth, could his new powers be assured.

   In the final scene of *The Dutch Courtesan* Franceschina is judged
and imprisoned. The temptation, in Freevill's words, to 'hazard
landing at this fatal shore' (V.iii.28) is resisted; the song of the
siren falls on deaf ears. Explaining how he managed to entrap
her, Freevill states: 'knowing that the hook was deeply fast,/I gave
her line at will till, with her own vain strivings,/See here she's tired'
(V.iii.46–8). The marine, watery creature is finally troped into a fish,
reified out of human existence, expunged from the text. And,

following the logic of the narrative, she now disappears anonymously and is not even called by her name.

NOTES

1. John Marston, *The Dutch Courtesan*, ed. M. L. Wine (Lincoln: University of Nebraska Press, 1965). All further references appear in the text.
2. While I do not address the contemporary material conditions under which prostitutes worked in the early modern period, the following have proved useful: Ian W. Archer, *The Pursuit of Stability: Social Relations in Elizabethan London* (Cambridge: Cambridge University Press, 1991), pp. 211–15, 231–4, 249–54; Paul Griffiths, 'The Structure of Prostitution in Elizabethan London', *Continuity and Change*, 8 (1993) 39–63; Ruth Mazo Karras, 'The Regulation of Brothels in Later Medieval England', *Signs: A Journal of Women in Culture and Society*, 14 (1989), 399–433; Wallace Shugg, 'Prostitution in Shakespeare's London', *Shakespeare Studies*, 10 (1977), 291–313; Jyotsna Singh, 'The Interventions of History: Narratives of Sexuality', in Dympna Callaghan, Lorraine Helms and Jyotsna Singh, *The Weyward Sisters: Shakespeare and Feminist Politics* (Oxford: Blackwell, 1994), pp. 7–58.
3. My argument about the psychological effects of naming has been stimulated by Stephen Greenblatt, *Marvelous Possessions: The Wonder of the New World* (Oxford: Clarendon, 1991), p. 82; Simon J. Harrison, *Stealing People's Names: History and Politics in a Sepik River Cosmology* (Cambridge: Cambridge University Press, 1990), pp. 90, 201.
4. For early accounts of these difficulties, see *Secret History of the Court of James I*, 2 vols (Edinburgh: James Ballantyne, 1811), vol. I, pp. 155, 168.
5. Jonathan Goldberg, *James I and the Politics of Literature: Jonson, Shakespeare, Donne, and Their Contemporaries* (Baltimore and London: Johns Hopkins University Press, 1983), p. 231. For more recent attempts to contextualise Marston's play, see Susan Baker, 'Sex and Marriage in *The Dutch Courtesan*', in Dorothea Kehler and Susan Baker (eds.), *In Another Country: Feminist Perspectives on Renaissance Drama* (Metuchen, NJ, and London: Scarecrow Press, 1991), pp. 218–32; Douglas Bruster, *Drama and the Market in the Age of Shakespeare* (Cambridge: Cambridge University Press, 1992), pp. 86–90.
6. *The Political Works of James I*, ed. Charles Howard McIlwain (Cambridge, Mass.: Harvard University Press, 1918), p. 7.
7. William C. Johnson, 'The Family of Love in Stuart literature: a chronology of name-crossed lovers', *Journal of Medieval and Renaissance Studies*, 7 (1977), pp. 95, 101; J. W. Martin, *Religious Radicals in Tudor England* (London and Ronceverte: Hambledon, 1989), pp. 216, 224. See also Chris Marsh, *The Family of Love in English Society, 1550–1630* (Cambridge: Cambridge University Press, 1993), *passim*.
8. *A Counterblaste to Tobacco* (1604), in James Craigie (ed.), *Minor Prose Works of King James VI and I* (Edinburgh: Scottish Text Society, 1982), p. 97.

9. *Daemonologie* (1597), in *Minor Prose*, pp. 30–1. See also *Basilikon Doron*, in *Works*, p. 20. On witches and poisons, and James's own experience of supposedly having been an intended victim of their arts, see Reginald Scot, *The discouerie of witchcraft* (London, 1584; STC 21864) pp. 116–20; David Harris Willson, *King James VI and I* (London: Jonathan Cape, 1963), p. 104.

10. *Basilikon Doron*, in *Works*, p. 50.

11. *A defence of the honorable sentence and execution of the queene of Scots* (London, 1587; STC 17566.3), sig. K4ᵛ.

12. William Kempe, *A dutiful inuectiue, against the moste haynous treasons of Ballard and Babington* (London, 1587; STC 14925), fos. 2ᵛ, 3ᵛ.

13. Leah S. Marcus, *Puzzling Shakespeare: Local Reading and Its Discontents* (Berkeley, Los Angeles and London: University of California Press, 1988), p. 74; James Emerson Phillips, *Images of a Queen: Mary Stuart in Sixteenth-Century Literature* (Berkeley and Los Angeles: University of California Press, 1964), pp. 7, 42, 67, 83.

14. Mary Anne Everett Green (ed.), *Calendar of State Papers, Domestic Series, of the Reign of Elizabeth, 1595–1597* (London: Longmans, Green, Reader, and Dyer, 1869), pp. 86–7, 94. See also David Norbrook, *Poetry and Politics in the English Renaissance* (London, Boston, Melbourne and Henley: Routledge and Kegan Paul, 1984), p. 137.

15. See Goldberg, *James I*, pp. 12, 14; Phillips, *Images*, p. 226.

16. George Geckle, *John Marston's Drama: Themes, Images, Sources* (London and Toronto: Associated University Presses, 1980), p. 175.

17. For a detailed study of this cult, see Elkin Calhoun Wilson, *England's Eliza* (Cambridge, Mass.: Harvard University Press, 1939).

18. Frederic Ives Carpenter, *A Reference Guide to Edmund Spenser* (Chicago, Ill.: University of Chicago Press, 1923), pp. 41–2. See also Goldberg, *James I*, pp. 1–2; Phillips, *Images*, p. 201.

19. See Giacopo Brocado, *The reuelation of S. Jhon reueled* (London, 1582; STC 3810), fos. 117ʳ, 124ᵛ, 142ᵛ; Heinrich Bullinger, *A hundred sermons vpo[n] the Apocalips* (London, 1561; STC 4061), pp. 349, 507; John Foxe, *Actes and monuments of matters most speciall in the church*, 2 vols (London, 1583; STC 11225), vol. I, pp. 397, 482; George Gifford, *Sermons vpon the whole booke of the Reuelation* (London, 1596; STC 11866), pp. 218, 246–7, 324, 326–7; T. L., *Babylon is fallen* (London, 1597; STC 15111), sigs. A3ʳ, A7ʳ, A8ʳ.

20. See Lyndal Roper, *The Holy Household: Women and Morals in Reformation Augsburg* (Oxford: Clarendon, 1989), pp. 108, 110.

21. Carol Z. Wiener, 'The Beleaguered Isle: A Study of Elizabethan and Early Jacobean Anti-Catholicism', *Past and Present*, 51 (May 1971), pp. 57–8.

22. *The Geneva Bible: A Facsimile of the 1560 Edition*, ed. Lloyd E. Berry (Madison, Milwaukee, and London: University of Wisconsin Press, 1969), fos. 117ʳ⁻ᵛ, 118ʳ.

23. See Norbrook, *Poetry*, p. 135; Roy C. Strong, *Portraits of Queen Elizabeth I* (Oxford: Clarendon, 1963), p. 138; Frances A. Yates, *Astraea: The Imperial Theme in the Sixteenth Century* (London, Boston, Melbourne and Henley: Ark Paperbacks, 1985), pp. 47, 80, 114. My argument

here has greatly benefited from Julia Gasper's excellent *The Dragon and the Dove: The Plays of Thomas Dekker* (Oxford: Clarendon, 1990), pp. 62–108.

24. Kempe, *A dutiful inuectiue*, fo. 3ʳ; Edmund Spenser, *The Faerie Queene*, ed. A. C. Hamilton (London and New York: Longman, 1977), Book 1, canto 2, verse 34.

25. James I, *King of England, Ane fruitfull meditatioun* (Edinburgh, 1588; STC 14376) sigs. Biᵛ, Biiiʳ; *The Poems of James VI of Scotland*, ed. James Craigie, 2 vols (Edinburgh: Blackwood, 1955 and 1958), vol. I, pp. 252, 254; *A Premonition to all Most Mightie Monarches, Kings, Free Princes, and States of Christendome*, in *Works*, p. 130.

26. Marcus, *Puzzling*, p. 162.

27. William Shakespeare, *Measure for Measure*, ed. N. W. Bawcutt (Oxford and New York: Oxford University Press, 1991), pp. 4–5; *Measure for Measure*, ed. J. W. Lever (London: Methuen, 1971), pp. xlviii–l.

28. Thomas Middleton, *The Phoenix*, ed. John Bradbury Brooks (New York and London: Garland, 1980), pp. 18–22.

29. John Marston, *The Fawn*, ed. David A. Blostein (Manchester: Manchester University Press, 1978), p. 32; *The Malcontent*, ed. George K. Hunter (Manchester: Manchester University Press, 1975), III.i.46–7, 76–8; V.v.24–5. See also Frank Whigham, 'Flattering Courtly Desire', in David L. Smith, Richard Strier and David Bevington (eds.), *The Theatrical City: Culture, Theatre and Politics in London, 1576–1649* (Cambridge: Cambridge University Press, 1995), pp. 137–56.

30. Philip J. Finkepearl, *John Marston of the Middle Temple: An Elizabethan Dramatist in His Social Setting* (Cambridge, Mass.: Harvard University Press, 1969), p. 222; Albert H. Tricomi, 'The Provenance of John Marston's Letter to Lord Kimbolton', *Papers of the Bibliographical Society of America*, 72 (1978), p. 213.

31. *The London Prodigal* (1604), in C. F. Tucker Brooke (ed.), *The Shakespeare Apocrypha* (Oxford: Clarendon, 1918), IV.iii. p. 132; Cyrus Hoy, *Introductions, Notes, and Commentaries to texts in 'The Dramatic Works of Thomas Dekker'*, 4 vols (Cambridge: Cambridge University Press, 1980), vol. II, p. 73.

32. Francis Beaumont and John Fletcher, *The Dramatic Works*, ed. Fredson Bowers, 8 vols (Cambridge: Cambridge University Press, 1966–92), vol. I, I.i.66, 68; Philip J. Finkepearl, *Court and Country Politics in the Plays of Beaumont and Fletcher* (Princeton: Princeton University Press, 1980), pp. 71, 73.

33. Edward Sharpham, *The Works*, ed. Christopher Gordon Petter (New York and London: Garland, 1986), pp. 183, 185–90, 203–4, 206, 217, 220, I.ii.117–18, I.iii.70–4; II.i.148–51; III.i.61–64, 110–12, 160–1.

34. Finkepearl, *Court and Country*, pp. 36–7, 69; James Knowles, 'Marston, Skipwith and *The Entertainment at Ashby*', *English Manuscript Studies*, 3 (1992), pp. 152–3.

35. J. W. Binns and H. Neville Davies, 'Christian IV and *The Dutch Courtesan*', *Theatre Notebook*, 44 (1990), 118–23.

36. The play went on to be staged twice at court in 1613, by which time a more accommodating political climate may have obtained. See Jill

Levenson, 'Comedy', in A. R. Braunmuller and Michael Hattaway (eds.), *The Cambridge Companion to English Renaissance Drama* (Cambridge: Cambridge University Press, 1990), p. 290.

37.   Anthony Nixon, *The blacke yeare* (London, 1606; STC 18582), sig. B2ʳ.

38.   Richard Dutton, *Mastering the Revels: The Regulation and Censorship of English Renaissance Drama* (Basingstoke and London: Macmillan, 1991), pp. 188, 268.

39.   Attitudes towards the Dutch were mixed, however. Anti-Dutch riots had exploded in the 1590s, and James saw the Dutch condescendingly as his clients as they owed him repayments: see Mark Thornton Burnett, 'Apprentice Literature and the "Crisis" of the 1590s', *The Yearbook of English Studies*, 21 (1991), 27–38; Willson, *King James*, p. 275.

40.   Leonard Tennenhouse, 'Representing Power: *Measure for Measure* in its Time', in Stephen Greenblatt (ed.), *The Power of Forms in the English Renaissance* (Norman, Okl.: Pilgrim Books, 1982), p. 140.

41.   Amanda S. Anderson, 'D. G. Rossetti's "Jenny": Agency, Intersubjectivity, and the Prostitute', *Genders*, 4 (Spring 1989), p. 103.

42.   My argument in this paragraph is indebted to Charles Bernheimer, *Figures of Ill Repute: Representing Prostitution in Nineteenth-Century France* (Cambridge, Mass.: Harvard University Press, 1989), pp. 2, 39, 52, 102, 252; Alain Corbin, 'Commercial Sexuality in Nineteenth-Century France: A System of Images and Regulations', in Catherine Gallagher and Thomas Laqueur (eds.), *The Making of the Modern Body: Sexuality and Society in the Nineteenth Century* (Berkeley and Los Angeles: University of California Press, 1987), p. 212; Alain Corbin, *Women for Hire: Prostitution and Sexuality in France after 1850*, trans. Alan Sheridan (Cambridge, Mass. and London: Harvard University Press, 1990), pp. 6, 23, 24; Jonathan Dollimore, 'Transgression and Surveillance in *Measure for Measure*', in Jonathan Dollimore and Alan Sinfield (eds.), *Political Shakespeare: New Essays in Cultural Materialism* (Manchester: Manchester University Press, 1985), pp. 80, 84; Helena Michie, *The Flesh Made Word: Female Figures and Women's Bodies* (New York and Oxford: Oxford University Press, 1987), pp. 59, 74; Angelika Rauch, 'The *Trauerspiel* of the Prostituted Body, or Woman as Allegory of Modernity', *Cultural Critique*, 10 (Fall 1988), pp. 82, 86–7.

43.   Michel Foucault, 'Of Other Spaces', *Diacritics*, 16 (1986), p. 24.

IV
Voicing the Past

9

Spectres and Sisters: Mary Sidney and the 'Perennial Puzzle' of Renaissance Women's Writing

Suzanne Trill

A spectre haunts contemporary feminist criticism of Renaissance women's writing: Virginia Woolf's mythic Judith Shakespeare. For a fictional character, she retains an uncanny influence in shaping our fantasies of the 'unknowable' Elizabethan woman. Seeking to solve the 'perennial puzzle' of 'why no woman wrote a word of that extraordinary literature when every other man, it seemed, was capable of song or sonnet', Woolf fashions the life of Shakespeare's sister through the powers of her imagination.[1] The story epitomises the effects of the social construction of gender upon literary creativity; in contrast to her famous brother, the 'extraordinarily gifted' Judith is uneducated, confined to the house, subject to her parents' vigilance and, against her desires, 'betrothed to the son of a neighbouring woolstapler'. But the force of her suppressed talent drives her to leave home and seek her fortune in London. Like her brother, Judith has a gift 'for the tune of words' and 'a taste for the theatre'; rather than finding success and admiration, however, she is laughed at and despised, becomes pregnant and 'killed herself one winter's night and lies buried at some crossroads where the omnibuses now stop outside the Elephant and Castle'. This tragic tale has served as a paradigm for interpreting women's, particularly Renaissance women's, relationship to (or, more precisely, absence from) literary history. Although the suicidal culmination of Woolf's tale is not borne out by the actual lives of women writers during this period, the constraints she outlines (education, restriction to the home, parental authority, 'arranged' marriages) have been established as 'facts' rather than 'fiction' by succeeding

191

generations of (primarily) feminist scholars.[2] Recently, however, the assumptions which underpin this portrayal have come under scrutiny and new questions are being raised about the methods by which we decipher the pieces of the puzzle that have been uncovered. As we discover further details about women's history and more writing by women is edited, anthologised and read, the question of how we interpret and categorise these texts becomes crucial: an 'alternative' canon is rapidly being established, but as one critic put it recently, 'are we as feminist critics fully conscious of the assumptions on which we have formed our tradition?'[3] Or, to put it another way, which women writers do we allow to 'put on the body which [Judith Shakespeare] has so often laid down' and on what criteria do we identify our 'sisters'? In this essay, I shall be addressing these questions in relation to an actual sister of a famous literary brother whose (angelic) spirit has cast a persistent shadow over critical accounts of her life and writing; that is, Mary Herbert, Countess of Pembroke, more widely known as 'Sidney's sister'.[4]

In the process of investigating the fluctuating evaluations of Renaissance women's writing over the last three hundred years, Margaret J. Ezell has recently discussed the latent assumptions permeating the myth of Judith Shakespeare. She suggests that 'anachronistic and deforming presumptions about literary practice, production, and genre' in combination with a linear, evolutionary model of 'narrative history', significantly distort our perception of Renaissance women's writing. Following in Woolf's footsteps, feminist critics have sought the individual, professional woman writer of published 'literary' (fictional) texts. All of these criteria suggest that the 'alternative' canon in fact unwittingly mirrors the construction of the pre-existing (male) canon. In contradistinction, Ezell perhaps rather over-enthusiastically proclaims that 'if we accept manuscript and coterie authorship and non-traditional literary forms as part of the female literary tradition, the canon of women's literature in the Renaissance and seventeenth century will no longer be silenced, but will speak with many voices'.[5] While her prophetic conclusion is, as it stands, more polemical than proven, the significance of Ezell's argument resides in the challenge this assertion presents to the image of early women writers as anomalies who, like the figure of Judith Shakespeare bequeathed to us by Woolf, were 'isolated, embittered, and embattled' individuals. For, whilst succeeding feminist critics have established that the constraints Woolf outlined operated as powerful injunctions against female literary creativity during this period, the material uncovered has also highlighted absences in Woolf's argument. Woolf's representation is, after all, partly determined by its own moment of production; despite her 'ignorance' about the lives of Elizabethan women, she has no difficulty in asserting their psychological make-up if they were to 'attempt the pen'. According to Woolf, a six-teenth-century female poet and playwright would have suffered 'a nervous stress and dilemma which might well have killed her. Had she survived, what she had written would have been twisted and deformed, issuing from a strained and morbid imagination' (p. 49). This representation is itself heavily influenced by late nineteenth-century preoccupations: Judith Shakespeare is surely suffering in a way comparable to women subjected to the rest cure in the nine-teenth century; denied an outlet for her creative energies, confined to the home and prohibited from reading, she scribbled on pages in the hay loft, eventually destroying both them and herself.

It is this image of the tormented women writer isolated from society and at war with herself which situates Judith Shakespeare as 'our sister'; for she symbolises 'Woman's' exclusion from social and literary history. Whilst the legitimacy conferred upon women's writing by recourse to genealogical metaphors of motherhood (in response to Woolf's assertion that 'we think back through our mothers if we are women') has received much critical attention, the implications of the term 'sister' requires further investigation.[6] Like our mothers, our sisters are hard to define; although literal mothers or sisters can be biologically determined, metaphorical female relations (like friends) are chosen rather than given. Whilst in a general sense simply being female might define one as a sister, being a member of the sisterhood has a very specific connection with a shared 'devotion' to 'the feminist cause'. To be a sister in this sense is to be primarily defined in relation to other women and particularly this definition often invokes a notion of the 'continuity' of female experience. However, historically the brother/sister rela-tionship has had a significant legal and economic influence upon women's lives, especially perhaps in the sixteenth and seventeenth centuries.[7] To be a sister in this sense is to be defined by reference to one's male relatives and serves to highlight difference rather than continuity. While Judith Shakespeare is only a fictional sister, the significance of her position lies in the fact that she symbolises the conjunction of these two definitions: she is both the sister of a famous brother (exemplifying difference) and 'our' sister (exemplifying continuity). It is, perhaps, for this reason that Woolf chose to transform Judith Shakespeare from her 'real' position as Shakespeare's daughter to her fictional status as Shakespeare's sister; for, in addition to the appealing alliteration of the latter title, it is only by identifying her as Shakespeare's sister that Woolf can highlight the specifically gendered differences between them. In so far as their respective identifications are based upon their more famous literary brothers there is an obvious parallel between the fictional Judith Shakespeare and the 'factual' Mary Sidney. But beyond this connection, how far does the model of a sixteenth-century women writer conjured up by Woolf's tale correspond to Mary Sidney's experience?

Although it is true to say that there were distinctly gendered differences in Philip and Mary Sidney's upbringing, in accordance with her social position Mary Sidney was still very well educated. From her translations we know that she could read and write French and Italian, and she would also have been taught Latin and possibly Greek.[8] Her *Psalmes* and her translations of Petrarch, combined with her translation of Philippe de Mornay's *The Discourse of Life and Death*, demonstrate that she was also conversant with a variety of poetic forms and rhetorical skills.[9] Although she spent much of her time at Wilton, Mary Sidney did travel; she spent some time at Court as one of Elizabeth I's ladies in waiting and, in later life, travelled to the continent. Like most other women of her class, Mary Sidney's marriage was an arranged one, but it seems to have been satisfactory. Her own family background, which aligned her with both the Sidneys and the Dudleys, in addition to her marriage to Henry Herbert, 2nd Earl of Pembroke mean that she can hardly be described as socially ostracised. Rather than writing in isolation, she was at the centre of a literary coterie and was associated with Spenser, Daniel, Abraham Fraunce and Nicholas Breton amongst others. Although not the most reliable of sources, Aubrey's comment that 'in her time Wilton House was like a colledge, there were so many learned and ingenious persons' is supported by other writers.[10] The evidence of a literary coterie makes it clear that Mary Sidney did not have to hide her writing by sneaking out to write in the hay loft, nor did she destroy it: the published editions of both *The Discourse of Life and Death* and *Antonious* are stated to have been written at Wilton. In addition to her own published works, she edited those of her brother; she also circulated in manuscript her translations of Petrarch and the

Psalmes, and wrote three 'original' poems, 'The Doleful Lay of Clorinda', 'To the Angell Spirit' and 'To the Thrice Sacred Queen'. Happily, 'Sidney's sister' did not meet a tragic death, but (rather mundanely and commonly for the period) died of smallpox in 1621.

If, then, Sidney does not conform to the model established by Woolf in her description of Shakespeare's sister, what kind of image of her has been established? Recent critical accounts have variously identified her as the swashbuckling countess fighting off pirates and maintaining the peace in Pembrokeshire, to the mournful Magdalene bereft at the death of her dearly beloved brother. Assessments of her writing veer from apologising for her hesitancy at the prospect of entering into print and for the genres in which she wrote, to identifying her as a woman adept at self-presentation who used the pen instead of the pike in advising the Queen politically in the psalms.[11] However, the most consistent lens through which Mary Sidney's life and writing have been viewed is that of her relation to her brother. While her identification as 'Sidney's sister' does not have the same straightforwardly negative and tragic consequences as the tale of 'Shakespeare's sister', it is certainly double-edged. On the one hand, her 'social capital' is founded upon her family connections and this gave her access to literary circles and a legitimate entry into the world of print; but, on the other hand, this connection has distorted our perception of her and her writing.[12]

While there has been a shift away from Frances Berkely Young's assertion that 'any criticism of the Countess of Pembroke must inevitably start with her connection with the *Arcadia*', the implicit association with her brother is still paramount.[13] Even Margaret P. Hannay's recent and impressively researched literary biography of the countess is entitled *Philip's Phoenix: Mary Sidney, Countess of Pembroke*. This title is justified by Hannay on the grounds that Sidney was represented in this way by her contemporaries; similarly, Gary F. Waller defines her as 'Philip and Robert Sidney's sister', stating that 'I describe her in that way deliberately, since it was a dual appellation and subjection she accepted unquestioningly'.[14] Despite his later apologia for the 'gender blindness' of his criticism, Waller consistently sees everything Mary Sidney did as refracted through the lens of her brother's life: perhaps unwittingly, he echoes M.M. Bulloch's assertion that Philip and Mary Sidney's 'minds seem to have been cast in the same mould' when he suggests that 'the Countess reflects the same intellectual contraries as her brother'.[15] Elsewhere, Waller's excessive insistence upon Mary Sidney's idealised love for her brother is analogous to Aubrey's scurrilous comments in his *Brief Lives*. Aubrey reports that 'there was such great love between [Philip] and his fair sister that I have heard old gentlemen... say that they lay together, and it was thought that the first Philip, Earl of Pembroke was begot by him, but he inherited not the wit of either brother or sister'. The conse- quence of the Sidney's relationship, according to Waller, is mani- fested in the realm of the mind rather than the body; Mary Sidney's translation of 'The triumph of Death', he suggests, 'reflects, one might speculate, her own deeply idealised love for her brother, the impossibility of its consummation and the realisation that his poetic inspiration for her is the only real and lasting fruit of her love'.[16] At least Aubrey's claims have the advantage of being easy to dismiss: Waller's assertions are far more insidious and have been reiterated unthinkingly in more recent editions and critical accounts of Mary Sidney's writing.

In the introduction to his recent student edition of the Sidney psalms, for example, R. E. Pritchard confidently claims that although Mary Sidney was happily married 'the real love of her life seems to have been Philip'.[17] But perhaps even more discon- certing is the way in which Pritchard appropriates some of the terms of feminist criticism in order to suggest that Mary Sidney's 'uneas[iness] at seeking to "match the matchless unicorn" her brother' is rooted in her 'femininity'. Echoing the feminist empha- sis on the constraints upon women's expression during this period, Pritchard asserts that Sidney's 'parade of poetic skill might be partly an indication of female capability, partly also an expression – particularly through any forced phrasing – of this act of presump- tion' (pp. 17–18). Pritchard's crude use of what might be termed the 'feminist critique template' and spurious linguistic analysis leads him to assert a correlation between Mary Sidney's 'femininity' and her expression. Yet his comments are not significantly less spurious than the means by which some feminist critics locate Mary Sidney's voice in her psalms; Beth Wynne Fisken, for exam- ple, suggests that one phrase from Sidney's psalms represents 'a poetic equivalent for her own small, personal voice, "my self, my seely self in me"'.[18] Furthermore, Pritchard's dubious conclusion that 'like some of Shakespeare's heroines' Mary Sidney, 'as mouth- piece for the Psalmist's (male) voices', could 'speak most for herself when speaking as another' (p. 18) is echoed by Tina Krontiris's suggestion that Mary Sidney speaks from 'behind the curtain' of the male-authored texts she translates: for 'to translate literally is to seek protection in the idea of conveying the author's meaning exactly'.[19] These critical comments highlight a crucial issue for feminist criticism; namely, what kind of female voice are we seeking? While the critical emphasis upon her brother has certainly distorted our perception of Mary Sidney, I would argue that our evaluation of the genres in which she wrote further obscures our recognition of the importance of her writing and perhaps precludes her from being situated as 'our sister'.

In her attempt to trace a 'female literary tradition', Woolf's analysis of sixteenth- and seventeenth-century women's writing is almost entirely negative: Anne Finch's poetry demonstrates her disturbed state of mind (she fails to achieve the transcendence necessary for true genius); Margaret Cavendish's writing, like Woolf's own notes in the British Library, 'poured itself out, higgledy-piggledy, in torrents of rhyme and prose, poetry and philosophy' (she fails to adhere to generic distinctions); and Dorothy Osbourne, though she had 'a gift . . . for the framing of a sentence,' fails because she 'only' wrote letters (pp. 56–60). But while Woolf evaluated these writers negatively, contemporary feminist criticism has reincorporated them into literary history precisely because of the consciousness of their sex that their writing displays. This prioritising of oppositional writing underlines contemporary developments in the feminist movement and feminist literary studies, which locate the value of texts by women in their expression of a specifically female experience: the most important of which, at least for identifying 'our sisters', is that of resistance to patriarchal demands. Early women writers, especially those who wrote or translated religious texts, are represented as simply having internalised dominant male prescriptions and are placed on the periphery of 'the female literary tradition'.[20] In *Silent But for the Word*, for example, Tudor women writers are represented as being 'on the margins of discourse' and as lacking 'an authentic female voice'.[21] More recent volumes reveal a hierarchy of oppositional writing which prioritises texts by women which actively resist patriarchal demands and place women writers and translators of religious texts at the bottom of this hierarchy: in *The Currency of Eros*, Ann Rosalind Jones argues that 'the most submissive response' by a woman writer in negotiating her entry into the world of print 'was to deal only with the domestic and religious concerns considered appropriate for women and to write without any ambition for publication'; in *Writing Women in Jacobean England*, Barbara K. Lewalski, although 'somewhat surprised' by 'the strong resistance...to the patriarchal construct of women as chaste, silent, and obedient' expressed in texts by women writers (including Anne Clifford, Elizabeth Cary, Æmilia Lanyer and Lady Mary Wroth), excludes less overtly oppositional writers, such as the writers of 'Mother's Advice Books'; even more explicitly, Tina Krontiris declares that her book, *Oppositional Voices*, 'is a study of female assertiveness in the literary field'.[22] My objection to these positions is founded not so much upon a desire to claim that religious translation was a subversive act, but rather that in seeking 'oppositional' writing, we distort the picture of women's literary history and run the risk of marginalising significant literary texts by women. For example, as a result of this emphasis upon resistance and, indeed, secular writing, there is a tendency even from feminist critics to lament the fact that Mary Sidney wrote but, paraphrasing Joanna Russ, 'it was only a translation': Betty S. Travitsky regretfully excludes Mary Sidney's *Psalmes* from *The Paradise of Women* because translations are 'essentially derivative' and Diane Bornstein bemoans the fact that Sidney did not produce her 'own meditations'.[23] These comments suggest that it is only by opposition that women can define themselves, but they simultaneously disclose a latent assumption informing feminist criticism; that is, that we are seeking identifiably 'original' and 'individual' female expressions. But what about women writers who do not fit this mould? Is it possible, for example, to re-evaluate Mary Sidney's writing, particularly her *Psalmes*? It seems to me that if one examines the importance of translation in the sixteenth century and explores the broader cultural significance of the psalms, it is possible to reassess the status of Mary Sidney's translations; although this still might not situate her as 'our sister,' it could help to extricate her from the shadow of her brother.

   Although Mary Sidney's most significant (literary) translations are her *Psalmes*, on the whole feminist critics have shied away from analysing them. The critical attention which her *Psalmes* have received primarily positions her as an adjunct to her brother, even though he only translated forty-three of them and she translated a hundred and seven.[24] There are, I think, three main reasons for this: first, the fact that they are religious translations; second, that they are perceived as yet another act of homage to her brother; and third, that they pose peculiar difficulties for identifying a specifically 'female' voice. By re-examining what is at stake in these underlying assumptions, it is possible to reassess Mary Sidney's position in the 'alternative' canon. The first assumption that requires reassessment is the notion that translation is a 'marginal' and 'feminine' activity. Translation was central to the Renaissance and it formed a significant part of men's education.[25] It seems to me, therefore, to be historically inaccurate to suggest that translation was inherently marginal or feminine: it may be true to say that some translations by women were marginalised, but, if so, I would argue that it is *because* they were women, not because the genre in which they wrote was itself intrinsically marginal. Particularly given the cultural and political importance of the psalms during the sixteenth century and the high poetic style of Mary Sidney's translations, their 'marginal' status needs to be reassessed. The psalms were regarded as a crucial discourse for the construction of Christian subjectivity during this period and, as I have argued elsewhere, there is a significant amount of evidence to suggest that there was a peculiar association specifically between women and the psalms during this period.[26] Consequently, it is equally possible to situate Mary Sidney's *Psalmes* within a 'female literary tradition', if one wished to do so. Simply to do this would be problematic, but it does indicate that Mary Sidney's interest in them should not be read merely as another act of homage to her brother.

The focus upon her association with her brother, combined with the critical emphasis upon women's exclusion from literary history, has warped our understanding of Renaissance evaluations of Mary Sidney's *Psalmes*, Elaine V. Beilin, for example, finds only one example of a contemporary male author praising Mary Sidney for her writing.[27] However, a number of other writers also praise Sidney's literary skills; significantly, they all praise her *Psalmes*. While this could be read as a means by which women writers were kept within their 'proper boundaries', as the often quoted comment from Edward Denny castigating Wroth's *Urania* suggests, writers such as John Donne and Samuel Daniel praise her poetry and highlight the importance of her *Psalmes* for the development of the English language.[28] Daniel dedicates both *Delia* and *Cleopatra* to Mary Sidney and in both dedications he makes reference to her *Psalmes*. The latter example is perhaps the most interesting; for, although Daniel's *Cleopatra* is reputed to have been 'commissioned' by Sidney and forms a pair with her translation of *Antonious*, he does not directly mention her translation of Garnier's play. Instead,

Daniel centres his claim for Sidney's literary fame upon her translation of the *Psalmes*.[29] In Daniel's representation, Mary Sidney's voice supplants those of David and her brother: it is her 'voyce' which is eternalised in her 'Hymnes'. Her name is revered through her translation of the psalms in a way which undermines the notion of the passivity and self-negation of biblical translation. Indeed, Daniel prophetically asserts that it is in the monuments of her *Psalmes* that Mary Sidney 'survivest' and through which she will be found by 'late succeeding ages, fresh in fame'.

Similarly, in her dedication to Mary Sidney prefacing *Salve Deus Rex Judaeorum*, Æmilia Lanyer alludes to Sidney's association with the psalms and, by virtue of that association, proclaims that her praises will be written in 'th' eternal book/Of endless honor, true fame's memory'.[30] Sidney is described as walking in Edenic bowers with Pallas who invites the women present to 'sit and to devise/On holy hymns' which are identified as 'Those rare sweet songs which Israel's King did frame,/Unto the Father of Eternity' (p. 79). Her companions sing the psalms of David 'with this most lovely lady', but in a version that is transformed into the heavens by 'her noble breast's sweet harmony', a phrase which suggests that Lanyer is referring directly to Sidney's own translations. Even more forcibly than Daniel, Lanyer emphasises Mary Sidney's displacement of her brother. Mary Sidney's exemplariness is compared and contrasted to that of her brother: Lanyer names her as 'sister to valiant Sidney' and praises him as a Protestant exemplar 'whose clear light/Gives light to all that tread true paths of Fame' (p. 80). Ultimately, however, in Lanyer's representation, Mary Sidney becomes the one who directs others toward divinity and who, by doing so, actually displaces her brother:

> And this fair earthly goddess which you see,
> Bellona and her virgins do attend;
> In virtuous study of divinity,
> her precious time continually doth spend.

> So that a Sister well she may be deemed,
> To him that lived and died so nobly;
> And far before him is to be esteemed
> For virtue, wisdom, learning, dignity.

(p. 80)

Although Lanyer invokes a comparison with her brother, this comparison is set up in order to establish Mary Sidney's superiority, as she surpasses her brother in the realm of 'virtue, wisdom, learning, dignity'. Lanyer clearly stresses Mary Sidney's role in the translation of the *Psalmes*. Although Philip Sidney's 'clear light' indicates the way to fame, it is his sister who achieves it, as she directs

> ... all by her immortal light
> In this huge sea of sorrows, griefs, and fears;
> With contemplation of God's powerful might,
> She fills the eyes, the hearts, the tongues, the ears
>
> Of after-coming ages, which shall read
> Her love, her zeal, her faith, and piety;
> The fair impression of whose worthy deed,
> Seals her pure soul unto the Diety.

> (pp. 80–1)

These dedications indicate the pivotal significance of the *Psalmes* for Mary Sidney's contemporary reputation: modern criticism, however, tends to devalue those translations in favour of her dedicatory poems. The reason for this is demonstrated in Margaret P. Hannay's assertion that it is in Mary Sidney's dedications that we 'hear' her 'own voice most clearly'.[31] Given the conventions of dedicatory address and the Genevan models on which Sidney bases her dedications, the 'clarity' of 'her voice' is questionable; yet, the majority of critical readings identify this poem as a personal lament for her brother's death. However, while the poem is personal (in that it is written from a sister to a brother), it is not only this: it was, after all, written to accompany a planned presentation copy of the psalms for Elizabeth I and was therefore written for a public audience. One critic argues that the 'indirectness' of Mary Sidney's expression and her use of 'the conventional stances of apology and humility' reflect 'her internalisation of cultural strictures against women speaking, and writing in public modes, which were assumed to be, morally, exclusively masculine domains'.[32] While the fact that Mary Sidney was female certainly accentuates the significance of the pose of humility and may serve to deflect contemporary criticism of her public expression, I am not convinced that she was as constrained by these prescriptions as many of her female contemporaries: the dedications she did write are both highly competent and confident; moreover, she did not preface her published translation of *Antonious* with a dedication of any kind, even though drama represents a potentially more public discourse than that of the *Psalmes*. This 'silence' could be read in many ways, but in neither case does Mary Sidney hide her authorship; both *Antonious* and *The Discourse of Life and Death* announce on their title-pages that they were 'Done into English by the Countess of Pembroke'.

In her dedications prefacing the *Psalmes*, Mary Sidney uses the male-defined conventions of this genre in order to justify her own expression and, consequently, subverts the constraints they represented. As a recipient herself of numerous dedications, she was well acquainted with the conventions of dedications, including the fact that self-deprecation could be read as an act of affirmation; or, as Bacon put it, 'excusations, cessions, modesty itself well governed, are but the arts of ostentation'.[33] If Mary Sidney's femaleness required an apologia, this was precisely because she was being 'ostentatious'. The major complicating factor in Mary Sidney's dedications is the critical stress upon the personal expression in the dedication to her brother; consequently, what she writes to him is assumed to be personal and 'genuine'. Yet, what she writes to her brother follows the conventions of dedicatory address and utilises the theories of Petrarchanism and Neoplatonism. Despite her claim that her poem to her brother is written in 'sad characters indeed of simple love', apparently denying its artistic merit, her style of writing and the content of her poem reveal her awareness of contemporary theories of aesthetic expression. Throughout 'To the Angel Spirit', Mary Sidney oscillates between an idealised representation of her brother, which demands her own self-abnegation, and an assertion of her sorrow, which produces a focus upon her own feelings, making them the centre of attention: by so doing, Mary Sidney places her brother in a position analogous to that of the idealised lady in sonnet sequences, or, indeed, in the conventionally female role of muse.[34] Importantly, the consensus of critical opinion when discussing both of these roles is that the central emphasis is not upon the lady, but upon the male writer. Correspondingly, Mary Sidney's dedication to Philip actually places great emphasis upon her sorrows and struggles. Although she does define herself in relation to him, she is not afraid to use the 'lyric I': 'infinites I owe', 'I call my thoughts', 'Truth I invoke', 'I render here', 'I can no more', and 'I take my leave'. She also uses the possessive pronoun 'my' in relation to her Muse, thoughts, woe, senses, day, life, heart. Like the contemporary poet-lover, her brother's absence places Mary Sidney in the position of one whose life seems empty – her day is 'put out, my life in darknes cast' – and in attempting to make an 'audit' of her woe, she is struck 'dumb'. Rather than representing a woman struck dumb by the prescriptive codes of her day, however, Sidney's poem reveals a keen awareness of self-presentation.

Although this self-presentation increases as the poem develops, the capacity for this development is apparent from the opening of the poem. Her work is addressed to Sidney 'alone', yet it is also dedicated to Elizabeth I and, at another level, the psalms themselves are addressed to God. Mary Sidney calls the *Psalmes* a 'coupled work, by double interest thine', which overtly suggests that she is disowning her role in their production and is giving all the credit to her brother. Yet, although she claims that 'what is mine' in the translations was inspired by her brother, she simultaneously 'dares' to combine her muse with his. Despite her claim that his muse is 'matchless' and that the psalms are now a 'half-maimed piece', she is bold enough to circulate them and present them to the Queen. By addressing her brother as a 'pure sprite' and 'Deare soul', Mary Sidney capitalises on the notion of having inherited his poetic gifts, 'thy secret power impressed'. While her apparent desire for her brother's approval is indicated in her invitation to him to 'behold' this 'finished' work, this statement simultaneously reinforces the fact that he is absent. By this method, Mary Sidney underlines her own completion of this work, and this point is further substantiated by her assertion that the work was 'left by thee undone'. Such remarks, which emphasise her role in the production of the text, undermines her later claim that '[to] thy rare works ... no wit can add'; not only did she do so in the *Psalmes* themselves, but also in her well-documented role as editor and publisher of his other texts. Mary Sidney's emphasis upon her brother's absence and her own completion of the *Psalmes* is also highlighted in her dedication to Elizabeth; first, she points out that they are now presented by only one subject rather than two, and second, she reiterates the fact that she completed the work: 'hee did warpe, I weav'd this webb to end'.[35] When Mary Sidney writes of her brother's works as 'Immortal monuments of thy fair fame' where 'will live thy ever-praised name', it validates her own involvement in this process; like contemporary dedications by male authors to their patrons, the glory belongs to both parties.

The ambiguity of Mary Sidney's position throughout 'To the Angel Spirit' reaches its culmination in the final stanzas: she claims her position on the basis of her relationship to her brother and thus establishes her right to write as a result of her role as her brother's chief mourner; however, this also identifies her as the inheritor of his poetic skills and thereby establishes her own fame:

> To which these dearest offerings of my heart
>   (Dissolved to ink, while pen's impressions move
>   The bleeding veins of never-dying love)
>
> I render here: these wounding lines of smart
>   Sad characters indeed of simple love
>   (Not art nor skill which abler wits doe prove)
>
> Of my full soul receive the meanest part.
>
> Receive these hymns, these obsequies recieve.
>   If any marke of thy sweet sprite appear
>   well are they born, no title else shall bear.
>
> I can no more: Deare soul, I take my leave:
>   Sorrow still strives, would mount thy highest sphere
>   Presuming so just cause might meet thee there.
>
> Oh happy change, could I so take my leave!
>
>   (78–91)

Earlier in the poem, Sidney referred to her 'heart tears' (20), the true tears that signify the concord of heart, word and action; now these 'tears' are 'dissolved to ink' and are the issue of 'the bleeding veins of never-dying love'. It is this love which positions her as Sidney's chief mourner and provides her with the space to express her self and her sorrow; specifically to express her self in 'ink'. The 'simplicity' of her expression denotes its truth, in accordance with the Protestant emphasis upon clarity of expression in relation to the word of God. This prioritises her expression over that of 'abler wits', for they are not able to approach her 'full soule'. Mary Sidney returns to the generic conventions of humility by stating that the *Psalmes* gain their worth from her brother's recognition and acceptance; however, as she has demonstrated earlier, she is fully aware of his absence. Despite the overt self-deprecation of this poem, in order for her *Psalmes* to bear her brother's eloquence, Mary Sidney's translations need have only a 'marke' of his 'sweet sprite'. Moreover, while her final exclamation indicates her desire to join her brother in 'thy highest sphere', rather than simply denoting her desire for self-abnegation these final lines focus upon the speaker and thus the ultimate emphasis of the poem falls upon her feelings and her conflict.

'To the Angel Spirit', in its representation of faith, doubt and reaffirmation of faith, emulates the psalms. The language Mary Sidney uses, both in her dedications and in the *Psalmes* themselves, combines the piety of psalmic discourse with the language of Petrarchanism and courtly love poetry. By merging these different discourses, Mary Sidney's translations demonstrate the significance of the psalms not only for the Protestant practices of personal confession and ritual praise, but also for the construction of a national 'English' identity.[36] Consequently, while a factor influencing Mary Sidney's decision to translate the psalms may well have been a desire to complete her brother's work, the end result (in both her own and other's opinions) was that she produced 'skillful songs' of the 'highest matter' in 'the noblest forme' which enhanced the status of English poetry.[37] Yet Mary Sidney's *Psalmes* remain peripheral to the 'canon' of women's writing. This seems to have little to do with the aesthetic qualities of Sidney's *Psalmes*, but far more to do with the fact that they are not 'oppositional' and, I think, because of the peculiar difficulties which the psalms present in the search for a specifically female voice. Although other critics have attempted to do so, it seems to me that any attempt to locate Mary Sidney's 'own voice' in the psalms is fraught with difficulty.[38] Beth Wynne Fisken suggests that 'our voices' are 'subsumed' by the psalmist's and asserts that Mary Sidney's *Psalmes* 'are centred in the world as we know it; God speaks to us in our own words'.[39] But this assertion effectively precludes any possible recognition of Mary Sidney's 'voice': the 'language' given to God in her *Psalmes* is not 'ours'; it is a variety of discourses produced in the sixteenth century, using images, metaphors and stylistic devices which are not at all what 'we' speak today. The words of these psalms are not 'our' words, they are the language of another time and, to a certain extent, of another person: it is these differences which reveal the 'individuality' of Mary Sidney's *Psalmes*, if not necessarily her 'own' voice. This does not mean, however, that the author's role in the production of the text is entirely negated; as Donne wrote, 'though some have, some may some psalmes translate, we thy Sydnean psalmes shall celebrate'.[40] For all the self-abnegation involved in the translation of biblical texts, an awareness of poetic merit forces a recognition of the earthly 'translators'.

To date, feminist criticism of Mary Sidney's *Psalmes* has either stressed the potential political commentary within them (based on the oppositional model of women's writing) or the confessional aspects of the psalms (based on the notion that religious discourses force women to internalise patriarchal prescriptions). But her contemporaries seem to have appreciated her translations as poetry, as poetry, moreover, which brings glory to God and to the nation. The dedicatory texts by Donne, Daniel and Lanyer identify the Sidneian *Psalmes* as translations which teach others how to sing and highlight their significance for the act of praising God.[41] These writers situate Mary Sidney as one who sings God's praises, and this is a position that her versions of the *Psalmes* accentuate. Although there is not space to explore this point fully here, it is important to note that whether Sidney's *Psalmes* focus upon individual or communal confession or provide political commentary, these issues are addressed through the medium of praise.[42] That Sidney's main purpose in translating the psalms was to praise God in poetic form is perhaps most clearly illustrated by the fact that she transforms the final psalm into a sonnet, which enables her self-consciously to conclude her text by drawing attention to the need to praise God and which consequently positions Mary Sidney herself as God's poet-praiser.

Ironically, while Mary Sidney's 'own' voice is not 'clearly' distinguishable in her *Psalmes*, her poetic skills are nevertheless negatively evaluated in relation to her brother's: critical discussions often unthinkingly reiterate Ringler's comment that Sidney's constant revisions position her as an 'inveterate tinkerer' who has to 'strive' to become a poet; by contrast her brother, like Shakespeare it seems, never blotted a line. Paradoxically, given the terms in which I defined 'sister' at the beginning of this essay, it is precisely in her identification as 'Sidney's sister' that Mary Sidney embodies the continuity of female experience, at least in the sense that she demonstrates the historical prejudices which consistently define women by reference to male relatives.[43] Furthermore, it is her writing which exemplifies difference and which makes her position as 'our sister' ambiguous; for although her writing is marginalised in anthologies of women's writing, it is more widely included in both new editions of established anthologies and anthologies of sixteenth-century verse in general.[44] This dichotomy highlights Mary Sidney's problematic position within the literary 'canon(s)': her example perhaps most acutely manifests the difficulties that Ezell articulates with regard to the construction of a 'female' or 'feminist' canon. However, by exorcising the ghosts of previous interpretative strategies and recasting the critical framework in which her texts are situated, we can perhaps reinterpret the puzzle of the past. If we are willing to re-evaluate the significance of translation in general and the importance of the psalms in Renaissance literary developments specifically, and are prepared to acknowledge the diversity of Renaissance women's literary production, Mary Sidney's *Psalmes* will be recognised as an important example of what a woman could achieve poetically. While the tale of Shakespeare's sister is not wholly applicable to Mary Sidney's experience, Woolf's emphasis upon androgyny and the need to escape the limitations of gendered roles are peculiarly appropriate when reading her writing. Although Mary Sidney cannot be easily assimiliated into a specifically 'female' literary tradition, her *Psalmes* manifestly demonstrate that at least one woman writer was able to produce both songs and sonnets in the sixteenth century.

NOTES

1. Virginia Woolf, *A Room of One's Own* (London: Panther 1985). For the tale of Judith Shakespeare, see pp. 46–7. All further references to this text are to this edition.
2. While Woolf expressed a desire for the scattered information about women's social and literary history to be compiled in one book, there are now numerous books on this subject. For recent bibliographies of Renaissance women's writing and critical studies of their work and social position; see, for example, *Women in the English Renaissance: Selections from English Literary Renaissance*, ed. Kirby Farrell *et al.* (Amherst: University of Massachusetts Press, 1988) and *Women in English Society, 1500–1800*, ed. Mary Prior (London: Methuen, 1985).
3. Margaret J. M. Ezell, 'The Myth of Judith Shakespeare: Creating the Canon of Women's Literature', *New Literary History*, 2 (1990), pp. 579–92 (pp. 579–80).
4. This phrase seems to originate with William Browne's epitaph 'On the Countesse Dowager of Pembroke' (Lansdown MS. 777, f. 43v), cited by

Margaret P. Hannay, *Philip's Phoenix: Mary Sidney, Countess of Pembroke* (Oxford: Oxford University Press, 1990), p. 206.

5. Margaret J. M. Ezell (1990), pp. 580, 585–6 and 592. See also Ezell's more detailed discussion of this topic in *Writing Women's Literary History* (Baltimore and London: Johns Hopkins University Press, 1993).

6. Woolf's use of metaphors of motherhood is, for example, re-examined by Linda R. Williams, 'Happy Families? Feminist Reproduction and Matrilineal Thought', in *New Feminist Discourses: Critical Essays on Theories and Texts*, ed. Isobel Armstrong (London and New York: Routledge, 1992), pp. 48–64. For a recent discussion of the implications of the term sister, see Christine Froula, 'Virginia Woolf as Shakespeare's Sister: Chapters in a Woman Writer's Autobiography', in *Women's Revisions of Shakespeare: On the Responses of Dickinson, Woolf, Rich, H.D., George Eliot, and others*, ed. Marianne Novy (Urbana and Chicago: University of Illinois Press, 1990).

7. For a discussion of the socio-economic effects of the brother/sister relationship in the Renaissance, see Maureen Quilligan, 'Lady Mary Wroth: Female Authority and the Family Romance', in *Unfolded Tales: Essays on Renaissance Romance*, ed. George M. Logan and Gordon Teskey (Ithaca and London: Cornell University Press, 1989).

8. For evidence concerning Mary Sidney's knowledge of Greek, see Theodore L. Steinberg, 'The Sidneys and the Psalms', *Studies in Philology*, 1 (1995), pp. 1–17.

9. For further details about Mary Sidney's literary biography, see Hannay (1990); Gary F. Waller, *Mary Sidney, Countess of Pembroke: A Critical Study of her Writings and Literary Milieu*, Elizabethan and Renaissance Studies, no. 87 (Salzburg: University of Salzburg, 1979); and Frances B. Young, *Mary Sidney, Countess of Pembroke* (London: David Nutt, 1912).

10. Hannay (1990), p. 101.

11. Hannay (1990), p. xi and pp. 84–105; Waller (1979); Tina Krontiris, *Oppositional Voices: Women as Writers and Translators of Literature in the English Renaissance* (London and New York: Routledge, 1992); Margaret P. Hannay, ' "Doo What Men May Sing": Mary Sidney and the Tradition of Admonitory Dedication', in *Silent But for the Word: Tudor Women as Patrons, Translators, and Writers of Religious Works*, ed. Margaret P. Hannay (Kent, Ohio: Kent State University Press, 1985), pp. 149–65.

12. As Elaine Beilin points out in *Redeeming Eve: Women Writers of the English Renaissance* (Princeton: Princeton University Press, 1987), p. 123. For a discussion of the concept of social capital and its use in feminist theory, see Toril Moi, 'Appropriating Bourdieu: Feminist Theory and Pierre Bourdieu's Sociology of Culture', *New Literary History*, 22(4) (1991), pp. 1017–50.

13. Young (1912), p. 123.

14. Gary F. Waller, 'Struggling into Discourse: The Emergence of Renaissance Women's Writing', in Hannay (1985), pp. 238–56.

15. M.M. Bulloch, *Mary Sidney, Countess of Pembroke: An Elizabethan Historiette* (Aberdeen: Belmont Congregational Church, 1895); Gary F.

Waller, ' "This Matching of Contraries": Bruno, Calvin, and the Sidney Circle', *Neophilologus*, 56 (1972), pp. 331–43 (p. 339).

16. *John Aubrey, Brief Lives*, ed. Richard Barber (London: Folio Society, 1975), p. 146. Waller (1979), p. 144.

17. R.E. Pritchard, *Mary Sidney (and Philip Sidney): The Sidney Psalms* (Manchester: Manchester University Press, 1992), p. 9.

18. Beth Wynne Fisken, 'Mary Sidney's *Psalmes*: Education and Wisdom', in Hannay (1985), p. 169.

19. Krontiris (1992), p. 66.

20. Ezell (1993), p. 52.

21. See introduction and Gary F. Waller, 'Struggling into Discourse: The Emergence of Renaissance Women's Writing', in Hannay (1985), pp. 238–56.

22. Ann Rosalind Jones, *The Currency of Eros: Women's Love Lyric in Europe, 1540–1620* (Bloomington and Indianapolis: Indian University Press, 1990), p. 29; Barbara K. Lewalski, *Writing Women in Jacobean England* (Cambridge, Mass. and London: Harvard University Press, 1993), p. 2; Krontiris (1992), p. 8.

23. Joanna Russ, *How to Suppress Women's Writing* (London: Women's Press, 1984); Betty S. Travitsky, *The Paradise of Women*, 2nd edition (New York: Columbia University Press, 1989), p. 13; Diane Bornstein, 'The Style of the Countess of Pembroke's Translation of Philippe de Mornay's *Discourse de la vie et de la mort*', in Hannay (1985), p. 134.

24. In *English Metrical Psalms: Poetry as Praise and Prayer* (Cambridge: Cambridge University Press, 1987), Rivkah Zim suggests that the Sidney psalms were largely the work of one man aided by his sister. Other examinations of the Sidney psalter focus almost entirely on Philip Sidney's contribution: Gary F. Waller, ' "This Matching of Contraries": Calvinism and Courtly Philosophy in the Sidney Psalms', *English Studies*, 55 (1975), pp. 22–31; Hallett Smith, 'English Metrical Psalms in the Sixteenth Century and their Literary Significance', *Huntington Library Quarterly*, 9 (1946), pp. 249–71; Richard Todd, ' "So Well Attyr'd Abroad": A Background to the Sidney-Pembroke Psalter and its Implications for the Seventeenth-century Religious Lyric', *Texas Studies in English Language and Literature*, 29 (1987), pp. 74–93, and 'Humanist Prosodic Theory, Dutch Synods and the Poetics of the Sidney-Pembroke Psalter', *Huntington Library Quarterly* (1989), pp. 273–93.

25. For further discussion of this point, see Suzanne Trill, 'Sixteenth-century Women's Writing: Mary Sidney's *Psalmes* and the 'Femininity' of Translation', in *Writing and the English Renaissance*, ed. William Zunder and Suzanne Trill (Harlow: Longman, 1996), pp. 140–59.

26. For a more detailed discussion of women's use of the psalms, see Suzanne Trill, ' "Patterns of Piety and Faith": the Role of the Psalms in the Construction of the Exemplary Renaissance Woman', unpublished PhD dissertation (University of Liverpool, 1993) and ' "Speaking to God in his Phrase and Word": Women's Use of the Psalms in Early Modern England', in *The Nature of Religious Language*, ed.

Stanley E. Porter (Sheffield: Sheffield Academic Press, 1996), pp. 269–83.

27. Beilin (1987), p. 125. Hannay (1990) and Mary Ellen Lamb, *Gender and Authorship in the Sidney Circle* (Madison, Wisc.: University of Wisconsin Press, 1990) discuss Mary Sidney's role as a patron in more detail.

28. Lord Edward Denny to Lady Mary Wroth, Salisbury MSS. 130/118–119, Feb. 26, 1621/22. Cited Hannay (1985), p. 5.

29. Samuel Daniel, *Delia and Rosamond Augmented* (1594), sigs. A2r–v.

30. Æmilia Lanyer, 'The Author's Dream to the Lady Mary, the Countess Dowager of Pembroke', from *Salve Deus Rex Judaeorum* (1611), in *The Female Spectator: English Women Writers before 1800*, ed. Mary R. Mahl and Helene Koon (Bloomington and London: Indiana University Press, 1977), pp. 75–82 (p. 79).

31. Hannay (1985), p. 149.

32. Beth Wynne Fisken ' "To the Angell Spirit..." ': Mary Sidney's Entry into the "World of Words" ', in *The Renaissance English Women in Print: Counterbalancing the Canon*, ed. Anne M. Haselkorn and Betty S. Travitsky (Amherst: University of Massachusetts Press, 1990), p. 265.

33. Francis Bacon, cited by Frank Whigham, *Ambition and Privilege: The Social Tropes of Elizabethan Courtesy Theory* (Berkeley and London: University of Calfornia Press, 1984), p. 102.

34. Mary Sidney, 'To the Angel Spirit', in *Silver Poets of the Sixteenth Century*, ed. Douglas Brooks-Davies (London: Everyman, 1992), pp. 299–302.

35. Mary Sidney, 'Even Now that Care', in *The Triumph of Death and Other Unpublished and Uncollected poems by Mary Sidney, Countess of Pembroke*, ed. Gary F. Waller, Elizabethan & Renaissance Studies, no. 65 (Salzburg: University of Salzburg, 1977), pp. 88–91, 1. 27.

36. Mary Sidney's dedication to Elizabeth makes its own claims for the significance of the Sidney *Psalmes*, see lines. 29–32.

37. Mary Sidney uses the phrase 'skillful songs' in psalm 47, l. 15 in *The Psalms of Sir Philip Sidney and the Countess of Pembroke*, ed. J. C. A. Rathmell (New York: New York University Press, 1963). In 'Vpon the translation of the Psalmes by Sir Philip Sydney, and the Countesse of Pembroke his Sister', John Donne claims that they represent 'The highest matter in the noblest forme' (11), in *Donne: Poetical Works*, ed. Herbert J.C. Grierson (Oxford and New York: Oxford University Press, 1985), pp. 318–19.

38. Margaret P. Hannay, 'House-confined Maids: The Presentation of Woman's role in the *Psalmes* of the Countess of Pembroke', *English Literary Renaissance*, Vol. 24, No. 1 (1994), pp. 44–71.

39. Beth Wynne Fisken in Hannay (1985), p. 182.

40. John Donne, 'Vpon the translation of the Psalmes', 49–50.

41. John Donne, 'Vpon the translation of the Psalmes', 22.

42. For a more detailed analysis of Mary Sidney's *Psalmes* and the art of praise, see Suzanne Trill, in Zunder and Trill (1996), and Trill (1993), chapter 5.

43. See Maureen Quilligan, in Logan and Teskey (1989), p. 62.

44.   Although Sidney's *Psalmes* have been explicitly excluded from *The Paradise of Women* and are rarely included in anthologies specifically devoted to women's writing, her *Psalmes* are now included in *Silver Poets of the Sixteenth Century*, ed. Douglas Brooks-Davies (London: Everyman, 1992); *Poems of the Elizabethan Age*, ed. Geoffrey G. Hiller (London, New York: Routledge, 1990); *The New Oxford Book of Sixteenth-Century Verse*, ed. Emrys Jones (Oxford: Oxford University Press, 1992); and *The Penguin Book of Renaissance Verse, 1509–1659*, ed. David Norbrook and H. R. Woudhuysen (London: Penguin Books, 1992).

10

What Echo Says: Echo in Seventeenth-century Women's Poetry

Susan J. Wiseman

I

The breeze that wafts the crowding nations o'er,
  Leaves me unpitied far behind
  On the forsaken barren shore
To sigh with echo and the murmuring wind;[1]

So Aphra Behn wrote in 'A Pindaric Poem to the Reverend Doctor Burnet On the Honour He Did Me Of Enquiring After Me and My Muse', her response to Gilbert Burnet's invitation to put her pen to work for the new, Protestant, rulers William and Mary. Her reply – a refusal – is couched in part in the voice of a woman rejecting the tempting overtures of a lover, a strategy which foregrounds the way the poem both echoes and answers a preceding voice. The presence of echo as a disembodied yet 'natural' and therefore authoritative voice, initiates play on agency and truth, lateness, mourning and political honesty which provoked the question this essay attempts to elucidate: How does E/echo work in seventeenth-century poetry, more specifically in poetry by women? This is not to argue that women universally or systematically use E/echo in any particular way, but rather that because women poets of this period are highly conscious of the gendering of voice, the play on absence and presence authority and powerlessness E/echo comes to offer in their poetry a voice which supplements and subverts that of the poetic subject.

Echo is both a figure and a kind of poem, even, as Jonathan Goldberg sees it, the structuring principle of lyric. He asks, 'What is this "play" of echoing voices, of acknowledged and unacknowledged repetition if not the stanzaic mode of lyric poetry?' and this essay develops his emphasis on the oscillation between acknowledged and unacknowledged speech so characteristic of E/echo.[2] The enigmatic force of the trope – or sound – derives precisely from that continuing uncertainty or undecidability about the nature and place of the voice of E/echo: is an echo the voice of Echo? Does the appearance of echo imply the entry of another subject or semi-subject into the poem? To whom can E/echo's words be attributed – to Echo? To the speaking voice? To the dominant voice of the poem?

The two major studies of Echo/echo, by Hollander and Goldberg, both concentrate on poetic echo effects. Hollander's reading of echo, though brilliant in its analysis of poetic echoing, nevertheless leaves aside ideological, contextual and gendered implications. As Loewenstein notes, 'if there is a myth and a literary history of Echo, there is also a literary history of echoing,' so it is worth attending, literally and contextually, to the kinds of thing Echo says, the implications of the voice and words of specific echoes.[3]

Echo, then, is understood in this essay as a presence somewhere between some*thing* and some*one*, which can reply when a proper or conscious subject cannot. The semi-subjective voice of echo seems to invite the anachronistic language of subjectivity to describe, for example, the splitting of the subject in 'hysteria' and in the 'dissociation' of multiple personality. Echo, considered as something connected to the human but culturally imagined as beyond the borders of the human, can be understood in these terms as a linguistic effect with implications for understanding the splitting of voice in lyric; echo can be seen as a presence when the subject is not present. Moreover, this power-play upon presence and absence gives E/echo 'her' distinctive authority as a supra- as well as non-human voice. As Freud wrote of echolalia and hysteric speech, echo's words are both archaic, emerging from ancient trauma, and present: 'involuntary … performances which have at one time had a meaning.'[4]

If the hysteric's body can be considered her 'silent speech', and the hysteric as a figure (in both senses) which is alternately subject and object, then E/echo, a voice without a body, can like the hysteric, be understood as oscillating between the status of subject and object. The E/echoic qualities of the poems examined here, and I would argue in the use of E/echo overall, are generated by this undecidability of status between subject and object.[5] Thus, although it is, of course, anachronistic to employ the term 'subject' to discuss the early modern poetic persona and the status of a trope, in this particular instance the term offers the most precise way to analyse the relationship between someone and something which E/echo puts in play.

II   TRACING ECHO: FROM ABSENCE TO AUTHORITY (AND BACK)

> . . . a voice without a mind.
> I only with another's language sport:
> And but the last of dying speech retort.
> Lowd Echoes mansion in the eare is found:
> If therefore thou wilt paint me, paint a sound.[6]

The particular properties of E/echo as semi-human are reworked by Renaissance texts from classical precedents. Aristotle's writing on music suggests echo's paradoxical reduplication and closing down of sound: 'echo is when some air is unified by the vessel that contains it and prevents its fragmentation, and the air rebounds [from it] like a ball.'[7] The mythic narratives initiate the process of endowing echo with naturalised authoritative, political and gendered meaning, in Loewenstein's terms mastering the 'uncanny materiality [of echo] by giving it a history'.[8] Probably the stories which were most actively reworked in the early modern period were two from Ovid's *Metamorphoses*. On the one hand, Echo was a chatterbox who kept Juno occupied while other nymphs sported with Jove – and so was punished (this is suggested in the garrulous Echo revived in Jonson's *Cynthia's Revels*). On the other, she fell in love with Narcissus, followed him into a cave where she pined away, became bones, and then nothing but spirit voice at one with nature, her body completely denied and, correspondingly, completely erased.[9]

This second, better-known, story suggests the complicated meanings of E/echo taken up by early modern poets; where Echo is implicated in the discontents of heterosexual desire, in the workings of courts and politics, bound up with loss and mourning and in the connected problematic of feminine desire. Echo's story and figure is reworked in the early modern period in a range of different ways but, most obviously, in relation to doomed erotic and amorous encounters and mourning for lost – but not relinquished – objects. However, in poems reworking the story, Narcissus tends to get the starring role. Thus, in Francis Beaumont's glancing reference to Echo's relationship with Narcissus, Echo comes in a poor second when Salmacis comments on Hermaphroditus's smooth face: 'Narcissus face was so,/And he was careless of a Nymph's sad woe.'[10] Echo (all voice) and Narcissus (all eyes) might be taken from Ovid, but the text invites us to ask what work they are doing and what valency they might have in their contemporary culture? Never simply 'a voice activated device', Echo's figure, neither someone nor something, yet gendered, occupies a textual position which invites a reading in terms of a play of authority and subversion, masculine and feminine.[11]

Although Echo's voice is secondary and her body is gone, her desires are heard. Indeed, it is the body's disappearance that makes her herself, a subject which is not a subject. With no body but some kind of residual 'personality' or set of qualities, Echo seems to be what Borch-Jacobsen describes as 'what happens to the subject… when there is no longer anyone there'; E/echo is 'there' once the subject has been displaced. She thinks, speaks, but provokes the question; 'Is this unconscious thinking therefore a thinking attributable to no subject?'[12]

Thus, a dynamic between agency and involuntary voice, presence and absence, between life and death, structures the continuum of meanings which Echo assumes in seventeenth-century poetry. Echo's involuntary versatility – or her disembodied promiscuity – makes her potentially a political figure precisely because she is, as the poet George Sandys puts it, immaterial and 'a voice without a mind' – as a kind of dead voice, she is also integrated with the landscape and therefore speaks as 'a daughter of God or a voice of nature'.[13] Through this association echo involuntary is frequently given some sort of agency.

Echo's authority and 'her' cultural significance as proximate to the subject but pointing towards the absence or extinction of the subject – both – is evident in the habitual figuring of E/echo as 'a dead thing' which foretells death. This supra-human, deathly, authority is illustrated by probably the best known instance of Renaissance E/echo, in *The Duchess of Malfi* where Echo is both person and function. Antonio walks among the 'ancient ruins' and an echoic voice, that of the Duchess but also that of E/echo, replies:

> *Antonio*: . . . but all things have their end
> Churches and cities, which have diseases like to men,
> Must have the death that we have.
> *Echo*:   Like death that we have.
>   . . . .
> *Antonio*: It groaned, methought, and gave
> A very deadly accent.
> *Echo*:   Deadly accent.
>   . . . .
> *Antonio*: Make scrutiny through the passages
> Of your own life, you'll find it impossible
> To fly your fate.
> *Echo*:   Oh, fly your fate!
>   . . . .
> *Antonio*: Echo, I will not talk with thee,
> For thou art a dead thing.
> *Echo*:   Thou art a dead thing.[14]

Echo's oracular iterations suggest a status as something close to the voice of nature, speaking with a prophetic authority grounded in culture (history, 'ruins') and nature (landscape). These unsourced words, spoken by ruins rather than a subject, but with the echo of a subject (now dead) who had been at the centre of the play, have for the audience a supra-human prophetic force. The authority of echo both exceeds that of the subjects of the court Antonio is part of, and yet incorporates the difficulty of primacy and secondariness (of gender versus status) in the relationship between the Duchess and Antonio. So Echo, arguably the one truth-telling voice in the play, takes on a natural and supernatural, also gendered and political implication.

In circumstances such as Antonio's encounter with E/echo amongst ruins, Echo is not exactly death, but she has a deathly authority and her murdering of words points towards death. In the mid-century Robert Coddrington's *Crumms of Comfort* (London, 1652) attempts to steer a middle way between the devotional 'tyranny' of Laud and 'Raunters, Quakers, Shakers Seekers &c with their Raptures, Visions and Revelations'.[15] Echo similarly appears in his meditations designed to prepare the Sinner for death:

Sinner: Are you there, with Death?
Echo: Here, With Death.
Sinner: Then, are you both together?
Eccho: Both together.[16]

Echo here is distinct from Death, but with death – almost like the
two processes in Freud's death drive, desire and extinction go
together.[17] Echo leads the sinner to death, and then speaks no
more. The tendency towards extinction, nevertheless replenished
with energy supplied from outside, enables Echo's answers to lead
the Sinner towards a conception of the end of Time and their own
extinction from 'I should have beleeved Time' to an understanding
that Death and Echo are 'both together' – coexisting with Echo as a
ghostly harbinger of death.

The tendency of such oscillation around agency and the involuntary, sense and nonsense, is to make Echo what Hollander calls 'a
kind of allegory' – meaningless, involuntary and yet filled with
meaning. Paradoxically, it is the involuntary nature of speech
which returns authority and discursive control to Echo. Bacon
figures this in terms of a kind of feminised access to truth, arguing:

of all words and voices Echo alone should be chosen for the
world's wife, for that is the true philosophy which echoes most
faithfully the voices of the world itself, and is written as it were at
the world's dictation.[18]

Echo's authority is not sourced in a person but in the whole of the
natural world whose authority, figured as masculine like that of a
husband, she, like a wife, repeats and makes audible.

Echo's status as deathly and as the voice of nature – a semi-
subject in each case – makes her also a royal figure, not human,
not god; knowing nothing and everything she announces both
death and kings. As Bacon's analysis of Echo suggests, it, or she,
is associated with death and politics, through being integrated with
landscape. Even as Echo tends towards death, then, the association
with a kind of authority sourced in a world far beyond that of
simple human authority in the realm of nature, next to God,
makes Echo available for repeated political figurations as a truth-
telling political voice. This can be found in pastoral, as in Browne's
Britannia's Pastorals where she appears in the Lady's song, speaking
on behalf of the whole nation:

> *Is* Henry *dead? alas!...*
> *....*
> Britaine *was whilome known (by more than fame)*
> *To be one of the Ilands fortunate;*
> *What frantic man would give her now that name,*
> *Lying so rufull and disconsolate?*
> *Hath not her watry Zone in murmuring,*
> *Filled every shore with* Ecchoes *of her cry?*[19]

Taking advantage of the association between echo and nature, the Civil War pamphlet-dialogue, *A Dialogue Betwixt London, and Echo* (1644) Echo uses the authority of unsourced invountary voice to endorse the royalist position:

> *London:* ... prethee, Echo tell
>   When will a happy Peace make England well?
>   That is now heart-sicke and like to die,
>   If Heaven send not Remedie.
> *Eccho*: Remedie.[20]

Echo goes on to say, 'Pray, Repent' and finally 'King', indicating one understanding of what Echo 'naturally' says. Although the nature of Stuart claims to kingship made Echo a suitable figure to voice royalist sentiment, Echo was by no means an exclusively royalist trope. Rather, Echo was deployed by several factions, to refract 'truth'; later in the war in *A New and True Echo From Old and Bold Authors* Echo found herself reiterating a presbyterian position in a pamphlet which 'echoed' the political writers of the past in relation to the contemporary controversy, bringing to bear resonant arguments about regicide.

Clearly, E/echo was used to naturalise a range of political positions in seventeenth century poetry. Bacon's domestication of 'her' as 'the world's wife', however, covers over the aspects of E/echo which are not controlled by the speaking voice: E/echo can only repeat words and yet can make meanings. The authority of her voice can not only foreground the competition of gendered voices in the lyric, but also tend towards a supra-human authority in which the echoes take over the poem.[21] The authority of E/echo as sourced in the natural world is, in seventeenth-century writing, bound up with a sense of E/echo as something potentially threatening to the subject, like the subject but not, and able both to invade the subject's consciousness and usurp their reason. In this guise echoes appear in *The Anatomy of Melancholy*:

> [Echoes] can counterfeit the voices of all birds and brute beasts almost, all tones and tunes of men, and speak within their throats, as if they spoke afar off, that they make their auditors believe that they hear spirits, and are thence much astonished and affrighted with it.[22]

The semi-subjective status of echoes here threatens and competes with the subject: the noises suggest external animation of the body as they 'speak within their throats', inviting interpretation as agents who wish to disrupt the subject's world, 'astonishing' them with the sounds of 'spirits'. This ability to take over from the subject is what will be discussed next, in terms of Echo as a second, gendered, voice in lyric poetry.

III GENDERING ECHO: ADDITIONAL VOICES, SECOND LANGUAGES

This section examines the expanding place of E/echo in three poems by seventeenth-century women. It analyses the twin aspects of E/echo as an authoritative and therefore potentially a political voice and an inhuman, semi-subjective voice which supplements and competes with 'official' forms of communication (such as the poetic voice and writing). This is played out vividly around the question of the secondariness of feminine poetic voice.

In lyrics E/echo stages gendered competitions or duets, implying a competitive dialogue of voice, though the source of the echoing voice can never be fully clear. In Abraham Cowley's 'Echo', Echo is posed as a voice giving life to the poet's love; where the mistress closes it down Echo multiplies sound with a hint of promiscuity – 'Hadst thou but Eyes, as well as Tongues and Ear,/ How much compassion wouldst thou show' where the mistress takes on the deathly, sound-murdering qualities associated with Echo, 'my barren Love alone,/Does from her stony breast rebound,/Producing neither Image, Fire, nor Sound.'[23] This rests on the convention of the lover's masculine single voice as the primary focus of the reader's attention and the poem's authority.

However, when two poetic voices – one male and one female – come into play, the lyric and mythic play of E/echo's presence and absence becomes complex. Henry Vaughan's poem to Katherine Philips takes up the question of the gender of the primary voice:

> Say witty fair one, from what sphere
> Flow these rich numbers you shed here?
> ...
> ...this made me (a truth most fit)
> Add my weak echo to your wit.
> Which pardon lady, for assays
> Obscure as these might blast your bays,
> As common hands soil flowers.[24]

The ironic play on primary and secondary voice is accentuated by the context – Katherine Philips was probably under 20 when these verses were printed. Even as Vaughan replies to her poem, the emphasis on his wit echoing hers calls attention to his status as a poet which undercuts the primacy his verse claims for her. And, of course, the very act of giving this primacy implies that in fact his authority is able to endow her verse with status. Echo here, as a displacement of and claim to primacy, is complicated by the gender of the authorising presence.

This suggests echo or Echo's function in lyric as part of a contention over meanings, and one in which the foregrounding of the gender of Echo as a subject/not-subject adds an extra dimension to the power struggles suggested in the first part of this paper. Echo's presence adds a gendered aspect to the question of vocal extinction in lyric – which, or whose, words will live and which will die? What will the intertextual voice preserve and what repress?

Evidently, the self-consciously secondary place of women's poetic voices in the period marks the dynamic of E/echo in the lyric; it is this secondariness which Vaughan's poem both effaces and parades. Yet, as suggested in *The Anatomy of Melancholy*, echoes can 'make their auditors believe that they hear spirits': E/echo's relationship to the poem can extend beyond the competition of primary and secondary voice to raise the question of another inhabitant or presence in the poem. Echo's tendency to extend and subvert language inheres in the particular ability to mimic and transform without having a body or a source for a voice and so she/it can become another personality, even a disorderly personality, inhabiting the poem. As Borch-Jakobsen asks of the personalities in the phenomenon of Multiple Personality Disorder, E/echo can produce the question, 'whom had I encountered? Had I really met some*one*?' For, like an additional personality with no body, E/echo can inhabit the poem as someone, or something, with 'no personal identity' but an ability to be there when the subject is not.[25]

Lady Mary Wroth's *Urania* is discussed elsewhere in this volume. The first poem in *Urania* is of interest here because it takes up the 'secondary' potential of both E/echo and the female poetic subject and E/echo's ability to take over (from) the subject. Her poem uses Echo as neither self, entirely, nor other, but the space between the two – a 'friend' to the female persona. The 'faire Shepherdesse Urania' takes a little path into the rocks, 'her eies fixt upon the ground, her very soule turn'd into mourning', and Echo rebounds her sorrows back to her:

> Unseene, unknowne, I here alone complaine
>   To Rocks, to Hills, to Meadowes and to Springs,
> Which can no Helpe returne to ease my paine
>   But back my sorrows the sad Eccho brings!
> Thus still encreasing are my woes to me,
>   Doubly resounded by that monefull voice,
> Which seemes to second me in miserie,
>   And answere gives like friend of mine owne choice.
> This onely she doth my companion prove,
>   The others silently doe offer ease:
> But those that greive, a greiving note doe love;
>   Pleasures to dying eies bring but disease:
> And such am I, who daily ending live,
> Wayling a state which can no comfort give.[26]

In a writer so conscious of family, status, voice and place in the world it seems significant that Echo – semi-personified – appears in the first poem in the book, spoken by Urania. The poetry of 'Urania' is framed by lateness, she is in mourning and her voice, like Echo's desire, is unheard: Echo is secondary to a voice which is itself mourning, secondary. Yet, of course, it is the first poem in a long story and, in calling attention to its belatedness by foregrounding its echoic qualities. In pinpointing the presence of two voices –

Urania's and Echo's – neither primary but both secondary, it puts in
play questions of presence and control, authority and echoing.

More play can be made with Wroth's use of Echo as a figure for
melancholy intertextuality, and the opening of the Urania with a
persona using a poem with the ultimate trope of lateness and
absence – a voice that simultaneously claims and disclaims authority, advances speech and refuses, speaks and does not speak.
Indeed, Wroth is reworking Sidney here: Urania herself appears
in Sir Philip Sidney's *New Arcadia*. Moreover, when Echo reappears
in Wroth's pastoral drama, *Love's Victorie*, she (or it) is once again a
helpful trope. Echo occurs when Philisses is about to meet Musella:
'No Echo shrill shall your deere secrets utter/Or wrong your silence
with a blabbing tongue'; 'since woods, springs, Echoes and all are
true/My long hid love, I'le tell, shew, write in you.' Echo, as in
Urania, is cast as a companion and though the speaker's words may
echo, the 'true' echo will not distort.

While E/echo suggests Wroth's literary genealogy and may be
self-referentially echoed in later texts, setting up a kind of self-
genealogy, within 'Urania's' poem E/echo is used to stage – and
resolve – the melancholic drama of the poetic subject:

> Unseene, unknowne, I here alone complaine
>   To Rocks, to Hills, to Meadowes and to Springs,
> Which can no Helpe returne to ease my paine
>   But back my sorrows the sad Eccho brings!
> Thus still encreasing are my woes to me,
>   Doubly resounded by that monefull voice,
> Which seemes to second me in miserie,
>   And answere gives like friend of mine owne choice.

As this extract indicates, the role of Echo in the poem shifts from
object, or mere landscape, to 'voice', and this shift brings with it a
transformation in the relationship between subject and Echo. In
being 'alone' and belated, secondary, mourning, the subject's
voice tends to produce itself as like echo. Like the Echo of the
Narcissus story, she is 'unseene, unknowne' and – her desire unác-
knowledged – complains the loss of her object in the *locus classicus*
of mourning E/echo. The echo replicates those sounds, initially
without agency; 'back my sorrows the sad Eccho brings!' apparently doubling rather than answering for mere nature 'can no
Helpe returne' and in reproducing woe, increases it. At this point,

though, Echo seems to shift closer to the position of a subject; 'monefull voice' and becomes a 'second' or 'friend of mine own choice'.

The secondary nature of the subject's voice ('unseene, unknowne') both apparently moves her towards the position of non-subject and, paradoxically, enables echo's appearance as an ally similar to the poetic subject in a reciprocal voicing – 'those that greive, a greiving note doe love'. Thus the animation of Echo endorses the subject's condition as a 'friend', comforting and restoring the subject.

At this point an analogy with the figure of the hysteric in psychoanalytic discourse may again be drawn; like the symptomatising hysteric, the subject at the opening of the poem is not fully 'at home' to herself but rather tends towards a leaking or evacuation of subjectivity into the unresponsive objects of the landscape around her. This evacuation of subjectivity propels the speaker towards sharing the echo's semi-subjective and landscape-bound status.[27] Notably, the poetic voice's complaint about lack of symbolisation or answer to grief, failure of the landscape to recognise and reply, is remedied by the reduplicative voice of Echo. Echo, in this case, repairs the failure of symbolisation in doubling – and thereby recognising and offering a symbolic language for – the subject's loss. In repeating the subject's words, E/echo is more alive than the other aspects of nature which 'silently doe offer ease'. Reiterating – 'those that greive, a greiving note doe love' – the Echo here perhaps replaces the mourned subject/object dynamic.

Such production of additional voices alongside the subject is discussed in much contemporary psychoanalytic discourse; Borch-Jacobsen, for example, sees this as a 'remake' (with sound) of the theory that hysteria was caused by trauma provoking the subject to split or 'dissociate'. He discusses Multiple Personality Disorder as the late twentieth-century form of the trance and, with his customary emphasis on the *cogito*, sees 'dissociation' and the movement between, or 'switching' of personalities as producing a momentary sense of 'I': as he puts it, '*je switche, je suis*'.[28] In the description of Multiple Personality Disorder (and hysteria) linguistic changes are central evidence; an additional voice or 'language' emerges, at a distance from the subject. Such a linguistic model allows us to address E/echo's potential to move far beyond the reduplicative potential of 'the world's wife' or 'a voice without a mind' to understand the figure and effect as a splitting of voices and an incursion of other voices, though not precisely subjects, into the poetic text. The subversive potential of echo within the lyric – both to extend and explode what is said – becomes clearer. E/echo considered this way, offers huge potential for the 'secondary' voice – whether feminine and, therefore, secondary/echoic or the voice of E/echo – to take over.

One of Aphra Behn's songs provides a clear example of echo as an additional occupant of the poem, extending and undermining the 'primary' voice. E/echo acts as an echo-chamber and, in doing so, comes to compete with the poetic voice. It illustrates the potential of E/echo not only to distort language and undermine authority, but to offer a supplementary yet also different language, adjacent to that of the subject and for the figure to build towards the establishment of a competing/supplementary E/echoic discourse. E/echo usurps any pretensions of the singing voice to sole poetic subjectivity:

Amyntas that true hearted Swaine,
Upon a Rivers Banck was lay'd,
Where to the Pittying streames he did Complaine
On Silvia that false Charming Maid.
While shee was still regardless of his paine.
   Ah! Charming Silvia, would he cry;
And what he said, the Echoes wou'd reply:
Be Kind or else I dy, Ech:—I dy
Be Kind or else I dy: Ech:—I dy.

Those smiles and Kisses which you give,
Remember Sylvia are my due;
And all the Joyes my Rivall does receive,
He ravishes from me not you:
   Ah Sylvia! can I live and this believe?
Insensibles are toucht to see My Languishments, and seem to pitty me:
Which I demand of thee: Ech—of thee
Which I demand of thee: Ech:—of thee.[29]

On the one hand, the poetic voice (third person and not conclusively gendered) tells a story of the exchange of kisses whereby two male lovers are brought into contact by their competition over a woman. The desire is tripartite, with one owing the other kisses exchanged through the woman, who never owns the kiss. The echo both collaborates with the structure in producing a soundbox fragmentation and multiplication of the desire and, on the other hand, truncates or kills Amyntas's words. The echo-effect of the ending plays on presence and absence, on the me/thee aspect of lyric address but Echo also more specifically serves to return the words to the speaker in a complementary and competitive sense. The ungendered framing voice introduces Amyntas's words and stages a scene where Echo – partly personified and presumably sung by a woman – retorts 'I dy'.

The echo works in at least four simultaneous ways. It is self-referential (the E/echo it/herself does 'dy', or though repeated fade away). It prophesies the death of the subject (probably Amyntas), it offers a punning prophesy of erotic fulfilment, and finally it gives a complication of who-loves-whom as the same words are repeated by different voices. In the second stanza E/echo works to further multiply and complicate the ownership of desire as with the words 'Of thee' E/echo repeats Amyntas's demand and turns back on him the question of between whom desire is, in fact, exchanged in this triangle. Thus E/echo, repeated, doubly doubles an already three-way chain of desire in such a way as, on the one hand, leaves Amyntas alone as a sole complaining voice (Echo repeats his words but is not figured as replying to him) and, on the other hand, suggests the endless multiplication of desire. Echo here takes on the life not only of a symptom of desire, but also an articulation of that desire, not within the precise structuring of syntax but in the guise of the linguistic fragment which can multiply and exceed the syntactically bound language of the poetic subject. In subverting the relationships of gender and desire and re-presenting them to both Amyntas and the reader, Echo makes a series of ideological as well as sonic interventions: simply by duplicating and multiplying words and fragments she, or it, foregrounds, even changes, the relationship between different members of the triangle.[30]

How, then, can we characterise such an implicitly present and disturbingly unsourced, automatic voice? In early Freud the notion of a symptom as a translation from one psychic order to another was central and, in certain ways, continued to be so in his understanding of the unconscious. The model of the psyche as unleashing other languages, understood differently from 'official' language offers a highly suggestive way to read or hear Echo in Behn's 'Song'.[31] Such a model of a translation or conversion of pain into symptomatic language, then retranslated into conscious capital L Language invites comparison with the operations of echo and with what Echo is permitted to say because it implies that L-language and a linguistically elaborated symptomatology coexist – and compete. This is not to say that, for example, in Behn's song or in *The Duchess of Malfi* or in Wroth's *Urania*, echo acts as the unconscious of the text; to do so might be to adopt the problematic model of female agency that Suzanne Trill outlines at the start of her essay (p. 191). Rather, it is to suggest that such vocalisation is a conscious linguistic placing and partial articulation, a hint towards, some additional, forbidden, or contradictory, implications. Another, or additional, text rather than an unconscious because what echo says (and how) is both fragmentary and highly structured in mathematical repetitions of sound. Certainly, this is how E/echo functions in Behn's 'Song' where the use of E/echo takes full advantage of the trope's characteristic potential to transform language, in this case in such a way as to invite into the poem a number of possible pairings of desire excluded by the (framed) subject whose single voice articulates desire; like in Wroth's poem, the appearance of Echo invites us to read in terms of a widening, echoic, frame of reference and licenses linguistic fragmentation, ambiguity and double-meaning.

The idea of the echoic fragmentation as part of an additional language articulating other meanings works elsewhere as a way of reading echo. It invites an understanding of echo as always already within the symbolic but operating as a voice which announces the inability of language – of 'official' and, indeed, its own language – fully to orchestrate and suppress meaning. This paradoxical status also indicates some of the political potential of echo, and that brings us to the final example. Behn's 'Pindaric to the Rev. Dr Burnet' offers an opportunity to place in a political context the aspects of E/echo outlined in section II and the potential of E/ echo to produce such an additional voice and even mode of symbolisation.

Behn's pindaric to Burnet is a poem written late in her career and in many ways it reflects ironically on the political consistency of that career. It offers an opportunity to place echo in the context of poetry which is interwoven with political discourse. The poem notionally responds to an invitation by Dr Gilbert Burnet to write in favour of the new regime of William and Mary which Burnet had been actively working to bring about. In October 1688 he wrote (to himself) that the 'whole matter will be brought to its full ripeness within a week or two; so that one of the greatest designs that has been undertaken now for many ages is brought very near a point.' He was worried about the outcome, which did indeed extensively change England/Britain's relations with Ireland and Europe, noting: 'I have a paper, which is now in the press, with a justification of the whole design.'[32] Burnet had clearly been active in producing this new regime; his pen and work had prepared the ground and this was known. Behn's poem addresses this fashioning of event as a kind of disruptive spirit, an ironic unfashionable echo.

Throughout her poem – the 'reply' to what she presents as his request – Behn counterposes voice (not writing) and writing. Burnet writes for 'Nassau' (William of Orange) whereas despite Burnet's solicitations, Behn will not. Casting the poem in terms of a refusal to write its very form is ironical as, indeed, written. Through Burnet's invitation Behn claims to be silent, while producing a justification of her position at some length. She replies to his invitation, gracefully interweaving the reasons why she should *not* write for 'Nassau'. Thus, as the poem develops it could be read either as grateful panegyric, or as irony.

Competition between singleness and multiplicity of voice is central to the poem's opening with the republican elections of Rome: 'When old Rome's candidates aspired to fame,/And did the people's suffrage obtain' suggests the part played by citizens in Roman government. As the poem progresses, emphasis shifts from the political scene of Rome where the voices of the populace were able (perhaps problematically) to determine who participates in government to the use of eloquence in sexual seduction. The recipient's apparent pleasure in being the 'choice' of Burnet's 'single voice' (with Burnet's singleness already ironically replacing the singleness of monarchical command) is recast through his use of 'wit', 'noblest eloquence', 'judgement' to become the persuasions of a seducer:

> A thousand ways my soul you can invade,
> And spite of my opinion's weak defence,
>   Against my will, you conquer and persuade.
> Your language soft as love betrays the heart,
>   And each period fixes a resistless dart.

> (st. 2)

228 Susan J. Wiseman

Language and masculine power, as in Behn's elegy on Rochester, are bound up together, though here the consequences are problematic. Not only has the scene shifted from Rome to the drama of a virgin's seduction (bringing with it a subtly effected shift of the nature of Burnet's enterprise), but punctuation and the organisation of thought – 'each period' – becomes an 'invasion' and, putting in play the language of rape, attempts violence on the poetic subject as well as echoing what a supporter of James might see William and Mary as having done. The answer ironises Burnet's 'divine command', framing the refusal in terms of a seducer's words: 'Against my will you conquer and persuade', 'Your language soft as love', while the listener is 'like a maid undone'. 'Official' or first-order language, especially writing, is incursive, violent, rapacious or seductive. Yet, of course, this is the replying/secondary voice's representation of a first voice that, for the reader, is absent.

The gratitude to Burnet is modulated through such irony and rapidly builds into the establishment of dual reading positions. The position of Burnet 'to' (though not, perhaps, 'for') whom the text is addressed can be imagined by the reader as either foolish and taken in by the praise, or as seeing the irony. The reader can imagine Burnet's position; they, too, can read it as panegyric and gratitude, but also as satire, at least irony. The position which offers the reader a strongest sense of 'knowingness' is to read it as both at once, as it were to read as 'official' and 'unofficial' readers simultaneously, and this is invited by the text's use of juxtaposition rather than contrast so that images and words can be read as either complementary, collaborative, or contradictory.

The establishment of the double position and the ironic usurpation of 'unofficial' meanings is played out in terms of the competition between Echo and writing. Loyalty means that the poet cannot write:

> The breeze that wafts the crowding nations o'er,
>   Leaves me unpitied far behind
>   On the forsaken barren shore
> To sigh with echo, and the murmering wind;

The complementary potential of echo found in Wroth and Lanyer reappears here, framed within a political discourse; E/echo complements the poetic subject even as it symbolises her melancholy and loneliness. But once again E/echo has the potential to take over, here characterised as a political potential to mourn and, therefore, remain faithful. This plays into the poem's invitation to double or ironic reading as E/echo's authority and loyalty challenges the longevity of the written word. All the fruit of Burnet's written labour is to immortalise a usurper; 'your pen shall more immortalise his name,/Than even his own renowned and celebrated fame.' Obviously, 'Nassau' is not the name of the King of England and, as the final words of the poem, they hold in place the ironic double-reading required by the rest. It is not conclusively or simply ironic about the achievements of Burnet's pen, but while the poetic subject gets nature, echo 'the barren shore' (margins, but still land), Burnet's panegyric celebrates only one individual.

Moreover, in contrast with the natural authority of (Stuart) echo, the poem suggests the power of writing to transform:

> O strange effect of a seraphic quill!
>   That can by unperceptible degrees
> Change every notion, every principle
>   To any form, its great dictator please:
> The sword a feeble pow'r compar'd to that,
>   And to the noble pen subordinate;

The pen transforms political truth, by degrees undermining the 'truth' of Stuart monarchy to the point where the way is prepared for 'Nassau'. Implicitly, then, the pen is the instrument of liars, here, and the sword of cowards; Burnet's lies have made way for the bloodless (cowardly) coup. 'Seraphic' here picks up 'writ divine' (stanza 1); the 'angelic' authority of Burnet over 'eloquence' and truth is transformed as the poem develops into its opposite – a willingness to produce a kind of linguistic black magic which turns truth into falsehood through the power of eloquence; later Burnet's strategies (and 'Nassau's') are associated with the trickery of the Trojan horse, 'Not all their numbers the famed town could win/ 'Twas nobler stratagem that let the conqueror in.' Thus writing is both valorised as powerful and undercut as dishonest and as having brought about the improper rule of 'Nassau' through trickery.

The voice which is claimed as dominating the poem and as participating in enforcing Behn's claimed though unobserved silence is Burnet's. Apparently respectful, the poetic subject distances herself from Burnet's false politics and writing in a sequence of associations from seduction to political lying, where Burnet is always implicitly in the wrong position. The organisation of the text as silent even as it speaks, not writing, puts into play the valorisation of voice. The 'shore' from which Echo speaks is also implicitly that by which James II departed; her loyal poem echoes his rule.

Echo operates twice in this poem, once as a figure for the poet and in a second, though related, way as the ironic presence of this (rather than Burnet's) voice. The ironic play between the compliments and their subversive possibilities make the echoic structure of the poem part of the reading process. To 'get it' the reader reads the official and the unofficial version. Unlike Behn's 'Song' the two versions are syntactically linked, the second, echoic, voice inhabits the poem in terms of its consistent irony. Thus, as echo takes over a poem, figuring it/herself as mourning, belated, near death and yet – strength in weakness – for those very reasons, naturally authoritative, true, it puts in play an unofficial discourse which, as this poem demonstrates, emerges in the political valency of ironic echo, the power of a female voice to reply while claiming silence and to echo, retrope and subvert political positions from within a discursive self-positioning as secondary. In doing this, Behn's text puts in place a political use of the subversive potential of E/echo as that always returning additional voice, and hints at the political potential of the trope for female political enunciation.

IV

While not being fully translatable her- or it-self, the operations of E/echo put in doubt the primacy and status of the poetic subject; E/echo competes with the poetic subject, multiplying voice in such a way as to put the origination or 'source' of voice in doubt.[33] It is this emptiness and its spooky potential that enables echo to become an authoritative and political figure in poetry. As Burton notes, the illusions of echo are in the mind: 'such illusions and voices … proceed most part from the corrupt imagination.'[34] It is, as Behn's poem implies, the listener or reader of echo who is to find its full reverberations. Yet, fragmentariness is bound up with echo's possibilities and modes of operation; any full translation of echo would, inevitably, be a mistranslation. For Bacon, not only does the world have the potential to distort sound, but the hearing has the potential to distort the sense of sound; for Bacon, the contract between echo and hearer is *per se* one of misapprehension.

However, the responsibility for this double mistaking – mistaking in both the making and receiving of sound – cannot be attributed. Each instance of echo is a provocation to the reader to make a sense that can be realised only allusively, not conclusively.

The diagnosis of E/echo as a particular voice is, inevitably, a misdiagnosis in suppressing the quality of E/echo which gives it its potential in the poetry examined here. E/echo is neither some*one* nor some*thing* and can, because of the trains of associations that set in play, be used as a political trope because of her associations with the natural world. Thus, Echo and what E/echo says, enables us to ask, 'what happens to the subject when there is no "personality", no personal identity, no "ego" (or "self"), no memory, no unifying pole of experience?... what remains when there is no longer any-one there, when "I", Ich, ego, have disappeared?'[35] Paradoxically, this quality of Echo is what makes it/her – not subject, not object, yet gendered – available as a figure of authority and politics. Obviously, one answer to who speaks as Echo, who is there when the subject is not, is the poetic voice, voice of the poem, and, as I hope I have suggested, this is precisely the potential of Echo for poets working self-consciously with gender: echo can be the poem's other voice, from nowhere. Such multiple poetic habitation allows Echo to speak as a sourceless voice to very specific social and political situations and, as in Behn's poem, to offer us a complex and unsourced route to the poem's sense of political truth.

ACKNOWLEDGEMENT

Thanks to the seminars at Newcastle-Upon-Tyne and Keele, 1994–5, for comments and particular thanks to Gordon McMullan.

NOTES

1. 'A Pindaric Poem to the Reverend Doctor Burnet On the Honour He Did Me of Enquiring After Me and My Muse', Janet Todd (ed.) *The Works of Aphra Behn* (London: Pickering, 1992), vol. 1, p. 267

2. Jonathan Goldberg, *Voice, Terminal, Echo* (London: Methuen, 1986), p. 24.

3. Joseph Loewenstein, *Responsive Readings: Versions of Echo in Pastoral, Epic and the Jonsonian Masque* (New Haven & London: Yale University Press, 1984), p. 2; John Hollander, *The Figure of Echo* John Hollander, *The Figure of Echo: a mode of Allusion in Milton and After* (Berkeley: University of California Press, 1981); Jonathan Goldberg, *Voice, Terminal, Echo*. Thanks to Julie Sanders, Susan Bruce, Roger Pooley and Tim Armstrong for discussion of tropes and gender.

4. Sigmund Freud, 'A Case of Successful Treatment By Hypnotism, (1892–3)', in James Strachey, ed., *The Standard Edition of the Complete Psychological Works of Sigmund Freud*, vol. I (London: Hogarth Press, 1966), pp. 115–31.

5. For discussion see also, e.g., Juliet Flower MacCannell, 'Things to Come', in Joan Copjec, ed., *Supposing the Subject* (London, 1994) pp. 106–32.

6. 'Echo', Ausonius trans. George Sandys, quoted Hollander, p. 9.

7. Aristotle, *De Anima* 419 b 4–421 a 6, in Andrew Barker, ed., *Greek Musical Writings* (Cambridge: Cambridge University Press, 1987), vol. II, p. 77.

8. Loewenstein, p. 9.

9. Ovid, *Metamorphoses* III; Ben Jonson, *Cynthia's Revels*.

10. Francis Beaumont, 'Hermaphroditus', in *Poems* (London, 1640).

11. Hollander, p. 8.

12. Mikkel Borch-Jacobsen, *The Freudian Subject* (London, 1988) p. 6; Mikkel Borch-Jacobsen, 'Who's Who? Introducing Multiple Personality' in Copjec, ed., *Supposing the Subject*, pp. 45–63, esp. p. 46.

13. Hollander, pp. ix, 6, 9; Amy Lawrence, *Echo and Narcissus: Women's Voices in Classical Hollywood Cinema* (Berkeley: University of California Press, 1991), p. 2.

14. John Webster, *Duchess of Malfi*, ed. G. B. Harrison (London, 1933; rpt. 1975), V. iii. Thanks to Gavin Lambert for discussion of echoes.

15. Robert Coddrington, *Crumms of Comfort* (London, 1652), #7r, #9r.

16. 'A Dialogue Between a Sick Sinner, Eccho, Death and Time' *Crumms* i2r-v.

17. Sigmund Freud, in James Strachey, ed., *Beyond the Pleasure Principle, Standard Edition*, vol. 18.

18. Francis Bacon, *Advancement of Learning*, II. xiii. Quoted Hollander, p. 10.

19. William Browne, *Britannia's Pastorals* (London, 1613), Book I, Song 5, p. 92; see also pp. 2, 101. Thanks to Michelle O'Callahan.

20. *A Dialogue Betwixt London and Echo*, np (London, 1644).

21. See Goldberg, *Voice, Terminal*, p. 5.

22. Robert Burton, *The Anatomy of Melancholy* ed. Holbrook Jackson (London: Dent, 1975), p. 427.

23. Abraham Cowley, 'The Mistress' (1647).

24. Henry Vaughan, 'To the most Excellently Accomplished Mrs K. Philips', in Alan Rudrum, ed., *Complete Poems* (Harmondsworth: Penguin, 1976) p. 326; Borch-Jacobsen, p. 46.

25. Mary Wroth, *The Countesse of Montgomerie's Urania* (London, 1621); *The Poems of Lady Mary Wroth* ed. Josephine A. Roberts (Baton Rouge:

Louisiana State University Press, 1983), p. 146. Thanks to Dr Helen Hackett.

26. Lady Mary Wroth, *Love's Victory*, ed. Michael G. Brennan (London: Roxburghe Club, 1988) The Forth Act, p. 137. Thanks to Marion Wynn-Davies for alerting me to this.

27. Elizabeth David-Menard, *Hysteria From Freud to Lacan* (Ithaca: Cornell University Press, 1989) p. 66; as David-Menard puts it, the body 'exists for a subject only as much as it is shaped by the symbolization of her desire', pp. 68–9.

28. Borch-Jacobsen, 'Who's Who', pp. 49, 62.

29. Janet Todd, ed. *The Works of Aphra Behn* (London, 1992), vol. 1, p. 54. See also 'Voyage to the Island of Love', p. 129.

30. Compare Æmilia Lanyer on the semi-animated garden of Cookeham. See Barbara Lewalski, *Writing Women in Jacobean England* (Cambridge: Harvard University Press, 1993) p. 238.

31. See *Hysteria From Freud to Lacan*, p. 64.

32. *Supplement to Burnet's History of My Own Time*, ed. H. C. Foxcroft (London, 1802), pp. 285, 286. Behn did write 'Congratulatory Poem to Her Sacred Majesty Queen Mary, upon her Arrival in England' – her poem to Burnet cannot be seen as pre-empting a career under William and Mary.

33. Goldberg, pp. 289–9.

34. Robert Burton, *The Anatomy of Melancholy*, I, pp. 427–8, 'The Symptoms of Melancholy: Immediate Causes Thereof'

35. Borch-Jacobsen, 'Who's Who', p. 46.

11

Restoring the Renaissance: Margaret Cavendish and Katherine Philips

Ros Ballaster

[T]here was no renaissance for women – at least, not during the Renaissance.'[1]

I INTRODUCTION

Joan Kelly's assertion of 1977 continues to be debated by feminist scholars, extending the discussion to wider contexts than Kelly's discussion of fourteenth- and fifteenth-century Italy.[2] This essay speculates on the possibility that the answer with regard to England may be yes, but only in the imagination and then retrospectively. Two seventeenth-century authors, Katherine Philips and Margaret Cavendish, develop a fantasy in their published works of the Restoration period of a Royalist return to Renaissance values in which women figure the possibility of a 'restored' economy of literary-social relations without the underpinning of a patriarchalist belief in the divine 'fatherhood' of sovereign power which the Civil War appeared to have removed from possibility. For Royalist women an interesting set of paradoxes was generated by the new political and ideological configurations of the 1660s. As Royalists they wished to see the restoration of an aristocratic court culture as the centre of power, but as women they had experienced new agency and power in the Civil War and Commonwealth years. Both Cavendish and Philips were Royalist sympathisers, who appear to have been writing throughout the Commonwealth years but appeared in print, mainly or solely, in the decade following Charles II's accession to the throne. Both lived in retirement for most of their married lives, Margaret Cavendish at her husband's estate in Nottinghamshire at Welbeck Abbey from 1660 to 1673, and Katherine Philips at her husband's home in the Priory, Cardigan from 1648 to 1664; for both the choice (and its availability) for aristocratic women between retirement and public display remains a constant preoccupation. Both were married to men considerably older than themselves. Margaret Lucas, the youngest daughter of Essex landowners, was in her early twenties when she became the second wife of a 52-year-old Cavalier aristocrat, William Cavendish, Duke of Newcastle, himself a playwright and patron of the arts. Katherine Fowler, the daughter of a London cloth merchant, married the 52-year-old kinsman of her stepfather, Colonel James Philips of Tregibby, when she was in her late teens. Yet, the differences between these two writers are as significant as their similarities. Where Margaret Cavendish shared her husband's politics and his interest in artistic production; Katherine Philips differed from her husband on both counts. Cavendish remained childless; Philips bore two children, albeit after the bulk of her writing had been completed. Both women wrote closet drama and poetry. Cavendish also wrote fiction and treatises in natural philosophy; Philips' letters were published after her death.[3] The most striking contrast between the two, however, remains Cavendish's active pursuit of what she termed 'fame' through the medium of print culture and Philips' public disavowal of the desire to be printed. In both cases this is a less simple process than it appears.

Margaret Cavendish visited England in 1653 in the company of her brother-in-law in order to petition the parliamentary Committee for Compounding for a wife's share in the estates of her exiled husband. She employed the long hours of waiting in London with preparing two collections for publication, *Poems and Fancies* and *Philosophical Fancies*. Cavendish exploited the expansion in print culture which was made possible by the decline of a centralised aristocratic court culture, but the magnificent folio volumes of her works which she sent to Oxford and Cambridge colleges appear to be print imitations of the private manuscript transcription of a Renaissance culture, not designed for purchase by the labouring or gentry reader. By contrast, Katherine Philips, as the wife of a leading Parliamentarian, had access to political knowledge that her origins as a daughter of a merchant would have precluded before the Civil War. Yet her poetry celebrates a world of private retirement and love between friends over the public ties of political loyalty and marital union. In 1664, Philips insisted that a book of her poems published by Richard Marriott be withdrawn. An unsigned preface to the 1667 *Poems by the most deservedly admired Mrs. Katherine Philips* (printed by Marriott) included a letter by Philips to Poliarchus (Sir Charles Cotterell) declaring that she 'never writ any line in [her] life with an intention to have it printed', and explaining that she has been forced to submit to his suggestion that she publish her verse in order to prevent badly transcribed versions from appearing.[4] While Philips eschews the public display that print culture entails, expressing her horror of having her 'imaginations rifled and exposed to play the Mounte-banks, and dance upon the Ropes to entertain the rabble' (p. 129), her interest in 'good copy' and the maintenance of accurate tran-scription through the medium of print suggests a more modern engagement with print than Cavendish's desire to see it simply reproduce the condition of the manuscript in circulation of earlier years. Indeed, Philips herself is aware that the advertisement and subsequent withdrawal of a text by the same publisher who even-tually produced the 'authorised' version (albeit posthumously) might be seen as a complex ploy to appear in print while appearing to deny the desire to do so. She is anxious to prove herself 'inno-cent of that wretched Artifice of a secret consent' (p. 129), while aware that no such proof can be forthcoming. Behind Philips' innocent surface then, lurks a shrewd understanding of the work-ings of the print culture of the new age ushered in with the removal of the sovereign power both she and Cavendish sought to see restored.

In the writings as well as the publication histories of both women we can trace a perceived need not to lose the literary-political free-doms women had experienced during the years when the Stuart monarchy had been in abeyance without denting the necessary ideological work of restoring the image of royalism. Both produce texts which self-reflexively present female artistry, however frac-tured and unstable, as an important ideological agent in the process of restoring Renaissance cultural relations.

The negotiation of a specifically female position in post-Restora-tion Royalist writing is brought about in the writings of Cavendish and Philips through the invocation of a nostalgic and selective image of Renaissance models reconfigured retrospectively for their own historical moment. The Renaissance ideal that repeatedly resurfaces is that of the mutually beneficial relation between poet and patron. Lorna Hutson persuasively argues in her article 'Why the Lady's Eyes are Nothing Like the Sun' that women writers in the Renaissance faced a peculiarly impenetrable aesthetic system in this 'humanist fiction of author and patron as authenticating one another in a relation of pure interpretative increase, a pure reproduction of each other's worth'.[5] Hutson draws our attention to the role of the image of woman in this hermeneutic exchange: as deluding diversion from the mutual relation of reflected knowledge but also as necessary mediator (or mirror) of mutual interpretative desire (homosocial if not homoerotic in its desire for a bond between men). The figure of the 'dark lady' of Shakespeare's sonnets 127 to 152 is emblematic of this tradition in Renaissance poetry.[6]

The idea of an interpretative community between men founded on the circulation of an idealised or demonised image of woman might be seen to have been fractured with the dispersal of cavalier royalists across Europe, their dispossession from their property and the attendant collapse of the great 'patronage' environments such as Wilton (centring on the Countess of Pembroke in the late sixteenth century) and the court (centring on Elizabeth I in the the same period and Henrietta Maria in the early seventeenth century).[7] Women could and did occupy the position of patron in Renaissance culture, and accordingly a discourse of heterosexual rather than homosocial desire was invoked to close the circuit of relations; but the one position in the triangle of poet, patron and poetic object that women rarely occupied was that of poet. Hutson's article focuses on the unusual precedent of Æmilia Lanyer's *Salve Deus Rex Judeaeorum* (1611) to elaborate the difficulties of adopting this posture for women in the Renaissance. Lanyer's poem seeks to imagine a multiplied exclusively female community of patrons in which the mutual object of desire that illuminates their relations with the poet and each other is the feminised body of the crucified Christ.[8]

Cavendish and Philips are also preoccupied with relations between the female poet and other women, but these are figured through dyadic rather than triangulated relations. The mediating 'object' (Christ for Lanyer, the 'dark lady' of Shakespeare's sonnets 127–152) collapses into the imaginary figure of the other woman, who is both a figure in the literary text and its generator. To demonstrate this complex dynamic, this article focuses on a work of prose fiction by Margaret Cavendish entitled *A Description of a New Blazing World* first published in 1666 with her *Observations on*

Experimental Philosophy and then as a separate volume in 1668 and a number of poems from the 1667 collection by Katherine Philips addressed to other women in her romance cabal. In both cases what appear to signal retreats into personal relations and an obscure system of private allusion can be read as a feminocentric reconfiguration of that largely homocentric Renaissance trope of the private relation between poet and patron as an expression of public power and mutual political interest. The ground then shifts from a masculine system of representation in which poetry acts as the public sign of social relations figured through private erotic desire, now transformed into a feminine system of representation in which writing acts as the private exchange between women of a shared desire for agency in the public world. In both cases, the contrast with a male contemporary (Andrew Marvell and Margaret Cavendish) or predecessor (John Donne and Katherine Philips) illuminates instructively these processes of conversion and trans-version of masculine models of the political agent in poetry.

II BLAZING WORLDS

Both Andrew Marvell's 'Last Instructions to a Painter' (1667) and Margaret Cavendish's *Blazing World* (1666) offer to their readers the image of a redemptive blazing figure at the centre of a great naval battle. Marvell's poem has long been recognised as a satirical rever-sion of Edmund Waller's 1665 'Instructions to a Painter' of 1665. Waller's poem celebrated the victory in the Anglo-Dutch wars of the English naval forces headed by James, Duke of York, off Low-estoft on 3 June 1665. James' wife, Anne Hyde, who visited Harwich in May, appears in the poem as a sea- goddess in the sort of masque entertainment associated with the Caroline court. Marvell's poem criticises James for calling off the pursuit of the Dutch after this victory, written as it is with the hindsight of a humiliating defeat in summer 1667 when the Dutch fleet managed to advance up the Medway and seize the *Royal Charles*, as well as fire the *Royal Oak* with its commander, Archibald Douglas, aboard. In Marvell's poem, Anne Hyde and Barbara Villiers, Charles II's mistress, are presented in an unholy conspiracy with Henry Jermyn, ambassador to France and rumoured to have married the dowager Queen Henrietta Maria; the triumvirate avert the attention of Charles and his brother, James, from matters of state to sexual debauchery. These images of monstrous femininity are countered in the poem by two figures of virginity: first, the bound virgin who appears to the King at the poem's conclusion arousing his lust rather than pity (a representation of Frances Stewart who was known to have refused Charles' attentions) and second, the young hero who dies on the deck of the ship, 'brave Douglas, on whose lovely chin/The early down but newly did begin' (ll.649–50).[9] It is clearly this latter figure of virtue who is an agent, albeit a self-consuming one, in redeeming England's reputation. Like Stewart, Douglas arouses lusts he refuses to allay; the 'nymphs' who watch him while he swims at night to harden his body for battle sigh that he flees 'love's fires, reserved for other flame' (l. 660). His death is described as the erotic consummation in battle that he has so devoutly wished:

> Like a glad lover the fierce flames he meets
> And tries his first embraces in their sheets.
> His shape exact, which the bright flames enflold,
> Like the sun's statue stands of burnish'd gold.
> Round the transparent fire about him glows,
> As the clear amber on the bee does close,
> And as on angels' heads their glories shine,
> His burning locks adorn his face divine.

> (ll.677–84)

Cavendish's *Blazing World* offers an equivalent scene of blazing martial success in naval conflict but at its centre stands a woman rather than the eroticised boy-figure of Douglas (who was, in fact, considerably older and a married man at the time of his death). Cavendish's fiction was published before Marvell's poem and before the 1667 defeat to which it refers, but it clearly has in its sights the 1665 victory at Lowestoft. Its heroine is an unnamed young lady who is abducted by a merchant who has fallen in love with her; he, however, dies in a tempest that has driven them off course, crossing over from the North pole to another world. In this new world, the blazing world, her worth is instantly recognised; the emperor falls in love with her, marries her and appoints her mistress of his kingdom. In the second part of *Blazing World*, the Empress discovers that her home country (ESFI: possibly England, Scotland, France and Ireland) is embroiled in a great war with most of the other nations in the world and determines to go to their aid. Not satisfied with simply preventing their defeat, she sets about making ESFI the 'absolute monarchy of all that world'.[10] Her method is simple but effective; she torches and terrorises her opponents through the remarkable properties of the 'firestone' which she has brought from the blazing world; it ignites on contact with water. The Empress carefully puts herself at the centre of this tableaux of blazing destruction. The morning of her great naval victory:

> the Empress appeared upon the face of the waters, dressed in her imperial robes, which were all of diamonds and carbuncles; in one hand she held a buckler, made of one entire carbuncle, and in the other hand a spear of one entire diamond... all her other garments were of several sorts of precious jewels; and having given her fish-men directions how to destroy the enemies of her native country, she proceeded to effect her design. The fish-men were to carry the fire-stones in cases of diamonds... and to uncase or uncover those fire-stones no sooner but when they were just under the enemy's ships, or close at their sides, and then to wet them, and set their ships on fire; which was no sooner done, but all the enemy's fleet was of a flaming fire; and coming to the place where the powder was, it straight blew them up; so that all the several navies of the enemies, were destroyed in a short time; which when her countrymen did see, they all cried out with one voice, that she was an angel sent from God to deliver them out of the hands of their enemies: neither would she return in to the Blazing World, until she had forced all the rest of that world to submit to that same nation.
>
> (p. 211)

For the disillusioned parliamentarian Marvell and the disappointed absolutist Cavendish alike, the male Stuart monarchy fails to meet the image of purity, power and transcendence that supports the fiction of authority required by a nation emerging from civil unrest and engaged in foreign wars. For Marvell a substitute is found in the figure of sacrificial civic virtue that challenges the egotism and intemperance of the King; Richard Braverman comments that 'Marvell adumbrates the "civic" mode that embodies a version of masculine desire and power grounded in a fraternal ideal that countervails the courtly-heroic paradigm.'[11] Royalist patriots such as Cavendish were also critical of Charles and his brother, James, disappointed as they were by Charles' apparent indulgence to rebels and failure to restore all properties seized from Royalists during the Civil War; moreover, the uncertainty of succession became increasingly apparent to them in the mid-1660s as the King's marriage to Catherine of Braganza proved childless. Cavendish's fantasy is one of the restoration of absolute and unified power in the figure of the female monarch, conjuring this image from the memory of the masque queen, Henrietta Maria, whom she had served in exile during the civil wars and perhaps also Anne Hyde at the waterside prior to the victory of 1665.

While the narrative of Marvell's poem points to the exhaustion of the Renaissance iconography of the idealised boy-hero in that Douglas's death does not avert political and military disaster, Cavendish revitalises the same Renaissance iconography by investing it in the figure of the female monarch/patron to suggest the possibility of absolute power in the fantastic space of writing if not the real.[12] The Empress is of course also a patron. In the first part of the fiction, the Empress engages in a series of enquiries into natural philosophy (Margaret Cavendish's own preoccupation), and then seeks a scribe to help her write up her own 'Cabbala', an explanatory system of signs for spiritual or secular 'mysteries'.[13] Her spirit advisers suggest she employ the 'soul' of the Duchess of Newcastle from the earth who 'although she is not one of the most learned, witty and ingenious, yet she is a plain and rational writer' (p. 181). 'Their meeting', we are told, 'did produce such an intimate friendship between them, that they became platonic lovers, although they were both females' (p. 163). The Duchess's soul commutes between her earthly home and the blazing world until the Empress is persuaded to make a spiritual visit to the Duchess and her husband; this results in an almost comic scene of triangulated desire when the two women's souls 'enter' that of the Duke. In the context of patronage relations this is an interesting moment:

> then the Duke had three souls in one body; and had there been but some such Souls more, the Duke would have been like the Grand Signior in his seraglio, only it would have been a platonic seraglio. But the Duke's soul being wise, honest, witty, complaisant and noble, afforded such delight and pleasure to the Empress's soul by his conversation, that these two souls became enamoured of each other; which the Duchess's soul perceiving,

grew jealous at first, but then considering that no adultery could be committed amongst Platonic lovers, and that Platonism was divine, as being derived from divine Plato, cast forth of her mind that Idea of Jealousy.

(pp. 94–5)

The triangular dynamic of Shakespeare's sonnets 127–52 in which two men (the poet, the young man) share one mistress (the dark lady) are caught in a circle of destructive mutual desire is here briefly evoked to be as briefly dismissed. As in the sonnets, the ambiguity remains as to whether the 'jealousy' of the poet/writer is directed to the heterosexual or the same-sex love object, but the explanation of 'Platonism' resolves the difficulty. The interest in 'Platonic' explanation in Cavendish serves as a form of discourse which recognises the lack of material ground for ideological representations.

Cavendish repeatedly associates women with the power of performance and illusion, most obviously in her so-called 'plays'. Her first volume of *Plays* (1662) must have been largely written during the Commonwealth period when the public theatres were closed. Private performances of drama may have taken place, but there are no records of any of Cavendish's plays being produced in this context. Cavendish seems to have exploited this environment to create plays with a vast temporal and geographical span that are almost impossible to produce on stage. In the absence of a material theatre the fancy is given free rein. The world of fancy and femininity for Cavendish is an aesthetic realm where fantasies of power can be played out despite the loss of material power in Cavalier/ Royalist culture, just as jealousy can be dismissed in an environment of souls where no material contact is possible.[14]

Cavendish's most actable play, *The Sociable Companions; or, the Female Wits* (in *Plays, Never Before Printed* [1668]) celebrates women's capacity to imagine resolution through verbal wit in the face of crisis. This intelligent comedy of intrigue engages directly with the financial difficulties that faced cavalier soldiers at the Restoration and, as such, it interestingly presages Aphra Behn's better-known and most successful play, *The Rover* (1677). Like Behn's cavalier soldiers in Madrid, Cavendish's cavaliers (Captain Valour, Will Fullwit and Harry Sencible) are a rascally, impoverished band, who retreat into drink and lechery. The army is disbanding and their property and estates have been sequestered, with little hope of return at the Restoration. Their friend, Lieutenant Fightwell, comments in the opening scene that 'all the Cavalier Party lost their Wits when they lost their Estates' (Act 1, scene 1, p. 8). It is their sisters, Peg Valourosa, Jane Fullwit and Anne Sencible, who provide that purpose:

Harry.   Why what would you have us do?
An.   Not to sit drinking in a Tavern most of your time; but to seek and endeavour to get some good Offices and Employments that may help to repair your ruins, and to maintain us according to our births and breedings.

(Act 2, scene 2, p. 30)

When the men show no sign of taking this sound advice, the women set about winning themselves wealthy marriage-partners from those men who have profited from the wars and their after-math: a lawyer, a doctor and a usurer. Peg, Jane and Anne embark on complicated confidence-tricks, trapping their husbands (drawn by lot) through mock paternity suits and cross-dressing disguises. In the process they win a wealthy wife for another cavalier, Dick Traveller, in one Lady Riches, whom the three men they appoint to be their own husbands have been courting. In this play, then, Cavendish trenchantly locates educated and nobly born women (however impoverished) as a vital source of regeneration and restoration in a culture that has lost and mourns the imagined securities of an earlier male authority.

That this privilege (of female agency through the exercise of fancy) is exclusive to upper-class women is equally clear. Not only is this freedom restricted to the nobly born, but it is also firmly confined to the 'fancy' itself, which appears to be the property of that class. Fascinated as she is by the splendid and extravagant display of a powerful aristocratic femininity, reminiscent of her former mistress Henrietta Maria's appearances in the court masque, Cavendish remains deeply suspicious of performance itself. The word 'act' in the title 'actor' clearly resonates for Cavendish as a suspicious privileging of materiality over the world of imagination. Actors turn the playwright's fanciful words into action. For Cavendish it appears a play, or the free play of fancy, is a play only when it is not played, turned into a performance; the female body as icon of absolute monarchical authority is only splendid when it is invoked in words not materially embodied.

III   'I'VE ALL THE WORLD IN THEE'[15]

The patron/poet relation is also reconfigured as Platonic exchange
of souls for Katherine Philips, but in the more explicit context of
her reworking of the love poetry of John Donne. Philips' love
poems to her female friends are written in conscious imitation of
the love poetry of John Donne, himself one of the first male writers
to produce a poem in the voice of a lesbian lover ('Sappho to
Philaenis', first published in 1635). This has led her commentators
to interpret her poetry in opposing ways: where Elaine Hobby
claims they express a 'closet', possibly sado-masochistic, lesbian
desire for women 'under cover' of the heterosexual invocation to
sexual union in 'masculine' love poetry, Lillian Faderman asserts
that the language of Donne is mimicked in order to reveal the
'higher' and 'purer' nature of the non-sexual union of female
souls in contrast to heterosexual fleshly and earthly lusts.[16] Interpretation of representations of female same-sex desire here hinges
on the discovery of the 'truth' behind the conventions, rather
than an exploration of the possibilities offered and exploited in
and through those conventions for the articulation of a sexual
economy (not necessarily or primarily physical but social, political
and desiring) that is 'different from' the heterosexual, and by extension, patriarchal, one. We must ask, then, in considering
these writings, to what extent the thematic departure from heterosexual to same-sex relations produces disturbances of gender conventions through the imaginary construction of a 'different'
economy of desire.

   Philips' passionate attachments to Mary Montagu, *née* Aubrey
(Rosania) and Anne Owen (Lucasia), two members of the coterie
circle of writers and royalist aristocrats surrounding the charismatic
Philips, are well documented through her own letters as well as her
poetry. Both Mary's secret marriage in 1652 and Anne's in 1662
prompted a flood of poetry and prose about the difficulty of maintaining same-sex friendship after marriage. Philips' poetry juxtaposes same-sex friendship and heterosexual marriage as competing
and incompatible modes of coupledom, most strikingly in her subversive transcription of Donne's famous image of the compasses in
his 'A Valediction: forbidding Mourning'. Donne represents the
female partner as a steady central foot in the twinned compass to
which the male partner is always attached as he wanders through
the public world: 'Thy soul the fixed foot makes no show/To move,

but doth, if th'other do.'[17] Philips, by contrast, makes no distinction between the two feet:

> And as in nature nothing's sett
> So Just as lines and numbers mett;
> So compasses for these being made,
> Doe friendship's harmony perswade.
>
> And like to them, so friends may own
> Extension, not division:
> Their points, like bodys separate;
> But head, like soules, knows no such fate.

('Friendship in Emblem,' Poem 29, p.108)

On the surface, heterosexual love and what Philips terms 'friendship' (almost invariably same-sex) appear to be in strict opposition to each other. 'Friendship' asserts:

> Friendship! that Love's Elixar, that pure fire
> Which burns the clearer 'cause it burns the higher;
> For Love, like earthy fires (which will decay
> If the materiall fuel be away)
> Is with offensive smoake accompany'd:
> And by resistance only is supply'd:
> But friendship, like the fiery element,
> With its own heat and nourishment content,
> (Where neither hurt, nor smoke, nor noise is made)
> Scorns the assistance of a forreign ayde.

(Poem 57, p.151)

Heterosexual love is carnal, murky, temporal; same-sex friendship is spiritual, eternal, 'Clearer than Crystall or the Mountaine-springs' ('A Friend,' Poem 64, p. 167). Yet the appropriation of Donne's image of the compass suggests a more uncanny link between the two modes of love, in which each is a version or 'copy' of the other. The Platonic discourse associated with 'friendship' would suggest in fact that heterosexual love is the weak 'copy' of the ideal form of same-sex friendship, yet the rewriting of an image drawn from an heterosexual love poem suggests that 'friendship' is the copy of an 'original' heterosexual love. My suggestion here would be that Philips' repeated reversals and mirroring distortions of one economy of desire with the other serve to destabilise the opposition of two kinds of love to the point where 'mimicry' of heterosexual courtship becomes subversion of the notion of a secure identity for lover and beloved in either heterosexual or same-sex love relations. We might equate this movement with Judith Butler's reclamation of 'drag' as a homosexual activity which subverts the secure notion of a distinction between inner and outer psychic space and hence undermines the assumption that the body expresses through specific acts the inner core of gender identity: '[T]he parodic or imitative effect of gay identities works neither to copy nor to emulate heterosexuality, but rather, to expose heterosexuality as an incessant and *panicked* imitation of its own naturalized idealization.'[18] In this process, neither heterosexual nor female same-sex desire can claim the status of original from which the other derives or departs, rather both are caught up in an infinite doubling *of each other*, a doubling that was also associated with the relation between lover and beloved in female same-sex desire in the poetry of both Philips and Donne. Philips' Platonic system of friends as 'each other's Mirrours' ('A Friend,' Poem 64, p. 167) uncannily repeats Donne's erotic depiction of Sappho's desire for Philaenis in which Sappho claims:

> My two lips, eyes, thighs, differ from thy two,
>   But so, as thine from one another do;
> And, oh, no more; the likeness being such,
>   Why should they not alike in all parts touch?

('Sappho to Philaenis', p. 128)

Both Philips and Cavendish construct utopian images of intra-female communities of reading; Cavendish presents herself as scribe to the Empress, while Philips' poems are gifts to her female friends. It is, however, a register of the new conditions of literary production and consumption of the Restoration that these communities are rapidly supplanted by a strenuous individualism on the part of the female writing subject. In the *Blazing World*, the Platonic exchange between Empress and Duchess rapidly becomes a question of individual intellectual property in the construction of imaginary worlds:

she [the Empress] sent for the Duchess, who being ready to wait on the Empress, carried her beloved world along with her, and invited the Empress's soul to observe the frame, order and government of it. Her Majesty was so ravished with the perception of it, that her soul desired to live in the Duchess's world; but the Duchess advised her to make such another world in her own mind; for, said she, your Majesty's mind is full of rational corporeal motions, and the rational motions of my mind shall assist you by the help of sensitive expressions, with the best instructions they are able to give you.

(pp. 188–9)

The Duchess then will not be 'empressed', pressed into allowing her imaginative productions to be ascribed to her 'mistress'; her creativity is her own property not the product of her relation with another. It is she who wishes to be 'empress', press the world into her images. The poet/writer, then, is recipient of the patron's generosity but does not 'return' by making her intellectual productions the property of the patron. *Blazing World* concludes with an epilogue which warns readers that 'if any should like the world I have made, and be willing to be my subjects, they may imagine themselves such, I mean, in their minds, fancies or imagination; but if they cannot endure to be subjects, they can create worlds of their own, and govern themselves as they please ... ' (p. 225).

So too Katherine Philips' poetry wrestles with the difficulty of inequality between the poet and the love object. Philips' poetry espouses a philosophy of absolute dyadic equality between Platonic friends against which her own experience is continually found wanting – she loves more and more possessively than Lucasia or Rosania. Married herself, she cannot tolerate their secret marriages. In a poem entitled 'To My Lucasia' she meditates:

> How much above the common rate of things
> Must they then be from whom this Union springs?
> But what's all this to me, who live to be
> Disprover of my own morallity?
> And he that knew my unimproved Soule,
> Would say I meant all friendship to controule.
> But bodys move in time, and so must minds;
> And though th'attempt no easy progress finds,

Yet quit me not, least I should desparate grow,
But to such friendship add some patience now.

('To my Lucasia,' Poem 43, p. 129)

What is presented as a dialogue of the souls of friends is revealed to
be a monologue. Like her Renaissance predecessors, Donne and
Shakespeare, Philips constructs tributes to a desired object, which
ultimately release a meditation on the generative capacity of the
writer rather than the object. It is her troubled negotiation between
collective and personal identity that preoccupies the poet and her
reader. The 'fiction' of a communality of women is maintained in
both Cavendish's and Philips' writing, only to enable an individu-
alist focus on the writer as voice for a feminine aesthetic, frequently
at the expense of the imagined interlocutor.

We can then make few claims for the feminism or proto-feminism
of these Royalist writers who carve out an elite space of romance
fantasy from which the privileged woman writer can speak. This
space is built on the apparent mimicry of the socio-literary relations of Renaissance culture in the changed context of the Restoration, a process which calls attention to its insubstantiality by
mourning the loss of material relations between poet and patron
centred in a court or aristocratic country house. The irony here, of
course, is that this is *itself* a nostalgic fantasy, an idealised construction of an 'imaginary' Renaissance order. Thus, Restoration writing
constructs the Renaissance as a prelapsarian space where relations
of power and authority are securely demarcated to the benefit of
both poet and patron – at the expense, however, of the representation of women. And here lies the final irony. Philips and Cavendish
present a fantasy version of a fully significant and signifying
mutually satisfying aesthetic Renaissance and claim their lineage
from it. Yet it is the myth of its dislocation – the fall of the Civil War
and the disturbance of patriarchalism – that is the enabling ground
of their own writing as *repetition* and yet *reconfiguration* of relations
of interpretation in the Renaissance. Women's alienation from political affairs enables them to continue to occupy aesthetic relations of
mutual mirroring between poet and patron/muse no longer available to men for whom the need to fancify relations of power is a
painful reminder of its loss.

NOTES

1. Joan Kelly, 'Did Women have a Renaissance?' (1977). Rpt in *Women, History and Theory: The Essays of Joan Kelly*, Women in Culture and Society Series (Chicago and London: University of Chicago Press, 1984), p. 19.

2. See Lisa Jardine, *Still Harping on Daughters: Women and Drama in the Age of Shakespeare* (Brighton, Sussex: Harvester, 1983); Stephanie Jed, *Chaste Thinking: The Rape of Lucrece and the Birth of Humanism* (Bloomington: Indiana University Press, 1989); Constance Jordan, *Renaissance Feminism: Literary Texts and Political Models* (Ithaca and London: Cornell University Press, 1990).

3. Tom Brown, now well known to have been a plagiarist and forger, published 'Letters of the late celebrated Mrs Katherine Philips' in his ed. *Familiar Letters* of 1697. In 1705 the *Letters from Orinda to Poliarchus*, Philips' letters to Sir Charles Cotterell, the trusted friend who had edited her *Collected Poems* of 1667, appeared in print.

4. 29 January 1663/4, Letter XLV, *The Letters*, vol. II of *The Collected Works of Katherine Philips*, ed. Patrick Thomas (Essex: Stump Cross Books, 1992), p. 128. The letter was extensively revised for *Letters from Orinda to Poliarchus* of 1705. See Appendixes 1 and 2 of Thomas (ed.).

5. Lorna Hutson, 'Why the Lady's Eyes are Nothing Like the Sun', in Clare Brant and Diane Purkiss (eds.), *Women Texts and Histories 1575–1760* (London: Routledge, 1992), p. 20.

6. See Eve Kosofsky Sedgwick, 'Swan in Love: The Example of Shakespeare's Sonnets', in her *Between Men: English Literature and Male Homosocial Desire* (New York: Columbia University Press, 1985), pp. 28–48.

7. On the Countess of Pembroke, see Mary Lamb, *Gender and Authorship in the Sidney Circle* (Madison, Wisc.: University of Wisconsin Press, 1990): on Henrietta Maria, see Sophie Tomlinson, 'She that Plays the King: Henrietta Maria and the Threat of the Actress in Caroline Culture', in Gordon McMullan and Jonathan Hope (eds.), *The Politics of Tragicomedy: Shakespeare and After* (London and New York: Routledge, 1992), pp. 189–207.

8. Æmilia Lanyer, *The Poems of Aemilia Lanyer*, ed. Suzanne Woods, Women Writers in English 1550–1830 series (Oxford and New York: Oxford University Press, 1993).

9. *Andrew Marvell: a Critical Edition of the Major Works*, ed. Frank Kermode and Keith Walker, The Oxford Authors (Oxford: Oxford University Press, 1990), p. 140.

10. Margaret Cavendish, *The Blazing World and Other Writings*, ed. Kate Lilley (London: Penguin, 1994), p. 214.

11. Richard Braverman, *Plots and Counterplots: Sexual Politics and the Body Politic in English Literature 1660–1730* (Cambridge: Cambridge University Press, 1993), pp. 88–9. For a reading more alert to the homoeroticism of the presentation of Douglas in this poem, see Stephen Zwicker, 'Virgins and Whores: The Politics of Sexual Misconduct in

the 1660s', in *The Political Identity of Andrew Marvell*, ed. Conal Condren and A.D. Cousins (Aldershot: Scolar Press, 1990), pp. 85–110.

12. For an innovative and inventive reading of the relation between absolutism and the female imagination in Cavendish, see Catherine Gallagher, 'Embracing the Absolute: The Politics of the Female Subject in Seventeenth-Century England', *Genders* 1 (1988): pp. 24–39.

13. On Cavendish's interest in natural philosophy, see Lisa Sarasohn, 'A Science Turned Upside Down: Feminism and the Natural Philosophy of Margaret Cavendish', *Huntington Library Quarterly* 47 (1984), pp. 289–307.

14. For Cavendish's understanding and presentation of fancy, see James Fitzmaurice, 'Fancy and the Family: Self-characterizations of Margaret Cavendish', *Huntington Library Quarterly* 53 (1990), pp. 199–210.

15. Katherine Philips, 'To my Lucasia', Poem 43, vol. I of *Collected Works*, p. 129.

16. Elaine Hobby, 'Katherine Philips: Seventeenth-century Lesbian Poet', *What Lesbians Do in Books*, ed. Elaine Hobby and Chris White (London: Women's Press, 1991), pp. 183–204: Lillian Faderman, *Surpassing the Love of Men: Romantic Friendship and Love Between Women from the Renaissance to the Present* (London: The Women's Press, 1985), pp. 70–1.

17. *John Donne: The Complete English Poems*, ed. A.J. Smith (Harmondsworth, Middlesex: Penguin Books, 1971), p. 84.

18. Judith Butler, 'Imitation and Gender Insubordination', in Diana Fuss (ed.), *Inside/out. Lesbian Theories, Gay Theories* (London: Routledge, 1991), p. 23.

REFERENCES

Braverman, Richard, *Plots and Counterplots: Sexual Politics and the Body Politic in English Literature 1660–1730* (Cambridge: Cambridge University Press, 1993).

Butler, Judith, 'Imitation and Gender Insubordination', in Diana Fuss (ed.), *Inside/out. Lesbian Theories, Gay Theories* (London: Routledge, 1991).

Cavendish, Margaret, *Blazing World and Other Writings: Margaret Cavendish*, ed. Kate Lilley, Women's Classics Series (London: Pickering Chatto and Windus, 1993).

——, *Plays, Never Before Printed* (London, 1668).

Donne, John, *John Donne: The Complete English Poems*, ed. A.J. Smith (Harmondsworth, Middlesex: Penguin, 1971).

Faderman, Lillian, *Surpassing the Love of Men: Romantic Friendship and Love Between Women from the Renaissance to the Present* (London: The Women's Press, 1985).

Fitzmaurice, James, 'Fancy and the Family: Self-characterizations of Margaret Cavendish', *Huntington Library Quarterly* 53 (1990), pp. 199–210.

Gallagher, Catherine, 'Embracing the Absolute: The Politics of the Female Subject in Seventeenth-century England', *Genders* 1 (1988): pp. 24–39.

Hobby, Elaine, 'Katherine Philips: Seventeenth-century Lesbian Poet', *What Lesbians Do in Books*, ed. Elaine Hobby and Chris White (London: Women's Press, 1991), pp. 183–204.

Hutson, Lorna, 'Why the Lady's Eyes are Nothing Like the Sun', in Clare Brant and Diane Purkiss (eds.), *Women Texts and Histories 1575–1760* (London: Routledge, 1992), pp. 13–38.

Jardine, Lisa, *Still Harping on Daughters: Women and Drama in the Age of Shakespeare* (Brighton, Sussex: Harvester, 1983).

Jed, Stephanie, *Chaste Thinking: The Rape of Lucrece and the Birth of Humanism* (Bloomington: Indiana University Press, 1989).

Jordan, Constance, *Renaissance Feminism: Literary Texts and Political Models* (Ithaca and London: Cornell University Press, 1990).

Kelly, Joan, 'Did Women have a Renaissance?' (1977). Rpt. in *Women, History and Theory: The Essays of Joan Kelly*, Women in Culture and Society Series (Chicago and London: University of Chicago Press, 1984), pp. 19–50.

Lamb, Mary, *Gender and Authorship in the Sidney Circle* (Madison, Wisc.: University of Wisconsin Press, 1990).

Lanyer, Æmilia, *The Poems of Aemilia Lanyer*, ed. Suzanne Woods, Women Writers in English 1550–1830 series (Oxford and New York: Oxford University Press, 1993).

Lilley, Kate, 'Blazing Worlds: Seventeenth-Century Women's Utopian Writing', in *Women, Texts and Histories 1575–1760*, ed. Clare Brant and Diane Purkiss (London: Routledge, 1992), pp. 102–33.

Marvell, Andrew, *Andrew Marvell: a Critical Edition of the Major Works*, ed. Frank Kermode and Keith Walker, The Oxford Authors (Oxford: Oxford University Press, 1990).

Philips, Katherine, *The Collected Works of Katherine Philips: The Matchless Orinda*, ed. Patrick Thomas, 3 vols: *Poems, Letters, Plays* (Essex: Stump Cross Books, 1990, 1992, 1994).

Sarasohn, Lisa, 'A Science Turned Upside Down: Feminism and the Natural Philosophy of Margaret Cavendish', *Huntington Library Quarterly* 47 (1984), pp. 289–307.

Sedgwick, Eve Kosofsky, 'Swan in Love: The Example of Shakespeare's Sonnets', in her *Between Men: English Literature and Male Homosocial Desire* (New York: Columbia University Press, 1985), pp. 28–48.

Tomlinson, Sophie, 'She that Plays the King: Henrietta Maria and the Threat of the Actress in Caroline Culture', in Gordon McMullan and Jonathan Hope (eds.), *The Politics of Tragicomedy: Shakespeare and After* (London and New York: Routledge, 1992), pp. 189–207.

Tomlinson, Sophie, '"My Brain the Stage": Margaret Cavendish and the Fantasy of Female Performance', in *Women, Texts and Histories 1575–1760*, ed. Clare Brant and Diane Purkiss (London: Routledge, 1992), pp. 134–63.

Wiseman, Susan, 'Gender and Status in Dramatic Discourse: Margaret Cavendish, Duchess of Newcastle', in *Women, Writing, History 1640–1740*, ed. Isobel Grundy and Susan Wiseman (London: Batsford, 1992), pp. 159–77.

Zwicker, Stephen, 'Virgins and Whores: The Politics of Sexual Misconduct in the 1660s', in *The Political Identity of Andrew Marvell*, ed. Conal Condren and A.D. Cousins (Aldershot: Scolar Press, 1990), pp. 85–110.

Afterword
Ann Thompson

The working title for this collection of essays, and for the series of talks in which they originated, was 'Renaissance Woman/Renaissance Man: New Voices'. I was able to attend only one of the talks when they were first delivered, but, as Gordon McMullan says in his Acknowledgements, I did manage to get to the conference at the University of Newcastle upon Tyne where most of them were delivered again and discussed by the whole group of contributors, with Charmian Hearne of Macmillan, during two unbelievably cold days in December 1994. Although we were all tired after a long term, and full of guilt about Christmas preparations neglected, this was a richly enjoyable event, intellectually and socially.

I did, however, find it a little disconcerting to be, by definition, about fifteen years older than anyone else present for the conference. By definition, because I was there (and am here), in the terms of the working title, as an 'old voice', not directly part of the group, but very pleased to be asked to participate in this project which includes work by younger scholars with whom I have been associated as teacher, employer, general editor, thesis supervisor, examiner, or just as the person who said 'Why not get X to do it?' when asked to recommend a speaker, writer or reviewer for a particular task. I suppose it is disconcerting because one of the good things about academic life in my own experience is that it is easy to forget distinctions of age and professional superiority as pupils, junior colleagues and research assistants metamorphose into friends, and it is unusual to be obliged to focus on generational differences. I don't feel quite ready to slip into the role of – What? 'Old fogey'? – in relation to the 'young Turks', and have to cheer myself up by remembering that, on the verge of retirement, Terry Hawkes still manages to be the *enfant terrible* of Renaissance studies. There may be life in it yet.

What, apart from being younger than I am, do these 'new voices' have in common? Is it possible or desirable to identify some distinguishing features shared by this generation of British scholars who are in the first five to ten years of their academic careers? How do they differ from my own or other previous generations? Listening to the papers in December 1994, I realised that this was not going to be an overtly polemical book. It does not come with a manifesto like some of the influential edited collections of the 1980s such as Jonathan Dollimore and Alan Sinfield's *Political Shakespeare*, John Drakakis's *Alternative Shakespeares* or Patricia Parker and Geoffrey Hartman's *Shakespeare and the Question of Theory*, all of which were published in 1985. There is no straightforward espousing of a new '-ism' here; no pressure on contributors to identify with any specific school of thought. (Not that I imagine that any of the 1985 editors applied pressure; more that the spirit of that time encouraged us all to indicate whether we were 'for' or 'against' particular positions.)

Nevertheless this next generation has grown up with all the new '-isms' – the various phenomena we now label 'literary theory': not just feminism and cultural materialism (perhaps, as Gordon says, the most obvious influences here) but New Historicism, Marxism, deconstruction, psychoanalytic criticism, postcolonial criticism, and so forth. They have at a basic level been obliged to acquire competence in these areas in order to be employable in today's highly competitive higher education market system. Even senior scholars who were decidedly 'against' these developments in the 1970s and 1980s (and who have never put themselves through the formidable relevant reading lists) see a knowledge of theory as a necessary professional skill these days, and 'an ability to teach literary theory' is mentioned frequently as desirable in the further particulars of job advertisements. At times the younger scholars are almost blasé about it, as when one speaker in Newcastle disarmingly said that her paper was too long so she would abbreviate it by skipping the 'boring theoretical stuff' in the first half on the grounds that 'you all know how it will go'.

This does not mean that this kind of shared knowledge and competence has been acquired at all unwillingly, or that it is being deployed cynically. These people are working on English literature of the Renaissance period, an area of literary study where 'theoretical' approaches have been particularly lively and influential. They take it for granted that in order to contribute to the field, they need to be conversant with the latest theory-based work from (at least) Britain and North America. They also take it for granted that these approaches must be incorporated into their teaching. While my generation worried about whether undergraduates could be expected to cope with this material, it does not occur to the next generation that they should teach other than by going straight to what they themselves find most interesting about Renaissance literature – which immediately takes them into the relationships of literary texts with their social and cultural contexts and into a heightened awareness of the role of the critic or teacher herself or himself in representing the text.

There really has been a significant shift in teaching practice, which became very apparent to me from my experiences during 1994–5 as a subject specialist assessor for the Higher Education Funding Council for England (the government funding body for universities and colleges). This involved going as one of a team (a different team each time) to a number of institutions of higher education in order to assess the quality of teaching and learning in English. After scrutinising the documentation sent by the English Department being visited (including course descriptions, reading lists, and so forth), older assessors would typically say 'This is too ambitious' or, more patronisingly, 'These students aren't up to these approaches'. But when they sat in the classrooms and watched the teachers at work, when they talked to the students and read their essays, they found themselves concluding, as often as not, that it *did* work and that the students were benefiting enormously from the demanding and stimulating teaching they were getting.

I think it is relevant to raise such an issue in this context because of what Gordon refers to in the Preface as the 'climate of considerable institutional change' in which young scholars are currently working. An important factor in this is that academic life in Britain is now much more subject to external and indeed internal regulation than it was a decade ago. In addition to Teaching Quality Assessment (TQA) as described above, we have the regular Research Assessment Exercise (RAE) every four years. Both these are national, external inspection systems operated by peer review. Universities and colleges have also been under pressure to formalise and improve their internal quality assessment mechanisms, ranging from course validation procedures to staff appraisal systems. These things have of course impinged on all academics, and we all complain about the increased bureaucracy and paperwork, but clearly the impact is different for me, as Head of a large Department, from what it is for the young scholars represented here. I am involved in implementing institutional changes; they are more simply subjected to them.

Young academics do feel under greater pressure than I did at their age (I would not quarrel with Gordon's statement in the Preface that they are aware of 'substantially increased obligations both in terms of teaching and administrative workload and of publishing output'), but perhaps the effects are not entirely negative. They are thoroughly professional about their teaching and aware that it matters, not only to the students (who have always appreciated good teaching and who now, rightly, have the opportunity to comment on bad teaching) but to their colleagues and to people outside their department. They are encouraged to be innovative and to share their ideas. Equally, their research is taken seriously: potentially productive staff, like all the scholars represented here, are likely to be given teaching relief or study leave at a much earlier stage in their careers than in the past; they are encouraged to give research papers and to attend conferences. Again, what they do is explicitly assessed, which may be a strain, but it is also explicitly valued, which may be an advantage and even a pleasure.

I believe there still are pleasures to be experienced in British academic life, despite the pace of change and our uncertainties about the future. The pleasure of intellectual engagement with cultural formations in early modern England is apparent throughout this book, and it is a pleasure which is patently enhanced by the simultaneous engagement with late twentieth-century modes of critical analysis. The pleasures of academic networking were important at every stage in the production of the book: we like talking about our work; we make and maintain good friendships with the people we work with; we like going to conferences; we even get paid for doing some of these things. I am flattered to be involved in this project and feel my own career to be justified and rewarded in so far as it has put me in a position where I can, in various modest ways, enable others. My confidence in the British higher education system, which has certainly faltered in recent years, is strengthened by the very fact that it has made room for these young scholars to begin to establish their careers. On the other hand, there would not be a lot of hope for it if it hadn't.

Index